Praise for *Catastrophe – Nakba II*

'The lips of the present give depth to history, and Fintan Drury certainly knows that there are several sides to every story. He rows the boat out – for some it will be a drowning experience, but for others it will be a pure lifeboat. The truth is polygonal but it eventually settles down into a single shape and this book will certainly contribute to where the shape finally falls.'

Colum McCann – Author of *Apeirogon*

'Bobby Sands said, "Our revenge will be the laughter of our children." He said this about the brutal British occupation of Ireland. An occupation that never sought to slaughter women and children. Twisted and psychopathic, Israel has brought evil to a new level. Fintan Drury doesn't shirk his duty as a human being. Here, he exposes the truth about Israel's genocide machine and their disgusting propaganda. This is a book that all of us should read.'

Kneecap – Musicians and social activists

'*Catastrophe – Nakba II* is a must-read for anyone trying to fathom the moral rupture that has permitted the slaughter, starvation and incineration of Palestinians in plain sight over the last year and a half. Fintan Drury lays bare all the lies, and puts the Israel-Palestine conflict in its proper historical context. He demonstrates clearly how the West has, for decades, not only allowed the state of Israel to breach international law and commit war crimes, but has provided the financial, military, diplomatic and *moral* cover to do so.'

Mary Costello – Author of *Academy Street*

‘Exploring the puzzle of Israel’s excessive brutality in Gaza, Fintan Drury explains how several Netanyahu governments contrived the total devastation of Gaza. Drury’s deeply researched analysis unravels the way cheap party politics in Israel plus global indifference to the Palestinians set the terms for this monumental tragedy. *Catastrophe – Nakba II* plucks out the heart of the mystery.’

Harold Aram Veeser – Professor of Post Colonial Literature, City College of New York and author of *Edward Said: The Charisma of Criticism*

‘Fintan Drury has written a challenging book. At times, it is an uneasy and uncomfortable read. But the whole point of this remarkable work is that we can’t be at ease with what has been happening. If we are comfortable with what has taken place in Gaza, we shouldn’t be. Many of us need to be challenged on why we have turned away. For those reasons, Fintan Drury has written, above all else, an essential book.’

Dion Fanning – Journalist and host of the *Free State* podcast

‘Fintan Drury has written a vital, unflinching account of a people under siege. This book demands to be read, and demands we bear witness. *Catastrophe – Nakba II* is devastating, courageous, and essential. It gives voice to those silenced, and documents horrors the world must not ignore. It’s both heartbreaking and necessary. Read it and don’t look away.’

Brian Conaghan – Author of *When Mr Dog Bites*

‘Fintan Drury joins authors and journalists like Ta-Nehisi Coates and Omar El Akkad in addressing what is happening in Palestine. Drury brings an Irish perspective to the history, which he recounts as if seeking the causal thread that has given rise to the current catastrophe. A masterful narrator, he delivers complex material with balance and empathy. *Catastrophe – Nakba II* is well researched, organised and deeply affective. It is a book for everyone.’

Carmel Mc Mahon – Author of *In Ordinary Time*

'Omar El Akkad wrote, "One day, when it's safe, when there's no personal downside to calling a thing what it is, when it's too late to hold anyone accountable, everyone will always have been against this." Fintan Drury has not waited until it is safe. He has not waited until it's too late. In this remarkable book, he has told the truth. The truth about Gaza and the West Bank and – most crucially for humankind – the truth about Israel's grotesque annihilation of a people and of all the things that make a human life worth living.'

Joe Brolly – Lawyer, journalist and host of the *Free State* podcast

In memory of my mother Róisín, an Irish Catholic born in Belfast in 1922, who died in Dublin in 2006 and for whom the lack of interest both of her country and her church in the plight of Europe's Jews in the 1930s and 1940s was a constant source of sadness and shame.

– Fintan Drury –

CATASTROPHE

NAKBA II

Fintan Drury

First published in 2025 by
Merrion Press
10 George's Street
Newbridge
Co. Kildare
Ireland
www.merrionpress.ie

© Fintan Drury, 2025

978 1 78537 559 0 (Paper)
978 1 78537 564 4 (eBook)

A CIP catalogue record for this book is available from the British Library.

All rights reserved. No part of this publication may be reproduced, stored in a retrieval system, or transmitted, in any form or by any means (electronic, mechanical, photocopying, recording or otherwise), without the prior written permission of both the copyright owner and the publisher of this book.

Typeset in Minion Pro 11/17
Typesetting and editing by JM Agency,
Kerry, Ireland

Front and back cover images: IMEMC (International Middle East Media Center). The International Middle East Media Center is an independent news organisation run by Palestinians living in the State of Palestine.

Cover design by Adrian Robb.
Map design by aux1 design.

Merrion Press is a member of Publishing Ireland.

'We shall try to spirit the penniless population across the border by procuring employment for it in the transit countries, while denying it employment in our country … the process of expropriation and the removal of the poor must be carried out discreetly and circumspectly.'

– Theodor Herzl,
Founder of Modern Zionism, 1896

'The Jewish people have an exclusive and unquestionable right to all areas of the land of Israel … Galilee, the Negev, Golan, Judea and Samaria.'

– Benjamin Netanyahu,
29 December 2022

Contents

Note to Readers

Most books on Palestine and Israel are by authors with extensive experience of the Middle East. Some are the work of academics who have studied the conflict through detailed analysis that is part of their professional DNA. Other books are the work of journalists who have lived in the area, met and interviewed some of the main protagonists and given their assessment based on that accumulated knowledge and experience. This is the account of a writer who spent only a couple of weeks in Jordan, Lebanon and the West Bank in the summer of 2024 and more time meeting and interviewing relevant parties elsewhere over the rest of that year; one motivated by a disbelief at the relative indifference of the institutional West to what was unfolding in Gaza and the West Bank.

This book is researched and written 'in the moment'; it is neither a historical nor an academic analysis. My training as a journalist seared in me the importance of objectivity, of taking time to research and consider events before deciding on the analysis you choose to offer. I believe in those principles, that reporting involves researching and informing, so the reader can better form their own opinion. This book is a bit different; it is written through the lens of someone who has long been suspicious of Israel, who considers it the primary aggressor in the conflict with Palestine and who, as a news reporter in the 1980s, wrote about the broader failure to understand the Arab world.

Catastrophe – Nakba II recognises the ruthlessness of Hamas and the embedded racism of its original intent when it was founded in 1987. But this book is a consciously pro-Palestine account of the events that led to its brutal assault of 7 October 2023 and the nature of Israel's response. It believes that since that fateful Saturday, Israel committed a genocide, one knowingly sponsored by some Western powers and supported by most others. The book's premise is that Israel remains intent on taking all of Palestine and at least a large part of southern Lebanon. Israel is an occupier that has, for decades, run political rings around the West's major powers and global powers and many of its institutions in the pursuit of its Zionist ambition. That *liaison dangereuse* has never been more in evidence and never yielded such harm as in the year after the Hamas attack of 7 October.

Catastrophe – Nakba II will be profiled in places as antisemitic; for some, the state of Israel represents such a uniquely important cause that it is reasonable to brand all those opposed to its unlawful expansion as such. The deliberate conflation of any criticism of Israel's state terrorism with being antisemitic reflects how entrenched many are in their belief that Israel is a state with rights beyond the international norm.

The purpose of this book is to underscore the case of those who support Palestine and to inform those open to persuasion of the merits of its case. The ambition is to provide a coherent and convincing narrative that shows how, while the Hamas attack of 7 October 2023 was the single greatest loss of life suffered by the Jewish people since the Holocaust, Israel's response is a genocide for which all those responsible must be brought to justice.

PROLOGUE

The 1948 Nakba and Seventy-Seven Years of Oppression

The Nakba (Catastrophe) happened when, after the end of the British Mandate, Zionist forces engaged in an operation that terrorised the indigenous Palestinian population, destroying their towns and villages in order to immediately set about expanding the borders of the new state of Israel as it was being brought into existence. Between 1918 and 1947, the Jewish population in Palestine rose from 6 to 33 per cent. Conflict was inevitable, and in 1947, UN Resolution 181, drafted by UNSCOP (United Nations Special Committee on Palestine), called for the partition of the region, with 56.5 per cent of the territory being granted to Jews even though they owned less than 10 per cent of the land at the time. Jerusalem was declared a special 'international' territory. The Arab leadership rejected this partition, but regardless, the resolution was passed at the General Assembly in November 1947.

This led to what became known as the Nakba – the word chosen by Palestinians to describe the utter carnage they then experienced. It involved the almost complete destruction of Palestinian society and the annexation of most of its territory. One of the worst massacres of the Nakba was when more than one hundred Palestinian children, women and men were killed in the village of Deir Yassin, outside Jerusalem. By the end of the Nakba in 1949, the Zionist campaign of terror had destroyed over 450 Arab towns or villages and at least 15,000 Palestinians had been killed. More than three-quarters of a million Palestinians were ethnically cleansed from their homeland by Zionist militia.

The state of Israel was formally declared on 15 May 1948. By then, almost 80 per cent of historic Palestine had been colonised, with the remainder divided into what are now the occupied West Bank and Gaza Strip. Displaced Palestinians numbered 750,000, and today, millions still live in refugee camps across Syria, Jordan, Lebanon, Egypt and Palestine itself. Though the international community agreed to establish a special agency, UNRWA (United Nations Relief and Works Agency), to represent their interests, Israel refused to recognise Palestinians as refugees because to do so would imply they had a homeland to return to; the legal right to return is an entitlement of all refugees under international law. About 200,000 Palestinians remained and lived in the newly created state of Israel, but it took 20 years before they were granted Israeli citizenship. Today, that cohort represents 20 per cent of the population of Israel, but, though they are citizens, their rights are limited – they live in an apartheid society, one that is in some respects more insidious and uncompromising than that which the ANC (African National Congress) had to fight against in South Africa.

In June 1967, at a time when Israel occupied the Gaza Strip, the West Bank, East Jerusalem, the Syrian Golan Heights and the Egyptian Sinai Peninsula, the Six-Day War arose as the ambition of the state of Israel met a coalition of Arab armies. This led to another forced displacement of about 300,000 Palestinians as more settlements appeared in the occupied West Bank and the Gaza Strip. A two-tier system was established, granting all the rights and privileges of being Israeli citizens to Jewish settlers, while Palestinians lived under a military rule that discriminated against them. Palestinians were prevented from any involvement in political or social activism. After the 1967 war, Israel held 78 per cent of the land of Palestine.

The hopeless inequity remained unresolved, with the Palestinians suffering humiliation upon humiliation without the international community showing any great interest. Israel had annexed East Jerusalem in 1980 but even that had been allowed to stand by its allies in the West. The First Intifada (Uprising) began in late 1987. It was prompted by the killing of four Palestinians, which led to street protests that triggered a brutal response by the Israeli security forces, including a 'break their bones' policy promoted by then Minister of Defence Yitzhak Rabin, which involved a range of violent measures, including summary killings. In his masterful history of Israel's settler colonial programme, *The Hundred Years' War on Palestine,* Rashid Khalidi references how the Intifada was led by young Palestinians, 'It was a spontaneous, bottom-up campaign of resistance, born of an accumulation of frustration and initially with no connection to the formal political Palestinian leadership.'[1]

The records of the Israeli human rights organisation, B'Tselem, show that over the twenty months of the Intifada, which ended in 1989, 1,100 Palestinians were killed by Israeli forces, 240 of whom were children. More than 175,000 Palestinians were arrested. Hamas was founded as the Intifada pushed for the establishment of Palestine's independence, and in 1988, the Arab League of Nations formally recognised the PLO (Palestine Liberation Organization) as the sole representative of the people of Palestine.

As a result of the Intifada and the international attention it garnered, the Oslo Accords were signed in 1993, resulting in the formation of an interim government called the Palestinian Authority, which had limited control over areas of the West Bank and Gaza Strip that remained occupied by Israel. With the accords, the PLO accepted a two-state solution but gave Israel control of 60 per cent of the West Bank and much of the territory's land and water resources. The accords offered little or no constraints on Israel's colonial ambition; Israeli settlements of Palestinian land in the West Bank gathered pace. The accords put the PLO at the centre of the Palestinian cause at a point where its credibility with its own people was in decline.

With the passage of time and the growing awareness that the Oslo Accords had offered Israel a diplomatic tool with which to play, the PLO (as the contracting party) increasingly lost the support of its constituency. The accords were seen as a misstep by an organisation that had been 'managed' into a very poor outcome for Palestine by a combination of international pressure and a failure to appreciate that Israel was not to be trusted and that its chief ally, the United States was not the honest broker it purported to be. By signing the Accords, the PLO had left the political hen coop wide open and, under scrutiny, it lost further credibility as it appeared to act in consort with Israel in shutting down political opposition to its administration of the agreement. Khalidi suggests that the PLO failed to appreciate Israel's hold on US Middle-East policy: 'Beyond the PLO's other misassumptions about the United States, its leaders failed to grasp the lack of American concern, even its disdain, for their interests and aims ... Most important, though, was their inability to understand how intimately the policies of the United States and Israel were linked.'[2]

The Second Intifada began on 28 September 2000, when the leader of Israel's Likud party, Ariel Sharon, visited the Al-Aqsa Mosque in Jerusalem in a show of territorial strength and ambition. This was just weeks after Ehud Barak and Yasser Arafat had attended a conference with US President Bill Clinton at Camp David. The summit had failed as Clinton and Barak attempted to force the PLO leader to accept the terms on offer as a full and final agreement: no commitment to the establishment of a Palestinian state, no changes in the status of Jerusalem and no resolution of the refugee issue.

When Sharon made his visit to Haram al-Sharif, he proclaimed that the Temple Mount was still in Israel's hands, and would remain so, as Israel imposed a security dragnet around the Old City, triggering inevitable violence that resulted in the death of half a dozen Palestinians. 'Unlike the First Intifada, this was a far more militarised uprising, spilling over into Israel itself ... Islamist resistance groups took up a renewed campaign of suicide bombings within Israel. The deadliest was perpetrated by Hamas: the bombing of Park Hotel in Netanya as Jews celebrated Passover. Thirty died and more than 140 were wounded.'[3] Israel responded with fierce intent by bombing cities, reoccupying the West Bank and parts of Gaza under a campaign it called Operation Defensive Shield.

Israel used the situation to justify reoccupying swathes of Palestine, built a large separation wall and promoted the resettlement of land it had lost under the Oslo agreements. Massive levels of settlement construction followed that effectively ended whatever level of independent life Palestinians had started to experience. When the Oslo Accords were signed in 1993, just over 230,000 Jewish settlers lived in the West Bank, including East Jerusalem. In early 2024, that figure had reached 750,000 people living on more than 120,000 hectares (460 sq. miles) of Palestinian land. This goes to the very heart of Israel's colonialist intent – settlements that are illegal under international law and that had stopped after the Oslo Accords are critical to its ambition.

The Second Intifada ended in 2005 when Israel left Gaza; the following year, elections were held for the first time and Hamas won a majority. As a result of this power shift, a civil war broke out between the Palestinian factions. Fatah, which was aligned with the Palestinian Authority, resisted as it could see its power leaking to Hamas. Later, when Fatah was expelled from Gaza by Hamas, it chose to focus its attention on the administration of the West Bank, where it still had the support of the majority.

In June 2007, Israel imposed a land, air and naval blockade on the Gaza Strip and between 2008 and 2021, it launched four separate military campaigns, killing thousands of Palestinians and destroying much of the strip's infrastructure. It is accepted that Israel used internationally banned weapons in some of those campaigns. It is documented that in 2014, over about a month and a half, its forces killed more than 2,100 Palestinians, most of them civilians, including about 500 children. 25,000 Palestinians were injured. That assault, called Operation Protective Edge by Israel, saw 20,000 homes in Gaza destroyed and half a million of its people displaced.

The 2014 assault was the single most brutal military campaign launched by Israel on Palestine until it initiated the new 'catastrophe', Nakba II, in October 2023, which continues to rage on unabated more than a year later. However, when reviewing what happened on 7 October 2023, it is the cumulative impact of Israel's conduct since the establishment of the 1967 boundaries, if not the 1948 Nakba, that warrants attention. That and how, perhaps uniquely, the West's main powers have for decades not just allowed one small state in the Middle East to breach international law but, at critical points over that time, sponsored its colonialist ambitions at a tremendous cost to the land's indigenous people.

It is worth noting that, even over the last decade and a half, with the four military campaigns of 2008, 2012, 2014 and 2021, Israel had launched offensives on one of the most densely populated and impoverished places on earth, knowing the terror it was wreaking but knowing, too, that the West would not care. Over that period, according to figures from the UN Office for Humanitarian Affairs, the Israeli military and the Palestinian Red Crescent, before the Hamas attack on 7 October, in Gaza alone, where Israel has sustained a blockade since 2009, those four assaults had taken more than 6,000 Palestinian lives, most of them civilians, at a cost of just over 100 Israelis, most of whom were soldiers.

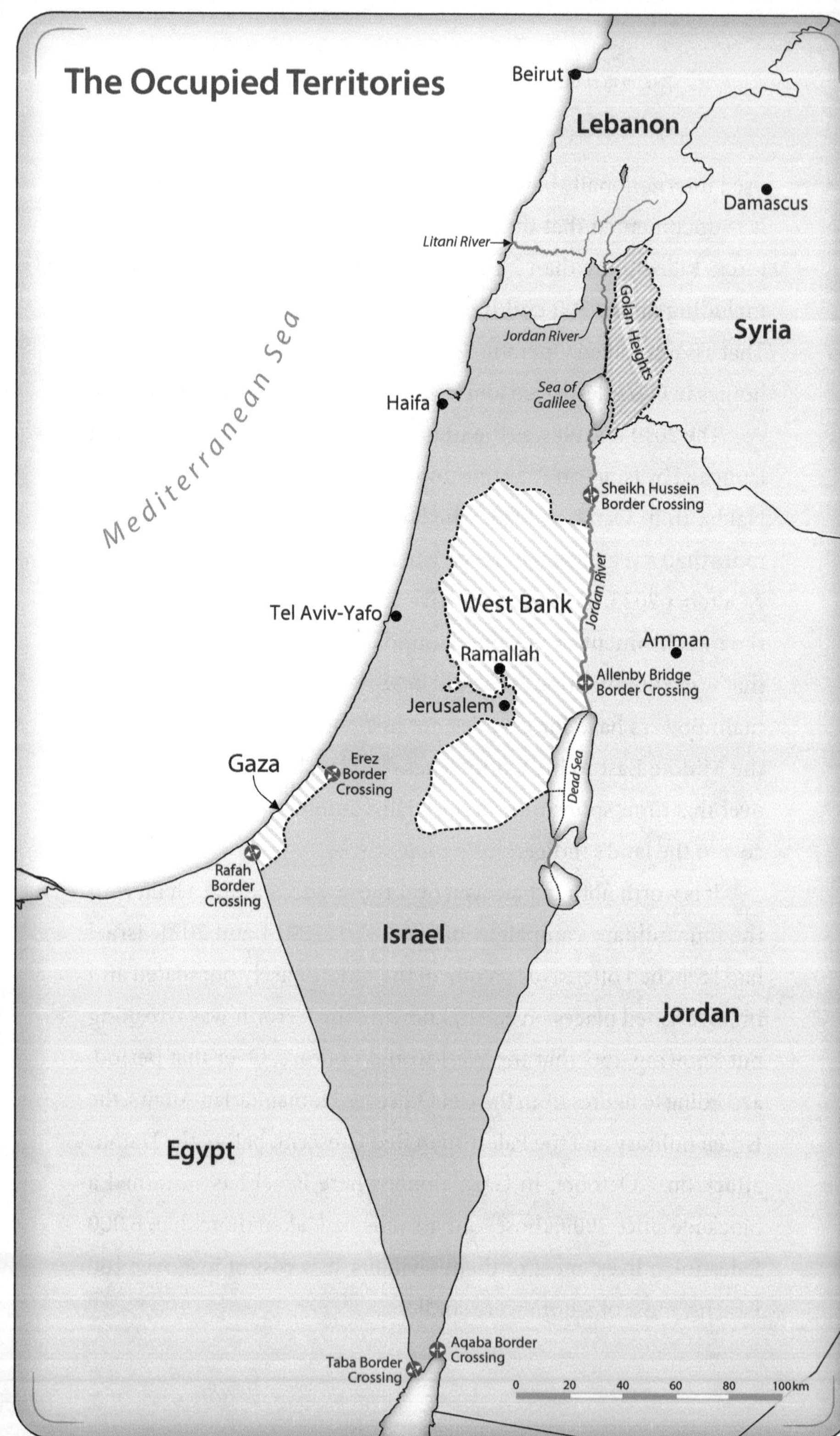
The Occupied Territories
Beirut
Lebanon
Damascus
Litani River
Syria
Golan Heights
Jordan River
Mediterranean Sea
Sea of Galilee
Haifa
Sheikh Hussein Border Crossing
Jordan River
West Bank
Tel Aviv-Yafo
Amman
Ramallah
Allenby Bridge Border Crossing
Jerusalem
Gaza
Erez Border Crossing
Dead Sea
Rafah Border Crossing
Israel
Jordan
Egypt
Aqaba Border Crossing
Taba Border Crossing
0
20
40
60
80
100km

INTRODUCTION

One Day, One Attack

In common with many, the first I knew of the Hamas attack of 7 October 2023, which left 1,300 Israelis dead, including 800 civilians, was a news alert on my phone. Citizens of more than thirty countries were among those killed, 46 of them American, while 251 civilians, again including some foreigners, were taken captive. The first news alerts didn't have that level of detail but, as instantly as it had appeared, images of the devastation of the Hamas attack were being distributed around the world by different social media outlets. It's how news travels now, much of it so mundane that it hardly qualifies as news – this event, however, most certainly did.

This news was very serious not because events of such violence have been that rare over the course of the longstanding conflict between Israel and Palestine but because, even with the earliest dispatches, it was clear that Hamas, the armed wing of the movement that has administered Gaza since 2007, had breached Israeli security and launched a large-scale attack on a music festival and kibbutzim on a Jewish public holiday. The numbers killed and the nature of the attack shocked Western media and commentators, as did the apparent ease with which it had been undertaken.

Israel had been forever telling the world of the quality of its sophisticated intelligence and its security services, yet now more than a thousand of its citizens had been killed on their own soil, in a place and at a time that was symbolic of Israel's sense of itself in the world. They had been killed by an enemy that the state knew offered a threat and yet it appeared that Hamas fighters had been able to breach border security, carry out the attack and withstand casualties of their own before returning to Gaza with hundreds of hostages. In the hours and days immediately following, the global reaction to what had happened, influenced by Israel's account, positioned the event as a terrorist act by Islamist militants determined to damage its place as the bastion of democracy in the Middle East. The absence of context, of any nuance, was perhaps understandable in the earliest days, especially in the West, where both the political class and much of the media have, for decades, seen the Middle East through an almost exclusively pro-Israel prism.

The limitations of that myopic lens had long been evident; without a deliberate attempt to widen its focus, it would be impossible to see Israel's long-running conflict with Palestinians other than how Israel and its greatest allies in the West want it to be seen. With regards to the coverage of the Hamas attack, there was nothing dramatically different to how biased it has always been; with this incident, we would be presented with a narrative, a perspective on events in the Middle East, no matter their provenance, that has been the same for generations. We would be offered an analysis largely based on the Western premise of Israel as a democratic oasis in a desert of autocracy, an almost uniformly good or positive view, certainly one dominated by Israel as the 'victim' – always the victim – whenever serious conflict occurs.

Through this lens, whoever was to blame for the brutality of the attack on 7 October 2023 had nothing to do with Israel; Israel was the completely innocent party. We've long been fed the narrative that Israel represents a piece of Western culture in the Middle East, a nation that thinks as we do, in a part of the world that much of the West feels threatened by, a place it neither understands nor has any great interest in doing so. This narrative has it that, in the Middle East, Israel alone understands us in the West as we think we understand Israel. It is a perspective where:

- Israel is a democracy.
- Israel has free and fair elections.
- Israel has a free media and allows freedom of expression.
- Israel is a strong trading partner of the European Union, the United States and Britain; it can be relied upon as a mature, functioning economy that wants to conduct its overseas business transparently.
- Israel is the home of the Jewish people, a place for Europe's Jews, those who survived the Holocaust and the offspring of those who did not, to make their own.
- Israel is a peaceful nation, an upholder of Western values in a part of the world where Islam predominates and where the threat of Islamic extremism is prevalent.

In short, for Western governments across Europe, the United States and Canada, Israel is, to all intents and purposes, a Western country that just happens to be located in the Middle East. Since its foundation, its geographic location has made it more interesting and valuable for some Western powers because it was seen as providing a footprint in a part of the world where Islam is the predominant faith, with – according to much Western commentary – an attendant risk of fundamentalism that is exclusive to it. This and its proximity to Iran gave Israel a special status that meant almost any actions it took to protect itself but also to advance its own national interests have for decades gone unchecked despite its predilection to breach international law in the expansion of its borders into territory where it has no entitlement.

For all these reasons, the West, without exception, rushed to condemn Hamas for its attack on 7 October with the not unreasonable mantra that 'Israel has the right to defend itself'. Sovereign nations do indeed have such a right but, knowing Israel's track record and that of its prime minister, Benjamin Netanyahu, the declaration could and should have been heavily caveated with the need for Israel's response to reflect its claimed status as a democratic nation and the need for proportionality. The absence of any guardrails around the offers of support by nearly every Western nation, most notably the USA, was fatal to prospects of the West exerting control on Israel's response as its campaign took on an unspeakably ugly character.

Israel's status across the institutional West meant there was, at the outset, little political motivation for any words of caution. Most Western media went on a full-scale attack on Hamas and, indirectly, the Palestinian people who, in Gaza, had voted them into government. The Western media was both a contributor to and a mirror of the public mood, one that had darkened as the Israeli government issued highly charged – and never verified – accounts of babies being beheaded and women being raped in the midst of the carnage that had ensued during the Hamas raids.

So, the international stage was set for Israel's response. The drumroll of alarm over the scale and nature of the attack on Israeli soil made it inevitable that innocent Palestinians – certainly those living in Gaza – would suffer. The unlimited embrace of Israel's right to defend itself made redundant any idea that the scale of its response should be proportionate, so the Gazans who would perish had only themselves to blame for allowing Hamas to represent their interests. What else could Israel do except take the fight to Hamas? The accompanying rhetoric reassured the West that Israel would continue to be the platform on which a coalition of interests to prevent the spread of Islam could be built. This was code for increased settlement of the West Bank and for putting Iran-backed Hezbollah in Lebanon on notice, and so the West, consumed by its fear of Islamism and the presumed threat of Iran, said little or nothing as Israel's government set its course.

When 7 October happened, the West's default position was to greenlight Israel to respond as it saw fit. The narrative was that the attack it had suffered was unprovoked and anything and everything Israel did in response was justified; its actions as a state that had been terrorised by the brutal, inhumane attack of an Arab terrorist group were appropriate. The Western institutional mindset was that Israel had not just the right to respond on behalf of its people but that it had a duty to do so.

It was presented as a simple case of cause and effect; whatever happened as a result of Israel's actions, the responsibility for it would rest with Hamas. By this analysis, in its brutal assault on young Israelis and overseas visitors celebrating a public holiday, Hamas had embodied the evil that supposedly lies uniquely within Islam and that, unchallenged, would represent an existential threat to the mores and culture of Western civilisation. Underpinning this assessment was that Israel alone in the Middle East understands that threat and is prepared to fight back; in protecting itself, it was, therefore, acting to protect us all, or those at least living in the West. That is how we were supposed to understand the events of 7 October 2023 and the devastation of Palestine that has ensued since.

◆◆◆

The prevailing narrative is one thing. The truth is quite different. The truth is that, through the most perverse irony, the state of Israel is engaged in an assault on humanity that is utterly devoid of reason other than it wishes to see the complete annihilation of the Palestinian people. On 7 October 2023, the Hamas attack reignited a Zionist dream that had, to the full extent of its ambition, been dormant for some time. This, then, is the counter-narrative, the account that places Hamas' attack in a wider context, one of decades of abuse of the Palestinian people by Israel. In November 1967, as the Six-Day War ended, French President Charles de Gaulle said that Israel 'is organising occupation on the territory it has seized. This cannot proceed without oppression, repression and expulsion and without the emergence of resistance to it, which in turn it [Israel] characterises as terrorism'.[4]

The decades of humiliation of the Palestinians were allowed by Western powers hopelessly compromised by what had happened to Europe's Jews at the time of World War II. Whatever Israel chose to do since its foundation was somehow justifiable on account of the Holocaust, so, without any apparent limitations, the West remained resolute in its support of the state of Israel. Even those nations that had worried at the choice of Palestine as the territory where Israel would be established trusted that those who'd been subject to such brutality at the hands of Nazi Germany would never visit such inhumanity on another people. Events over the twelve months between October 2023 and October 2024 – and beyond – showed the world the leaders of those countries today were mistaken in that belief.

What happened on 7 October 2023 was neither the start of something nor the cause of anything; it was, just as de Gaulle had prophesied, the result of decades of intense oppression of Palestinians by Israel. Yet, as the state responsible set about the complete destruction of Palestine, the West allowed it to happen. Some of the West's most powerful nations did a great deal more than eschew intervention, they chose to sponsor Israel at levels that allowed it to elevate its military response from seeking retribution for 7 October to a campaign of genocide. Without that support, Israel could not have progressed the ambition of its government to wipe out the entire Palestinian people.

There is a great irony in the fact that Hamas' strength was, at least in part, down to the misjudgement of Israel and its prime minister. The attack was further evidence of Benjamin Netanyahu's delusional sense of self as a master political strategist. In his leadership of previous governments, he attempted to drive a wedge between the Palestinian power blocs in the Gaza Strip and the West Bank. Convinced the Palestinian Authority, led by Mahmoud Abbas since the death of Yasser Arafat in 2004, was the real existential threat to the state of Israel, he chose to support Hamas with funds that were routed through Qatar. Netanyahu believed the real risk of the establishment of a Palestinian state lay in the West Bank, not Gaza. Funding Hamas was, he thought, the smart 'play'. Hamas said that the funds were needed to pay public salaries and for medical purposes. It had led the government of Gaza since the elections of 2006 and, while it would have needed funds for its administration of the strip, it was clear that some of the funds Israel was routing to Hamas through Qatar would be used for other purposes. US officials confirmed that the West was well aware of what was going on: 'We deferred completely to the Israelis as to whether this was something they wanted to do or not.'[5] Other allies, such as the EU's head of foreign policy, Joseph Borrell, knew it too: 'Hamas was financed by the government of Israel in an attempt to weaken the Palestinian Authority led by Fatah.'[6]

The Palestinian Authority also knew and attempted to prevent the move but, in August 2018, the deal was approved by Israel's security cabinet at a meeting chaired by Prime Minister Netanyahu. US officials involved have said that the Israelis wanted to keep Hamas in power in a weakened form in Gaza as they were considered the lesser threat compared to Fatah; the funding of Hamas continued until the change of government in Israel in 2021.

Netanyahu's successor as prime minister, Naftali Bennett, said that he'd consistently warned of the risk that Israel was strengthening its enemy with the funding, which was why he had immediately ended the transfers when he assumed office. 'I stopped the cash suitcases because I believe that horrendous mistake – to allow Hamas to have all these suitcases full of cash, that goes directly to reordering [*sic*] themselves against Israelis. Why would we feed them cash to kill us?'[7]

◆◆◆

It was months after the 7 October attack when I recalled the horror my mother often expressed over the fate of the Jewish people in 1930s and 1940s Europe. We'd had many discussions about it where she'd expressed the view that there had to have been enough people in positions of power who knew about the camps. Her faith was important to her but she thought Pope Pius XII had been cowardly, a charge she also levelled at Ireland's Taoiseach (prime minister) Eamon de Valera, in whose cabinet her father had twice served as a cabinet minister. Those conversations sometimes ended with her gratitude for modern communications and how she felt assured that nothing like the Holocaust could ever happen again.

I have spent much of my professional life in business, but my training and experience as a news journalist, which was my life in my twenties, are deep-rooted. So, as early 2024 gave way to spring and the onslaught on Gaza continued, I became increasingly fascinated with events and the dreadful reality on the ground. I wanted to understand it, to see where the truth might lie. I did this on my laptop, on my phone, watching every news channel I could, reading

The Guardian, *The New York Times*, *The Middle East Monitor*, *Middle East Eye*, and I took out a subscription to *Haaretz*, the Israeli daily newspaper I'd trusted as a journalist in the 1980s and found to still be a largely balanced and considered source of news. I read books that I had read before and I found new writers and new titles, some revelatory, about the decades-long conflict between the rights of the Palestinians and the sense of entitlement of the Israelis.

I followed two social media platforms pretty much 24/7, and I marvelled, in equal measure, at both the professional and citizen reporting from Gaza. As 2024 was a presidential election year, I talked with people in the US about the differences, if any, between the Democrats and the Republicans on Israel and Palestine. It appeared that Israel was one of the very few issues most agreed on, both in the presidential contest and across the Congressional campaigns. Britain would have an election too, one where, post the carefully engineered campaign alleging antisemitism against his predecessor, Labour's new leader, Keir Starmer, wouldn't be found wanting in his support of Israel.

Increasingly, across the West, Palestine again seemed isolated, not with the public but with the institutions that represented them. After some years of improved awareness and some political support for the Palestinian cause, much of Europe either stayed silent or, in the case of some of its bigger players, actively sponsored Israel's campaign. It was left to a few – Ireland and Spain chief among them – to consistently voice concern and regularly ask some of the hard, if obvious, questions.

In May, as I became more astounded by events, I sensed an emerging narrative prevailing in the Western media, one that was using the horror of 7 October to further Israel's ambition to retake all of Palestine, so I decided to go to the region to interrogate it and find out the truth on the ground. I had been on enough protest marches; I knew I could make better use of my time, my gifts and my experience through active investigation of the facts. Gaza was off-limits, but Lebanon, Jordan and the West Bank offered sources and access that could confirm (or otherwise) my belief that Israel was a rogue state and that it had, over the course of 2024, been allowed by the West to play that role with consummate ease.

That it could do so, in full public glare, with everything from drone strikes on Gaza, the theft of a few sheep by 'settlers' in the West Bank or the incursion of a handful of Israeli soldiers into the blue zone on the Lebanese border being published on social media, was remarkable. It was shocking that week in, week out, its campaign of terror continued with ever-increasing numbers of civilian casualties while the world (knowing what was happening, as it was happening) went about its business, largely indifferent to the deliberate annihilation of a whole people.

Those who refuse to see the long-embedded settler-colonial intent of the state of Israel or those for whom the scale of its onslaught since 7 October 2023 is explained by the Hamas attack forcing Israel's hand seem to be ignoring the evidence. In its pursuit of armed combat against Palestine, Israel has consistently displayed a complete disregard for the welfare of civilians. In the twenty-first century, whenever Israel has attacked Palestinians, the ratio differential of mortality statistics in the two civilian populations is, by a distance, the highest of any conflict in the world.

Israel's recklessness toward civilians is well documented. In 2008, in Israel's Operation Cast Lead in Gaza, the overall ratio of civilian losses was 255 Palestinians to one Israeli, with a total of 318 Palestinian children killed, while all Israeli casualties were adults. With Operation Protective Edge in 2014, the equivalent figures were 244 to one, with 551 children killed in Gaza and one Israeli child fatality. Even allowing for the indisputable evidence of Israel's disregard for Palestinian lives in previous attacks, the scale of the figures for Nakba II is unimaginable. It is a genocide.

◆◆◆

This time, unlike the Holocaust of my parents' generation, there was no credible basis on which anyone could say that they did not know, that they did not understand what Israel was doing or that they had somehow missed it. We therefore do not have the excuse that if only someone had brought the scale of the abuse to our attention, we would have done something about it. The institutional inertia in most countries was staggering; the active sponsorship of Israel's campaign by some of the more powerful nations in the Western world, chilling.

What brought tens of millions onto the streets of global capitals on pro-Palestine marches every week was the scale of the horror and the eyewitness reporting of the loss of life and wilful destruction of place by Israel in Gaza. The injustice inflamed passions. I had marched and chanted 'from the river to the sea, Palestine will be free' countless times, surrounded by equally enraged citizens, without appreciating just how impossible that aspiration is with Israel positioned as it is, as the protector-in-chief of 'Western values' in the Middle East. I was among hundreds of thousands of Irish people, one of tens of millions of Europeans, who knew what was afoot was egregiously wrong, but who might have struggled to explain why. We were horrified by the scale of death and destruction, but unsure of the backstory, so we protested and our hearts ached for the people of Gaza, but maybe, truth be known, we didn't know our Hamas from our Hezbollah or our East from our West Jerusalem.

We are emotional creatures; a great deal of the public action through huge-scale street marches and campus protests across the globe represented a visceral reaction to what people were seeing and reading about Israel's campaign. From early in 2024, the consensus among protesters was that the world was witnessing a genocide. I felt certain of it and that I knew its source but, though I was reasonably informed, I still didn't know the history well enough to appreciate its scale and Israel's labyrinthine hold on the West. The information is there, all of it (brilliantly written by skilled academics, historians and writers) but this new, tragic phase in Israel's assault on humanity needed to be set in that context to better inform those whose hearts were with Palestine, all those whose senses bristled with hurt for the people of Gaza and the West Bank and with anger at those among our political leaders who'd chosen to support Israel.

However, even when, later in the year, the UN found its voice and the international courts ruled as they did, Israel continued its onslaught in Gaza and its accelerated theft of land in the West Bank, knowing the risk of meaningful sanction was practically nil.

With each passing month, it became clearer that Israel's actions were not at all about the Hamas attack of 7 October; something more profound was afoot and understanding that history and its importance to those in power in Israel in 2024 is fundamental to appreciating what a second Nakba represents for the people of Palestine.

◆◆◆

When I spoke with people who were involved or affected by the events, there was an overriding sense of despair at the ease with which Israel was conducting its siege of Gaza. The younger generations were particularly alert to the trauma; a group of young mothers in Beirut, women with no links to Palestine, talked with me of their horror at what was happening and the complicity of the United States. One spoke of her daughter's awkwardness at discovering, while on holiday in Greece, that two girls in her group were Israeli; she'd felt compelled to express her dislike of Israel's actions. These young mothers were less sure their parents' generation would speak so clearly of the horror unfolding in Gaza, preferring to keep quiet as long as it was at a distance. Just days later, the Israeli bombs started to fall on their own city as, in the south of Lebanon, the IDF (Israel Defense Forces) increased the pressure on Hezbollah.

In the summer of 2024, there was real surprise in Lebanon, Jordan and the West Bank that, in these times of instant global access to events, any nation could engage in such an openly genocidal campaign without sanction. For most, there was disbelief at how, given the clear evidence of its conduct, more than eight months after the Hamas attack, the West's most powerful nations still supported Israel's actions. There was anger at the decision of some to directly sponsor Israel's campaign against Palestine by providing it with an endless supply of arms. This had continued long after there was no basis left to argue that Israel's security remained threatened.

With those who really knew the facts, no matter how well informed, the question asked most often was about the absence of alarm, of real outrage. Across those with the deepest understanding, including those with little time for Hamas, the question I heard asked most frequently about Israel's actions was, 'Where is the outrage?'

In late July 2024, I was at the headquarters of UNRWA in Amman, Jordan. UNRWA was established by the United Nations in 1949 to deal exclusively with the needs of the Palestinian people. Juliette Touma, its head of communications and a veteran of its work in Gaza, where it administers much of the territory's public services, asked me that question a number of times. She asked it plaintively – disbelieving that Israel's campaign was unchecked by some of the most powerful nations in the world.

UNRWA directly employed 13,000 people in Gaza in the provision of health care, education and social services. Its work meant it had some involvement in the delivery of operational elements in the governance of Gaza by the political wing of Hamas. It has been targeted by Israel; many of its employees have been killed while the Israeli government and its agencies have been determined to undermine the organisation's wider reputation, its status and the value of its corporate testimony. Yet, UNRWA's scale and its reach across Gaza over the course of Israel's campaign meant it had unique, informed and critical insights into the events that followed the Hamas attack of 7 October 2023. Its testimony to events will be essential if we ever want to understand the sheer scale of Israel's destructive intent. Where is the outrage? Juliette Touma asked again and again:

> Really, where is it? Last night I spoke with one of my colleagues in Gaza City – he's a teacher and he told me that for the third night in a row, he would sleep in the car with his wife and his two children. This man has already lost family members, his home is destroyed and he and all our colleagues are living through a catastrophe of unimaginable proportions, yet the world seems largely disinterested! That's life now for him and thousands of other UNRWA workers and they're the lucky ones; 200 were killed by Israel's bombing over the last ten months.[8]

Touma and other UNRWA personnel knew that people were protesting, out marching in their tens of thousands, but they still felt the absence of an all-consuming outrage at what Israel was doing. UNRWA staff were not just seeing what the world could see with the constant flow of information on social media; they were there, they were working, living – and dying – there as Israel conducted its campaign of terror. Bearing witness as these people did, the relative lack of interest of the international community was impossible for them to understand. The absence of complete outrage mystified them.

UNRWA does more than help to administer critical services in Gaza. It provides services and administers the installation of fifty-eight Palestinian refugee camps across Palestine, Syria, Lebanon and Jordan, where people eke out different levels of existence depending on where they are located. Since October 2023, those in the camps in Gaza and the West Bank knew that whether their camp was a tented town or multiple rows of cement-block houses, it could be targeted by the Israeli air force and its ground artillery. The intention, the idea, of a 'refugee camp' had no meaning and was of no relevance to Israel and those who supplied it with arms. Over the course of Nakba II, every place, every single person in Gaza represented a legitimate target for the IDF. In tandem, the brutal theft of more land in the West Bank increased.

My neutral Irish accent sometimes leads people overseas to think I'm an American, which can leave me open to certain assumptions being made. As Samir from East Jerusalem, who has lived all his adult life in the overcrowded Amman New Camp, known locally as Wihdat, asked, 'Why has America given Israel so much? Why does Biden want to support Netanyahu with billions of dollars of weapons when he knows – they know – that thousands of innocent civilians are being killed in Gaza? Why do the American people allow this?'[9] The camp, established in 1955 on the southern outskirts of Amman city, is a permanent home to over 60,000 Palestinians, many of whom are children of refugees of the first Nakba. The United Nations estimates that 34 per cent of its residents live below the poverty line and that it has the highest rate of chronic health issues of all ten UNRWA camps in Jordan.[10] There is a quiet disbelief that another catastrophe is being unleashed on those still living in Palestine. My assumed status as an American had prompted the question, one asked more in sadness than anger. It was Samir's way of questioning the absence of outrage.

◆◆◆

A few days later, I was in Ramallah, the administrative capital of the West Bank. Abdullah, a Palestinian taxi driver in his mid-sixties, despaired of the West ever stepping in and stopping Israel. He spoke eloquently about the sense of abandonment that had been his life experience and how he saw little prospect of that changing. There was a rawness to his perspective and a certainty that things were going to get considerably worse. There was also a striking sense of humour. Abdullah explained that the authorities had, the previous day, warned of a worsening security situation and advised people to stock up on essentials. He explained that, as his wife was away, he'd chosen only to bulk-buy what he could not survive without: 'a kilo of tobacco,' he laughed through a small cloud of smoke as he paused his narrative.

We were driving from the checkpoint on the Israeli side of the famous Allenby Bridge that connects Jordan to the occupied West Bank, en route to Ramallah, when his personal story transported me to the reality of life in Gaza. I was curious at the casual way he'd said that his wife was 'away' and when I asked about her, his explanation transported us right into Gaza and to the horror of that place right then, in the summer of 2024. Abdullah explained that she was in Cairo with her critically ill daughter-in-law and baby grandchild. She had two children by her first marriage, including a son who was based in Gaza with his wife, their 5-year-old son and 3-month-old daughter. They lived in a small one-room unit in Khan Younis camp. Abdullah told me,

> One morning, after they brought the baby to the UNRWA clinic for a check-up, my stepson and his little boy went into the

> house while his wife stayed outside breastfeeding the baby. The camp was bombed and their place was hit. When the mother came round, she was covered in rubble and the infant she was feeding was nowhere to be seen. My wife's son and his boy, her grandchild, were dead, instantly I'm sure, but here's the most remarkable thing, his wife had a fractured pelvis, skull and many other serious injuries but the infant, her 3-month old that was in her arms when the blast happened was found on top of a mound of rubble, just metres away, crying but without so much as a scratch.[11]

Those Palestinians whom I spoke with in the West Bank were outraged by the brutality of Israel's campaign in Gaza but many saw too that it was providing cover – internationally at least – for Israel to significantly increase its accretion of their land. The West Bank, for so long the centre of the world's limited attention span for the Palestinian cause, had been shifted to the periphery by the scale of Israel's actions in Gaza. From the roof of his home in Al Bireh, Munif Treish, a member of its city council and head of a long-established family in the Ramallah area, showed me a road that cut through the illegally occupied land that was built for the use of Israelis alone. The new tarmac road that ran all the way to Jerusalem was policed and only Israeli settlers or members of its security services were permitted to use it. Treish, an engineer, pointed at various settlements across the landscape, some of which I later saw at close quarters; the land that was stolen, settled and heavily fortified was always in the most fertile and accessible areas. The Treish family had, for generations, been battling against the settlement of their own land; a decade before, one of Munif's sons had returned from America to fight in the courts to prevent his land from being stolen. Munif's overwhelming emotion was sadness.

Abdullah felt the same, though both men, neither of whom was young, felt the absolute imperative of going on living the best lives they could and, through a quiet resolve, trying not to allow the injustice to defeat them. It is an admirable quality but one that has to be very difficult to sustain. The relentlessness of Israel's pursuit of that which does not belong to it has repercussions for those whose land it is; the need for vigilance and for resources to fight the settlers means that many cannot compete with the Zionists. It also means a level of exhaustion – emotional more than physical – that makes it difficult to think of anything other than your own cause or at least of the horror that is being played out in your own community. The hurt was intense; the sense of outrage deeply felt, if quietly expressed.

Abdullah knew that millions of people were protesting around the world, but, for him, that didn't amount to a uniform sense of anger over events that the world was able to follow in real time. Abdullah had no doubt about Israel's intentions and didn't believe anyone with any understanding of history could come to any other conclusion than Israel wanted the complete annihilation of the people of Palestine. The outrage he felt was less with Israel than with those who pretended not to know its intent: 'The West doesn't see what it doesn't want to see; there is no surprise in that, no surprise that Israel's cause comes first.'[12]

◆◆◆

Israel is widely considered a democracy, at least in the West. In terms of political administration, it exhibits many of the relevant characteristics of one but, despite this, it cannot be described as such. Its real structure is an ethnocracy, a state that's controlled by a dominant ethnic group with the ambition to further only the interests, power, and resources of that group, which controls the full apparatus of the state and works toward that end.

This distinction is critical to understanding the direction Israel has taken over recent decades. It has become increasingly self-assured, more emboldened that the Zionist dream can be realised. Zionism is an ethno-nationalist project that, by its nature, involves racism and authoritarian governance with a commitment to take and hold – through violence if necessary – all land that it believes belongs to that ambition. The ongoing 2023–24 genocidal campaign in Gaza, Israel's accelerated annexation of land in the West Bank and its manufactured row with Hezbollah to allow it to enter Lebanon all represent the actions of an ethnocracy. The Netanyahu government, elected in late 2022, was a coalition of interests that took Zionism closer to the heart of Israeli political intent than any of its predecessors in recent decades. From the outset, among its priorities was the expansion of settlements in the West Bank, with a full annexation to be given consideration. This was part of its stated plan; such disregard for the rights of Palestinians or for the international rule of law long predated the Hamas attack of 7 October 2023.

In Paris in September, I spoke with an Israeli school teacher, Aaron, who had left Tel Aviv with his wife and two small children as the scale of Israel's assault on Gaza became ever more visible.

He and his wife feared that, had they stayed, their sons would be educated in a system that encouraged ethnic superiority.

> The staff room was silent on Gaza, on its destruction, even on the prevention of aid getting through to its beleaguered people. When you're a moral person, the pride you may feel as a citizen of Israel has to be impacted by such an absence of concern over what's done in your name and what children are being taught to see as normal or correct.[13]

Aaron and his wife experienced a sense of growing isolation in their home city, which had started to seem alien. They loved their country but, over the last decade, felt sure the principles they lived their lives by, the mores they'd inherited from their parents, were being threatened. The apathy of colleagues, their lack of interest in even discussing the need for aid to get through to people in Gaza made the silence in the teachers' room representative of this change, one Aaron sensed was as much about fear of speaking up than necessarily signalling support of Israel's offensive. The absence of outrage among young Israelis seemed to him to represent the result of a deliberate control of education and media: 'Israel is very different now to a decade or two ago; the IDF is different to when I did my three years mandatory service twenty years ago. Truth is a casualty.'[14]

◆◆◆

Michel is an experienced Lebanese public servant. We sat for hours one July morning in Beirut discussing the risk that Israel's campaign of terror on Gaza could spill over into Lebanon. The informed view was that it would not, that Hezbollah represented an enemy of greater scale than Hamas and that any engagement by Israel ran the risk of Iran becoming involved, which Michel believed Israel's allies would not allow. The plight of the Palestinians upset him, but Lebanon's own scars are not fully healed and its economy is beyond fragile, so the sympathy was tempered, although when Israel's insatiable appetite for land was discussed, it was elevated.

I should have been in Tyre, a coastal city in southern Lebanon only 20 kilometres from the border with Gaza, but my sources in UNIFIL (United Nations Interim Force in Lebanon) – the UN peacekeeping force on that border – asked that I would not travel, as a higher security threat had arisen. I spoke with Michel again the next day after Israel had bombed a suburb of Beirut just two neighbourhoods away from where we'd met. It had also moved more troops to the border, mischievously claiming that its northernmost communities were coming under unprovoked and sustained rocket fire from Hezbollah. Michel recognised the changed dynamic but remained optimistic that it would not escalate. 'Lebanon doesn't want any level of war with Israel; Palestine's is not our cause to fight but if Israel tries to take land that belongs to Lebanon, then that changes everything – there can be no compromise on that.'[15]

One

Israel 2023

Coalition

The thirty-seventh government of Israel was sworn into office on 29 December 2022, almost two months after the general election, which returned what was generally regarded as the most right-wing Knesset (parliament) in the history of the state. What was also a feature of the newly elected Knesset was the scale of the success of religious parties, some of whom had found their way into the seven-party coalition formed by Likud leader and six-time prime minister, Benjamin Netanyahu. One immediate fear among secular Jews was that the religious parties in government would attempt to weaken the judiciary through 'an "override clause" that would allow the Knesset to overturn [certain] court decisions'.[16]

The election and the formation of the government that followed represented a marked shift to the right in Israeli politics, described as 'authoritarian' by the daily newspaper *Haaretz* and with Benjamin Netanyahu at its head, the country was being led by a figure for whom it was important to leave a mark. There were a number of reasons for him to believe that assuming the role for the sixth time might prove his last opportunity to do so. He was 75 years old at the time but those reasons were about more than his age; what was considerably more likely to constrain his influence on Israeli politics was that he was facing criminal indictments that could lead to him being forced from public office. The charges of receiving bribes and engaging in fraud were serious and dated back to his fourth and fifth terms as prime minister.

Early in 2023, Netanyahu and his closest allies in the new government set about formulating plans to reform the judiciary. The Supreme Court had the right to declare Knesset legislation unconstitutional, but the proposed reforms would have permitted parliament to overturn such a ruling, effectively rendering the Court powerless on legislation. The new administration's plans included making the appointment of judges a matter for the government by changing the composition of the independent Judicial Selection Committee. Netanyahu, who was facing criminal charges that predated the formation of the new government, argued that the proposed changes, and others, were necessary because the judiciary had too much influence over public policy. The Attorney General ruled that Netanyahu must absent himself from the debate to remove any idea that his intentions were influenced by the criminal charges he faced. While he may not have been in the room, his hand was still evident as his coalition brought forward a raft of bills concerning Israel's judicial system and the balance of powers.

Minister of Defence Yoav Gallant opposed the government's intentions and, when he found himself isolated, took the unusual step of making public his disagreement with Netanyahu. On 25 March, he invited journalists to his office and warned that the legislative battle on the government's planned changes to the judiciary had the potential to undermine the state. Gallant told reporters, 'the breach within the nation has penetrated deep into the IDF and the defense establishment – this is a clear and major threat to the security of Israel.'[17] Netanyahu tried to fire him but, as that became public, the country's largest trade union, Histadrut, called a national strike and the scale of public protests stayed his hand. Gallant, having warned of such civil unrest, repeated that it would only offer opportunities to Israel's opponents and chose to stay in government. The strong public reaction had influenced Netanyahu to at least pause the pace of his reforms.

Presidential Fears

Yoav Gallant wasn't the only politician in high office concerned about the government's intent on judicial reform. Israel's president, Isaac Herzog, a lawyer and member of the political establishment, had also spoken of how divisive the planned legislation was. The president was alarmed by the huge levels of public protests but he was also being pressed by different interest groups across the most powerful elements of Israeli society.

> Anyone who thinks that a genuine civil war, with human lives, is a line that we could never reach – has no idea … the abyss is within touching distance. Today, I say to you what I told them:

> civil war is a red line! I will not allow it to happen! At any price. By any means … I heard real, deep hatred. I heard people on all sides, for whom, God forbid, the thought of blood in the streets is no longer shocking.[18]

That the president felt compelled to issue such a warning – in a nationally televised address just three months after the confirmation of the appointment of Benjamin Netanyahu as prime minister for the sixth time – was telling.

The immediate backdrop to Herzog's public intervention was the growing public protests, but there was also an institutional backlash, including from the powerful security community. In mid-February, the Commanders for Israel's Security wrote to the president. The letter, signed by 400 former security officials, including former heads of Mossad and Shin Bet, warned Herzog that Israel's 'standing amongst nations, security, economy, and its essential bond with Jewish People in the diaspora' would be damaged.[19]

The former IDF chief, Dan Halutz, said that Israelis wouldn't want to serve in the military if the government's plans were advanced, warning, 'soldiers and officers who recognize that there is a dictatorship here, will not want to become mercenaries of a dictator'.[20] The explicit reference to a political move toward a dictatorship was made by others who appealed to Herzog to intervene. Nadav Argaman, a former head of Shin Bet, Israel's internal security agency, said the threat was real and should not be minimised. In an interview with an Israeli TV channel, he used what was very strong language for a longtime Israeli public servant: 'It's a regime change, legally turning Israel into a dictatorship.'[21]

The president unveiled a counter-proposal, 'The People's Framework', the aim of which was to replace the government's plans to radically overhaul the judicial system, which, he said, would give too much power to the executive branch of government. Herzog urged both sides not to destroy the country in a political battle about the powers of the judiciary, but rather to seize the opportunity for what he described as 'a formative constitutional moment'.[22]

President Herzog's plan, drafted after wide-ranging consultations across the legal, political and public spheres, offered what he believed was a real chance for a broad national agreement on reform. The proposal was tied to the principles of the Declaration of Independence and would, he argued, strengthen in law the independence and autonomy of the judicial system. This message was directed at those legislators who seemed determined to diminish the independence of the judiciary. As a lawyer and former government minister, Herzog appeared to understand what was afoot and appealed directly to the people to recognise that the risk to democratic principles was profound. 'This framework protects each and every one of you, citizens of Israel. This framework protects the Jewish and democratic State of Israel.'[23] The president's views of his country's principles may have been somewhat rose-tinted; most high office holders think only the best of their nation, but his decision to make such an impassioned plea suggested the president may have had real concerns about Israel's political direction. A different chasm was around the corner, and even if he had been able to envision its nature, he could not have imagined its scale. The president's address was uncompromising, especially from someone who fully understood the limitations of his office; Israel is, technically, a unitary democracy where the office of president is largely ceremonial. Whatever horror he foresaw ahead for Israel clearly concerned him to the point where he undertook his much-vaunted public consultation and announced his framework with a televised address that attempted to accrue to himself and to his office a leadership position for Israeli society.

The president, a 64-year-old veteran of the Knesset who served as a government minister on four occasions and led the Labor Party in opposition to Netanyahu's government for five years between 2013–18, is no political neophyte. The process he undertook and the manner in which he announced it were meant to carry weight. Prime Minister Netanyahu dismissed it out of hand, if quite diplomatically, knowing he could rely on some of his ministers to speak more critically for him. Minister of Transport Miri Regev said the president's proposal appeared to have been written by the head of the Supreme Court and 'insults the intelligence of the public. It takes a clear side, against the nation and the sovereign'.[24]

Herzog's 'People's Framework' addressed critical aspects of the relationship between Israel's branches of government. It proposed greater constitutional emphasis on the state's Basic Laws (there are fourteen that are quasi-constitutional), a revised approach to the selection of judges and a judicial review over Knesset legislation, a revision of the authority of legal advisers to the government and also the Attorney General. Israel has no written constitution nor a Bill of Rights, so it is the Basic Laws that allow the courts to determine the state's position on a wide range of fundamentals, from LGBTQ freedoms to 'ruling on issues in Israel's occupation of the Palestinian territories'.[25] This was the reason Herzog's proposals were so important, because, absent a written constitution, the emphasis on the primacy of the Basic Laws could have manacled the ambitions of Netanyahu and his cohort.

The president's plan would have instituted a rigid system for the passage of Basic Laws, giving them greater constitutional status without being subject to judicial review. In light of events since, it's noteworthy that the framework also proposed that the right to freedom of expression, opinion, protest, and assembly would be explicitly protected in Israel's Basic Laws: Human Dignity and Liberty. That was in sharp contrast with the proposed legislation of Netanyahu's government prohibiting the Supreme Court from protecting basic rights, including those particular freedoms.

Herzog offered the approach for the people to adopt; it was then for the citizens to 'own' it in order to strengthen the democratic integrity of their nation. 'Most citizens of Israel want a framework that will bring both justice and peace ... Most citizens of Israel want a broad consensus. Most citizens of Israel want to live good and secure lives.'[26] The proposal to strengthen basic rights was a challenge to Netanyahu, and it brought into relief that the government's intent was oppressive and potentially harmful to democracy and needed to be replaced by a framework for consensual reform. The president was not overstating the government's intentions to weaken the position of the Supreme Court, describing its plans as 'a disaster', 'a nightmare'.[27]

It was no great surprise that Netanyahu rejected the proposal within hours. In contrast, Yair Lapid, head of Yesh Atid, the leading opposition party, congratulated Herzog and promised to consider it with 'respect for his position, the seriousness with which it was written and the values on which it is based'.[28] The government coalition of seven parties had a majority of eight in the Knesset and

Netanyahu's Likud had thirty-two seats compared to the twenty-four of Yesh Atid, the largest party in opposition. Benny Gantz, leader of the second largest party in opposition then, National Unity, said the party accepted the president's framework 'as a basis for legislation instead of the existing dangerous legislative outline that the coalition is advancing'.[29]

While civil war may have been unlikely, the president's appeal to halt the government's assault on the separation of powers resulted in a legislature that was effectively split down the middle on the merits of what he proposed. Netanyahu's government was undeterred and, in July 2023, brought the legislation to change the balance of the Supreme Court before the Knesset. Israel's parliament may have been pretty evenly divided but Netanyahu knew he had the numbers and both his own personal legal jeopardy and the wider needs of his right-wing and religious coalition meant that, as the different stages would be voted upon, there would be only one outcome.

When the Knesset considered the first major step in the government's plan to weaken the judiciary, the bill passed by a vote of 64-0. All members of the governing coalition supported it, while all opposition members left the chamber in protest. The bill stripped the Supreme Court of the power to declare government decisions unreasonable. It represented the most significant intervention in the independence of the state's judiciary ever. However, It was only the first element in the Netanyahu government's plan for a radical overhaul of the whole judicial system, and it had split the country, with hundreds of thousands taking to the streets in protest.

◆◆◆

Some months later, in August, another group emerged to publicly question the government's plans to shift ever more power to the legislature, reducing the independence of the judiciary. As the public mood became increasingly fraught, there was another significant intervention, one focused on Jewish Americans and one that drew attention to more profound failings in the governance of the state of Israel. A group of more than 400 Israeli academics, intellectuals and other public figures wrote an open letter to the Jewish community in the United States, warning them of the real intentions behind Netanyahu's proposed judicial reforms. The letter was uncompromising in its view that Israel was on the brink of political actions that would undermine any claim it might make to being a democracy. Given the letter's content and, most especially, its source, it should have elicited global attention, but it did not. It was, in some respects, to prove prophetic; the letter warned in the most explicit terms that the purpose of the reforms being touted by the government was 'to tighten restrictions on Gaza, deprive Palestinians of equal rights both beyond the Green Line and within it, annex more land, and ethnically cleanse all territories under Israeli rule of their Palestinian population'.[30]

This was not a call by a group of radical idealists; one hundred of the signatories were academics in Israeli universities, including prominent historian Benny Morris and former Knesset Speaker Avraham Burg. The letter said there was a direct link between the government's efforts to reform the judiciary and its illegal occupation of Palestinian land; it was time for the Jewish community in the US to break its silence. The correspondents believed an increasing denial of 'equal rights' was at the heart of the government's wish to enforce such radical change, and argued that without equal rights for all, be it one state, two states, or other possibilities, equal rights for all citizens must be upheld. 'Palestinian people lack almost all basic rights, including the right to vote and protest. They face constant violence: this year alone, Israeli forces have killed over 190 Palestinians in the West Bank and Gaza and demolished over 590 structures. Settler vigilantes burn, loot and kill with impunity.'[31]

The letter, with David Feldman, the Director of the Birkbeck Institute for the Study of Antisemitism, among its signatories, said Israel was operating a 'regime of apartheid'. The tone of the letter was a great deal more forceful than even President Herzog's in his national appeal four months previously. It asked the Jewish community in America to push their representatives to work toward ending the occupation of Palestinian land and curtailing military aid to Israel; it further called for the impunity Israel enjoyed in international organisations, including the UN, to be ended. Furthermore, the signatories stressed that Israel's human rights organisations should be supported and that their work should be promoted within communities. The letter endorsed the need for the school curricula to provide an objective and honest account of Israel's historical and contemporary behaviour.

In January 2024, the Knesset's decision had to go before the Supreme Court, which ruled by an 8 to 7 vote that the new legislation was unconstitutional. The outcome represented a defeat for Netanyahu, especially as the Court also found it had the right to 'intervene in those rare and exceptional cases where the Knesset exceeds its constitutional legitimacy'.[32] By then, of course, the whole political landscape had changed and the concerns raised by the hundreds of thousands who'd taken to the streets, by the senior members of the security community and by the open letter to the Jewish community in the US had been replaced by the language of war. The language of Israel under attack and the circumstances and behaviours that had brought that about were no longer, in Israel, generally considered appropriate for public debate. The country was at war.

Prime Ministerial Jeopardy

It is difficult to know whether personal or political reasons were more compelling for Netanyahu in advocating a reform of the judicial system that aimed to reduce civil liberties and diminish the independence of the judiciary. The criminal charges of fraud, bribery and breach of trust that he faced were so serious that those who were opposed to the changes his government advocated had grounds for suspecting his motives were exclusively personal. They could argue that he was taking steps to hinder state prosecutors from bringing him to justice; by then, he had already forced through a bill that changed the circumstances in which a sitting prime minister could be declared unfit for office, restricting the reasons to physical or mental incapacity and requiring two-thirds of the cabinet to vote for such an outcome.

Investigations into his behaviour in public office had started in 2016, arising from claims that he had, not infrequently, performed official favours for wealthy businessmen in exchange for gifts that ranged from cigars to securing positive media coverage from those who controlled elements of the Israeli press. The full list of 'gifts' was more akin to the kind of allegations often made against minor-league mafia bosses than a prime minister but, by early 2018, the investigation team made a formal recommendation that he be prosecuted. The indictment was issued in November 2019 and the trial began in May 2020.

The District Court trial had been expected to last a year, but progress has been slow due to the global pandemic and problems with a number of witnesses. The trial involves three different cases, numbers 1000, 2000 and 4000, but with only one court hearing all three at once rather than sequentially, delays have slowed the prospect of an outcome. The details of the charges include taking large financial gifts from Hollywood producer Arnon Milchan, on behalf of whom, it is claimed, Netanyahu pressured Israel's Ministry of Finance to amend the tax exemption rules for returning expatriates; as well as helping Milchan advance his interests in two Israeli TV channels. The indictment also accuses him of lobbying the US government to help Milchan renew his American visa and claims that, after an intervention with then US Secretary of State John Kerry, it was extended for ten years. It has been reported that the US refused a request by Israeli investigators to interview Kerry on the matter.

In Case 2000, the charges include that he considered enacting legislation to promote the commercial interests of one newspaper in Israel over another in return for positive coverage, while Case 4000 claims that over a five-year period, the telecom mogul Shaul Elovitch and his wife gave Netanyahu's family gifts in the hope that he would not obstruct the Elovitches' business interests. Case 4000 is the most serious. Netanyahu is charged with giving Elovitch regulatory benefits in exchange for favourable coverage. The charges are detailed and are reported to include recordings that are incriminating of Netanyahu and Elovitch, who is also charged. As two former allies of the prime minister who managed the alleged criminal activities for him have turned state witnesses, the expectation in Israel has always been that this case would be the most difficult for him.

In 2008, when then Israeli Prime Minister Ehud Olmert was indicted for multiple cases of suspected corruption, Benjamin Netanyahu, who was then in the opposition, called for a general election, saying, 'a prime minister who is neck-deep in investigations has no public or moral mandate to make crucial decisions … the right thing to do is for the government to go home'.[33] At the time, Olmert was also 'neck-deep' in peace talks with the Palestinians, which, even as he announced he would not seek re-election, he committed to seeing through in the hope of establishing a new basis for peace. It was a peace that few in Israeli politics wanted then and one that is unimaginable now.

In 2018, Netanyahu addressed the nation shortly before the police released their findings, saying, 'I feel a deep obligation to continue to lead Israel in a way that will ensure our future … You know I do everything with only one thing in mind – the good of the country. Not for cigars from a friend, not for media coverage, not for anything. Only for the good of the state. Nothing has made me deviate, or will make me deviate, from this sacred mission.'[34] On the first day of his trial in May 2020, he addressed the people and again claimed that he was the victim of a conspiracy woven against him by the then Attorney General Avichai Mandelblit, State Prosecutor

Shai Nitzan and Police Commissioner Roni Alsheich. Years earlier, when he'd received the file, Mandelblit had forcefully defended the integrity of the process: 'Let me be clear – police aren't persecuting anyone, the state prosecution isn't persecuting anyone and judicial officials don't seek to govern or to persecute … The only thing we pursue is justice and the rule of law.'[35]

The conspiracy suggested by those on the prime minister's side was about his potential removal as someone determined to protect Israel's interests and his replacement with a weak, puppet prime minister who would be controlled by conspirators determined to bring the decades of conflict with the Palestinians to an end, effectively bringing about the establishment of a Palestinian state. The contrast with how both Yitzhak Rabin and Ehud Olmert had offered to resign – Rabin in April 1977 and Olmert in 2008 – was used by many critics of Netanyahu as evidence of his desperation to, at all costs, hold on to power. With echoes of the conduct of those supporting his political soulmate, Donald Trump, Netanyahu's supporters claimed the indictments were proof of a deep-state conspiracy against him.

The charges he faced were serious and if he was found guilty, it would very possibly lead to him spending time in prison, a horrifying prospect for a man known for his liking of the best things that life can offer. It was not just that he wanted to hold on to power; he liked the trappings that went with it. With Netanyahu, the desire to stay in control went beyond politics to more mundane things like the lifestyle that he was long accustomed to. It's perfectly reasonable that any political leader would want to look their best, but Netanyahu is reluctant to acknowledge the lengths to which he has gone in that regard; in 2016, he took legal action to prevent his laundry bills when in office from being made public under freedom of information. In 2020, his office denied a *Washington Post* report that he and his wife, Sara, always brought extra bags of dirty laundry on trips to the White House, even though the paper said 'officials spanning the Trump and Obama administrations'[36] had confirmed the story. In June 2019, Sara Netanyahu was convicted by a court in Jerusalem of misusing thousands of dollars of public funds on lavish meals for private use.

Netanyahu was no novice in the business of indictments; in the 1990s, he'd faced serious corruption charges, but a combination of circumstance and a reluctance on behalf of the state led to those charges being dropped by the office of the attorney general. This time, two of the three indictments were more serious and any chance that they would not be prosecuted had evaporated before his government set about its radical reform of the courts.

◆◆◆

The Hamas attack of October 2023 provided Benjamin Netanyahu and his inner circle with the perfect opportunity to put domestic political considerations aside in order to appear to focus all attention on protecting Israel from external peril. The means used to garner the West's support for that endeavour was the ever-reliable conjuring of Israel as the bulwark on which the defences against the wider threat of Iran and Islamists could be built. So, for Benjamin Netanyahu, politically, professionally and personally, the Hamas attack was a godsend. And the attack was not unexpected. In 2019, at a UN

Watch conference on the Great March of Return – a series of protests staged regularly between 2017 and 2019 on the Gaza-Israel border demanding the right of Palestinian refugees to return – a retired British colonel, Richard Kemp, who was bombastically supportive of the conduct of the IDF, had warned that Hamas' intention was 'to get through the border fence … to send people in very large numbers into Israel with the intention of getting into the Israeli communities – places like Nahal Oz which is a few hundred meters from the border – and slaughtering Israeli civilians and abducting Israeli civilians and torturing them'.[37] It was pretty much exactly what Hamas was to do four years later.

There is evidence that in the months and weeks before the attack, the Netanyahu government had been warned by Israel's own renowned security services that an attack was imminent. Egyptian intelligence, which controls who crosses its border with Gaza, said it had alerted the Israelis to the possibility of a major attack but Israel 'underestimated' the warnings.[38] It's a matter of public record that the leaders of Israel's opposition parties were briefed ahead of time, so it seems inconceivable that the government did not receive at least the same information, some of which referenced kibbutzim being targeted and the range of tactics that the intelligence services believed were being considered by Hamas.

It is generally accepted that, whatever the awareness of the government, Israel's own intelligence service, Aman, 'had strategic and tactical warning that Hamas was planning a large-scale attack, and numerous junior analysts and border sentries raised the alarm on multiple occasions. Their warnings were ignored'.[39] The only explanation offered since was that the nature of the planned attack seemed so audacious as not to be credible. This despite the fact that, even on the day before and early on the morning of 7 October, IDF 'spotters' – a team of exclusively women officers that monitors activity along the Gazan border – had warned of the suspicious movements of Hamas suspects. Senior officers were reported to have refused to listen, which the women spotters claimed 'stemmed partly from arrogance but also from male chauvinism'.[40]

Experts agreed that assumptions and biases within Aman and more widely in the Israeli administration left it prone to the attack. In late 2022, one intelligence unit had filed a report called 'Jericho Wall' that detailed how Hamas fighters would 'breach the border using paragliders, drones and rockets' and later another reported a rehearsal exercise being staged in Gaza City, one which the officer referenced as preparation 'not for a raid, but an invasion'.[41]

What state, especially one that claims to always be fully prepared for any and every 'terrorist' eventuality, would not take such intelligence seriously? What government of a state that projects itself as being under constant fear of attack would not take every precaution around such briefings so it could limit, if not prevent, the danger? What political leadership would risk the lives of hundreds of its civilians by determining that the concerns of its own intelligence services were groundless? Israel has a history when it comes to ignoring such warnings: in 1973, just such a situation occurred when it failed to recognise the threat of Egypt and Syria attacking in what was to become the Yom Kippur War.

What is certain is that the intelligence service had enough information to consider a Hamas attack of the nature that occurred to be at least possible, but either Aman had failed to push its concerns to the political masters or it had not been heeded. One intelligence report to Netanyahu said, 'The enemy perceives the summer of 2023 as a historic weak point for Israel.'[42] One year after the attack, Netanyahu's government was still refusing to launch an investigation into the intelligence failure, in contrast to the approach taken by the Israeli government after the failures in 1973.

The level of narcissism required for the government to have chosen not to act, not to prepare, would seem to make it impossible to conceive of such a wanton act of political expediency. Yet it is certain that some very real security concerns were ignored. Why would a government, aware of a possible attack, not prepare for that scenario? Just six months before the 7 October attack, Netanyahu himself seemed convinced that there was no real threat, that 'Hamas was deterred from undertaking a significant attack',[43] and while its scale could hardly have been anticipated, Israel would not have required something of such magnitude to justify a military response.

There were conflicting views of the threat but the political imperatives at the time meant a general lack of coherence prevailed. The focus was on political reform, on shifting the balance of power toward the legislature, undermining the judiciary and vesting more control over the state's affairs away from the principle of a separation of powers fundamental to its boast to be a Western democracy in the Middle East. This could be why the briefing of opposition leaders in the weeks leading up to 7 October that had referenced Hamas breaching Israel's boundaries was ignored by the political class. Given the public backlash to those planned political reforms, is it possible that a gamble was taken on a potential attack happening but, as Netanyahu had said months previously, possibly not a 'significant' one?

What seems certain is that there was relative indifference to the risk and that Israel's real focus, in autumn 2023, was on radical political reform and on the West Bank where, with ministers like Bezalel Smotrich and Itamar Ben-Gvir aggressively pushing the case for an increased rate of settlements, the Zionist ambition could be reborn.

Two

7 October 2023

The Attack

On 7 October 2023, the people of Israel suffered the horror of a violent attack by the Palestinian guerrilla army, Hamas. Institutionally, their state had also suffered the ignominy of a breach of its much-vaunted security when Hamas, with the support of some other smaller militia, crossed its borders and inflicted terror and heartbreak on civilians as well as on the IDF. The death toll was put at around 1,300, most of whom were civilians, though the security forces suffered the loss of a reported 370 lives. The attack also led to 251 people being taken hostage, again mainly civilians. It was the bloodiest attack on Israeli soil in the state's history and was immediately presented by its politicians as the most grievous assault on Jews since the Holocaust. Many Israelis questioned how their government, one that had always promoted the need to be 'armed and loaded' and had boasted about its preparedness for all eventualities, had allowed such an attack to take place.

The immediate backdrop to the attack was a heightened level of tension between Israel and Hamas, which had been administering Gaza since elections in 2006, as well as controlling it militarily. Ahead of the attack in the West Bank, during the first nine months of 2023, the number of Palestinians displaced by Israeli-backed 'settlers' was unprecedented. This was where Netanyahu's attention was focused. Far-right elements in Israel were stoking tensions over the status of the Al-Aqsa Mosque in Jerusalem, knowing its importance to the Muslim population. There had been a dispute over a border incident that resulted in the death of five Palestinians only three weeks before the 7 October attack and while Israel would deny Egyptian claims about giving them a clear warning that something very big was going to happen, according to the chairman of the US House of Representatives Foreign Relations Committee, Republican Michael McCaul, a strong supporter of Israel, repeated warnings were given to Israel. McCaul's claim was reinforced by an Egyptian intelligence official who was quoted as saying they had repeatedly warned 'an explosion of the situation is coming, and very soon, and it would be big. But they underestimated such warnings'.[44]

Regardless of the warnings, what happened on 7 October 2023 should not have come as a surprise to anyone. The Hamas attack wasn't unprovoked or without cause. The violence, killing, and terror waged on Israelis that day were as inevitable as they were distressing; the only question would have been about the precise nature and timing of the attack. The history between Israel and Palestine is poisonous and widely known but not well understood, given the weight of the Israeli lobby across most of the West. Still, the Hamas attack, while rooted in a generational abuse of their human rights, was provoked in large measure by an increasingly Zionist ambition of the state of Israel since the turn of the twenty-first century.

The attack was not just related to past disagreements or long-held feelings of historic injustice, no matter how grave. The grave injustice with which Israel had behaved was on such a scale and over such a long period that it would be easy to focus only on the preceding history. It would be a mistake for Palestinians whose forefathers had suffered at Israel's hands and the West's complicit embrace to think it was only about the past; in fact, it was much more about the here and now, not the decades-long injustice but the reality of life for Palestinians in 2023, whether in Gaza or the West Bank.

The Nakba, the Intifadas, and all the elements of the long and painful history of Palestine were and are relevant, but what Palestinians were actively dealing with, what they wanted to address and what Hamas went on the military offensive over on 7 October were the injustices of that time.

Whenever Israel protests that its genocidal campaign was a response to 7 October 2023, it's important to situate how things were on 6 October of that year.

The Day Before

On Friday, 6 October 2023…

- Israel controlled most of Palestine in complete defiance of international law.
- Israel kept the people of Gaza under a blockade. Palestinians were without electricity for an average of 13 hours a day

and more than 96 per cent of the groundwater in Gaza was considered 'unfit for human consumption'.[45] Israel controlled the supply of food and other critical supplies, meaning, before the Hamas attack, 80 per cent of the population of Gaza relied on humanitarian aid.[46]

- Israel was continuing the policy of blocking most of Gaza's population from travelling through the Erez crossing into Israel, the only means by which they could get into the West Bank and, from there, travel abroad. In 2023, the daily average of those allowed through was a little over 5 per cent of the number that could move about prior to the Palestinian uprising (Intifada) of 2000.
- Israel continued to support the illegal settlement by its people and by Jewish immigrants of large tracts of Palestine in the West Bank.
- Israel had built an extensive infrastructure in the West Bank for the exclusive use of Jews.
- In 2023, Israel had already killed around 250 Palestinians by October, including almost 50 children in its most aggressive settler push across the West Bank for almost two decades.[47]
- Israel's interest in holding its security services to account for excesses or to discipline settlers who stole land and attacked Palestinians was non-existent; the state actively supported increased levels of occupation.
- Israel's security services and its prison service were arresting increasing numbers of innocent Palestinians, including hundreds of minors, and holding them without charge in appalling conditions.

- Israel was engaged in the flagrant abuse of human rights by its own agencies. Less than 1 per cent of complaints of abuses by Israeli forces filed by Palestinians in the West Bank between 2017 and 2021[48] and 7 per cent of complaints of settler violence between 2005 and 2022 led to indictments.[49]

That was how life was for the people of Gaza, for the indigenous Palestinian people across the land occupied by Israel, on 6 October 2023. Twenty-four hours later, on 7 October, the attack by the Hamas armed militants was presented to the world as an arbitrary act of terror, one that was unprovoked and unconnected to anything else. Israel presented itself as 'broken', 'shattered', by an 'act of terrorism' so grievous it knew most of its Western friends would condemn it and would offer their full support for whatever military response it considered necessary. Yet, even in the hours after the scale of Hamas' attack was becoming clear, the Israeli government could never have anticipated just how disinterested the West's big powers would be in proportionality, never mind that anyone would have the courage to question why it was that Hamas existed at all. The idea that in the midst of the horror just inside Israel's border, anyone in Downing Street, the White House or the Elysee Palace would ask how life was for the Palestinians on 6 October and for the decades before was unlikely but the complicity of much of the West in what ensued over the following year will be a cause for shame forever.

Institutionally, the West had long ignored the horror visited upon the Palestinians by Israel, so now, as Israel contorted itself in paroxysms of anguish at the brutality of the Hamas attack, what the Palestinian people had been enduring for decades had no relevance.

The only thing that mattered was Israel's right to defend itself as though such a right – inalienable as it is – belonged only to one side of this particular political chasm. It was as if the lived experience of being a Palestinian in any part of Palestine, the daily life of those who remained from the time of the 1948 Nakba through to the youngest of their descendants, was of absolutely no relevance.

◆◆◆

On Saturday, 7 October 2023, Hamas and its allies breached not only the geographical border but the veneer of righteousness with which the state of Israel had tried to cover its Zionist ambitions. Israel caught its breath for only a few hours to see how its allies, its sponsors in the West, would respond, but it need not have paused at all. Most of the world reacted predictably; those countries that are allies of Israel, irrespective of events or circumstances, decried Hamas, profiling its attack as a blatant, unprovoked act of terrorism. Some, however, while lamenting the loss of civilian lives, did reference Israel's abuse of the Palestinians over generations.

Israel has often been put on notice of an attack, especially by its Arab neighbours. Saudi Arabia had warned Israel that its continued occupation would lead to a major event of resistance. Not long before the attacks, Jordan's King Abdullah II spoke of the risks, saying Palestinians had 'no civil rights; no freedom of mobility'.[50]

The nature of the Hamas attack provided the almost perfect basis on which to launch a full-scale military response. Its timing, in a US election year, offered even more scope for Netanyahu and his right-wing, hardline government to pursue the Zionist agenda with untrammelled ambition. The only real complication that arose was Hamas' success in taking 251 hostages, some of whom were not Israeli. With the world reacting in horror at the nature of the attack, the targeting of civilians and the, however exaggerated, details of the brutality involved, Israel's government, led by a prime minister whose tenure was threatened, knew it could respond almost as it wished. The taking of such a large number of hostages didn't deter those in charge from reacting in a manner that signalled their underlying intentions. Hours after the Hamas attack started, the Israeli air force started bombing Gaza; a week later, the IDF launched its ground operations, and by the end of the month, its full-scale invasion was underway.

Netanyahu's Moment

Netanyahu's personal needs were to become more evident over the course of the aggression in Gaza but not because of the utterly disproportionate use of force or the levels of killing and destruction that Israel conducted. The extent to which he desperately needed the conflict to continue was most manifest in how, for months on end, he undermined the considerable efforts being made by international agencies and some of his own people to reach a hostage deal with Hamas. In late November, just seven weeks after the Hamas attack, 105 hostages were released, 24 of whom were not Israelis, and there was optimism that more would follow; but it was not the portent of more substantive progress that some hoped at that time.

Securing a full deal on hostages would involve some form of ceasefire, which could bring political uncertainty for Netanyahu, so instead of using the momentum of that first exchange, he took an approach that undermined any prospect of a complete hostage deal being realised. There was personal political capital in prolonging the destruction of Gaza; a return of the hostages that were still alive would make it more difficult to justify continuing the bombardment, and without a war to prosecute, the possibility of Netanyahu being able to stay in power was fraught.

Gaza presented a 'cause'. It enabled his political ambition by facilitating his need to survive and it facilitated the ambition of the most right-wing elements in his government to extinguish the rights of Palestinians forever. Netanyahu, among the most soulless and pragmatic of politicians, would allow that objective to play out exactly as it did during the year that followed. It was well into 2024, as the destruction of Gaza continued unabated, with the numbers of deaths – mainly civilians – reaching barely believable though, according to reputable international observers, likely under-recorded levels, that elements in the Israeli media started to focus on the apparent lack of interest Netanyahu had in finding a solution to the hostage problem within the overall crisis.

In July 2024, the respected Israeli daily newspaper *Haaretz* documented how, ever since the conclusion of the November deal, the prime minister had continually thwarted the Israeli negotiating team in its efforts to find a solution. Sources in the report, some of whom were directly involved in the process, referenced how he and people on his behalf had leaked confidential information, fomented hardline opposition to any deal, undermined Israel's negotiators and sought to subvert any progress they reported.

As early as January 2024, Qatar, which had a formal mediation role, identified Netanyahu as a problem in the efforts to reach a positive outcome. Its spokesman, Dr Majed Al Ansari, said remarks he'd made were 'irresponsible and destructive to the efforts to save innocent lives, but are not surprising'.[51] This view was reflected in commentary closer to home as, throughout 2024, families of those with relatives still being held became suspicious of their prime minister's motives.

In the West, the inherent prejudice against Muslims – and therefore against Arabs – made it easy for the Israeli government to always suggest that the failure to progress matters was down to the other side, to those representing Hamas. In much of the Western world, even in countries where they are a significant percentage of the population, Muslims are often portrayed as representing a threat to a Christian-centric societal model. Large tracts of Western media, some unconsciously, portray Muslims as a threat to a peaceful society. In the United States, the problem is acute. University of Georgia research showed that criminal attacks committed by Muslims received 357 per cent more US media coverage than those committed by non-Muslims.[52] This is despite the fact that, statistically, white and right-wing acts of violence or 'terror' in the US represent almost twice the figures as the number of attacks by Muslim extremists. What was especially interesting was the hugely disproportionate coverage of 'terror' attacks in the US when the person responsible was both a Muslim and not a US citizen. Research established that Muslims accounted for 12.5 per cent of such incidents over a ten-year period but it accounted for a massively greater level of coverage. This underlying racist attitude fuels the Western narrative of exceptionalism that is most clearly evident in the behaviour of the United States; but, more widely, the idea that Muslims (and Arabs) are a threat to the West keeps simmering beneath the surface.

After 7 October 2023, Benjamin Netanyahu played to this prejudice, knowing how easy it was to bring to the boil that sense of righteousness, the particular proprietorial sense that many in the Western world feel about civilisation. It is why his invocation of Amalek – the Hebrew name for an enemy nation of the Israelites – in the aftermath of the Hamas attack was so toxic. While it was to become part of the ICJ (International Court of Justice) case against him, Netanyahu used it in a speech and in a letter to soldiers involved in the ground invasion, knowing its power to mobilise Israeli public opinion in support of a completely disproportionate response. It worked.

An opinion poll conducted by the International Program in Conflict Resolution and Mediation at Tel Aviv University in late October 2023 showed that Israeli Jews were either unaware or unconcerned by the scale of the suffering being endured by Gazans. Just less than 2 per cent of the respondents said they believed the IDF was using too much firepower and nearly 58 per cent said they were using too little.[53]

The government's tight control of the media meant that the Israeli public was not getting the same level of insight as was evident internationally but domestic public opinion hardly changed. In a poll conducted by the Israel Democracy Institute in December 2023, Israeli Jews were asked to what degree Israel should take into account the suffering of the civilian population in Gaza when planning the continuation of the campaign there. Over 80 per cent responded with 'to a very small extent' or 'to a fairly small extent'.[54]

Even in late January 2024, when getting aid through to Gaza was first considered urgent, another poll found that 72 per cent of Israelis said, 'the entry of humanitarian aid into the Gaza Strip must be stopped until the Israeli prisoners are released'.[55] In May 2024, the Pew Research Center published results of a survey it had conducted in March that found 39 per cent of Israelis believed Israel's military response to Hamas in Gaza had been 'about right', while 34 per cent thought it had 'not gone far enough' and, even allowing for increasing awareness of the scale of the devastation being suffered by Palestinians, only 19 per cent thought it had 'gone too far'.[56]

Domestically, Netanyahu and his supporters continued the campaign for a rebalancing of the powers between the branches of government, even as those opposed to it argued that the full suite of legislative changes threatened the independence of the judiciary. At any time, moves to give the government more control over the appointment of judges and allow it to remove independent legal advisors from different government ministries would have engendered considerable criticism, but what made them even more contentious was that these moves came as Israel was engaged in the campaign in Gaza and its prime minister faced criminal indictments.

The more sinister, more troubling interpretation of what really lay behind the government of Israel's ambition to reel in the independence of the judiciary went beyond how it might undermine a successful conviction of its prime minister. While Netanyahu cared chiefly about his indictment, the greater risk with the planned judicial overhaul was that it would help those at the centre of the country's political elite, those of true Zionist persuasion, realise the ambition of its founder, Theodor Hertzl, that Jews would take over all of Palestine in the formation of the state of Israel.

The reform would also increase, as Netanyahu's own minister of defence, Yoav Gallant, had warned, the risk of a completely divided and therefore exposed Israel. Writing in the autumn of 2024, Eran Yashiv, professor of economics at Tel Aviv University, expressed bewilderment at the West's failure to see what was happening. 'They also don't understand that if Netanyahu remains on the scene, there will be no more free elections in Israel. In the "best" case, there will be restrictions on certain populations, such as the Arabs, while in the "worse" case, elections will be postponed under the pretext of a perpetual state of emergency.'[57]

The founder of modern Zionism, Theodor Herzl, regarded as the 'spiritual father of the Jewish state',[58] had no compunction in setting out how the Jewish people should go about taking the entire land of Palestine for themselves. While he had previously expressed an openness to annexing other places for Israel's homeland, in time, he came to believe there was no other course but to found the Zionist state in Palestine. 'We shall try to spirit the penniless population across the border by procuring employment for it in the transit countries, while denying it employment in our country … Both the process of expropriation and the removal of the poor must be carried out discreetly and circumspectly.'[59]

One hundred and thirty years on, this 'ideal' is echoed in the approach of Benjamin Netanyahu, Bezalel Smotrich, Itamar Ben-Gvir and others in Israel's coalition government, although it appears the need for the kind of 'discretion' or 'circumspection' that Herzl had counselled for is gone. The uber confidence with which many Israeli leaders today approach the business of cleansing Palestine of Palestinians is more trenchant and considerably less cautious. 7 October presented them with a perhaps unique opportunity to push for the ultimate outcome: the expansion of Israel's borders and the removal of the Palestinians once and for all.

THREE

Another Nakba

One Word, One Meaning

In stark contrast to what the last quarter of 2023 and 2024 represented for the political elite in Israel, for all Palestinians, it's a period that's best described as another catastrophe, another Nakba. The use of the word Nakba is particular to the Palestinian experience, to the genocidal intent they experienced at the hands of Zionists in 1948. That period was, for them, nothing short of a 'catastrophe', a time when, with the establishment of the state of Israel, they lost their homeland. That the rights of the Palestinians were set aside by the world, especially by the Western powers that chose to promote Israel's rights exclusively, added to the anguish. The Israeli narrative around what happened then is a work of fiction; to believe it would mean believing that, until their 'return' from exile, the land of Palestine was empty – that they were a people without a land, and the land was without a people.

For Palestinians, other setbacks were to follow: in a further act of colonialism in 1967, Israel 'conquered' and occupied the

West Bank, Gaza, Sinai and much of the Syrian Golan Heights. The brutality of its expansionism was undeterred by different UN resolutions that have had no material impact on Israel's avarice for land that is not theirs to take and has involved further trauma for the people whose land it is. Still, for Palestinians, the Nakba refers only to what happened in 1948. The Palestinian scholar, Raja Shehadeh, explains why:

> The Arabic word for defeat is 'hazimeh' … A defeat usually means that a society or a nation suffers a setback, has its values called into question … This is what happened in 1945 to Germany and Japan after the Second World War … both soon developed into powerful nations. But the case of Palestine is different. What happened in Palestine was the utter dissolution of the nation. The people were forced out of their homeland and dispersed … Yet they were not classified within the UN Refugee Convention as refugees. That would have implied that Palestine was their country, to which they should be allowed to return. On both counts that was not how the Israeli authorities saw it. With the creation of Israel, Palestine ceased to exist … To describe what befell the Palestinian nation in 1948 a word stronger than defeat with a different connotation was needed … the word that came to be used was nakba, because what had happened was no less than a total catastrophe.[60]

Since October 2023, Israel has conducted a campaign of terror against the people of Palestine aimed at their obliteration. It is another Nakba or catastrophe. The main difference to 1948 is that, this time, for the Palestinians of Gaza, the West Bank and the camps scattered across the region, there has been no surprise at the determination with which Israel has pursued its wish to remove them. The Palestinian diaspora living all over the world, which is larger in number than the Palestinians who are, or were, surviving in historical Palestine, can only watch from a distance as, in 2024, Israel tries to fulfil the full extent of its genocidal intent that was thwarted in 1948 and 1967.

On 8 June 2024, there was extensive coverage in Western media of the successful 'extraction' by the IDF of four Israeli hostages. It was newsworthy that these innocent civilians were found and released from captivity within the Nuseirat refugee camp in Gaza. It was absolutely correct that Western media focused on the joy of their family and friends on their safe return to Tel Aviv but what was also marked was the absence of attention given to the wider story. The military operation had, even according to an IDF spokesman, taken place 'in the heart of a residential neighbourhood in Nuseirat where Hamas had kept the hostages in two separate apartment blocks'.[61] The resulting loss of civilian life was estimated at over 250 Palestinians, including 64 children and 57 women. It was widely reported that US intelligence had assisted with the operation, which involved an overnight bombardment of Nuseirat that targeted housing, the local marketplace and the Al-Awda Mosque. The camp was a Hamas stronghold, which, along with the known presence of civilian hostages taken on 7 October 2023, gave some military legitimacy for the attack; but the scale of the offensive, and the brutality of IDF troops on the ground further undermined any idea that Israel was conducting its war on Gaza professionally. The 'extraction' of four Israelis had come at a hugely disproportionate cost of human life and yet most Western media coverage of the story betrayed a disturbing indifference to that truth.

What Israel has done since October 2023 and how it has been sponsored by many Western powers in its genocidal campaign against the Palestinian people is barely believable given that, less than a century ago, European Jews suffered unimaginable trauma as the Nazis attempted to exterminate them. It is the horror of the Holocaust that explains, in part, why so much Western media and large parts of its institutional framework have refused to hold Israel to account for its conduct; the historically recent Holocaust means that somehow Israel must be treated differently from any other nation. There are other strategic considerations, too, but a large part of the latitude granted Israel is borne of a fear that to criticise it represents some dormant Western-wide dislike of the Jewish people.

Israel has long used that horrific spectre as a means of reducing criticism of its actions, deliberately deploying the tactic of smearing those who would dare to criticise it as being antisemitic, as Jew-hating. Some of the world's brightest Jewish minds (philosophers, academics, writers, politicians) have for decades attempted to counter the patently false narrative promoted by the Israeli establishment and its Western allies, which is that ever to challenge Israel or its political direction, ever to question its behaviour, is to be an antisemite.

With all its immense military strength, its endless supply by Western allies of new weaponry and its phenomenal success in lobbying for political support in legislatures across Europe and the USA, Israel's most powerful tool is the whispered branding of those organisations, movements, or individuals that refuse to support them as 'antisemitic'. With the support of large parts of the Western media, it is often a difficult charge to contest. In autumn 2024, 237 British journalists claimed the UK's major broadcasters had abandoned journalistic principles in covering Gaza 'when it comes to holding Israel to account for its actions'.[62]

Despite the bias in reporting within the West, the overwhelming evidence is that Israel's intent is to rid the land of Palestinians. What transpired over the last quarter of 2023 and all of 2024, but also in its history, particularly since the Six-Day War, makes this clear. It is equally clear that there are those in the West for whom Israel has a special entitlement to extend its current boundaries, to displace whoever is in its way and to face no consequences for its active colonialism. There are those with influence and considerable support who would rather set history to one side, deny the rights of the indigenous population and allow Israel to control all of Palestine. It is racist; it is a political position that considers Israel's behaviour since October 2023 to have been a justifiable response to a violent attack on its soil by terrorists and one that sees Israel as the first line of the West's defence against Islamism. This is a hopelessly corrupted perspective overladen with injustice and one that carries the certainty of grave regional instability for decades.

When it comes to racism, intolerance and the destruction of other people, Hamas, too, has 'form'. Its original charter, the Covenant of the Islamic Resistance Movement, agreed in 1988, established it as the Muslim Brotherhood in Palestine fighting the oppressors with 'the struggle' defined as being against the Jews in order to establish an Islamic state in all of former mandatory Palestine.[63] It went further. Just as with the Zionists, the realisation of such an independent outcome was not enough; the charter also called for the obliteration of Israel. It sought the destruction of Israel and the annihilation of the Jewish people. This original charter, which represented an incitement to genocide, was amended in 2017, removing openly antisemitic language and clarifying that Hamas' struggle is against Zionists and not Jews. Arguably, the most critical change was that, under its new charter, Hamas accepted the idea of a Palestinian state that would only be based in territories occupied by Israel since the Six-Day War of 1967 (Gaza, the West Bank and East Jerusalem).[64] It remains the case that the more recent (2017) Hamas charter does not explicitly accept the existence of the state of Israel, something that is regularly referenced in the West – correctly so. What is absent, though, is a similar focus on the obduracy and entitlement of Israel's counterclaims, even though they are contrary to international law. Likud, the party Benjamin Netanyahu has led for the past twenty years (he had also led it between 1993 and 1999), used the slogan 'between the Sea and the Jordan there will only be Israeli sovereignty'[65] on its foundation in the 1970s, something Netanyahu repeated at the UN General Assembly just days before the Hamas attack of 7 October 2023. The slogan was the mantra by which Israel went about its business since the end of the Six-Day War. When some of Palestine's strongest advocates – including many Jewish scholars – call for an acceptance of the 1967 borders, they do so knowing, even though it is a concession for the Palestinians, what the cost would be to the Israeli occupiers. For Israel, it would mean losing the progress made toward establishing its sovereignty over Palestine. Since the Six-Day War, 100,000 hectares of land in the West Bank have been seized by more than 700,000 'settlers', at least 50,000 dwellings and structures demolished, and millions of Palestinians displaced.

Over much of its existence, Hamas' approach has been racist and violent. To acknowledge this is not to provide cause for Israel's conduct. Israel – we are told repeatedly – is a democratic sovereign state, so it should be reasonable to have different expectations of it to those of what it, and others, choose to dismiss as a 'terrorist group'. But we have known for many years that we can have no such expectations; though there isn't a true democracy anywhere that would want Israel as its doppelganger.

This point goes to the heart of the paucity of Israel's belief that 7 October gave it reason to engage in the barbarism it unleashed on the people of Palestine. It did not. But beyond that, to really understand the emergence of Hamas and the support it received from Gazans requires an acceptance that when, for decades, a people are denied their land, oppressed, subject to arrest and imprisonment without charge, tortured, find that their food and water supply is being deliberately destroyed and that they are denied freedom of movement, it is inevitable that some will gravitate to armed resistance and that the majority will support them in that effort. Hamas is a guerrilla army determined to overthrow those oppressing its people, breaking international law in the process. It did – as all such forces do – choose a point and moment of weakness of the oppressor to attack it at source. It dared to cross into Israeli territory and unleashed a devastatingly successful attack. It was an institutional humiliation for a state that considered itself impregnable to such a military intervention.

The counter-narrative to the one that simplistically describes Hamas as bad, as a bunch of terrorists, and Israel as a respected state within the college of global democracies has to begin with seeing Hamas not as a terrorist group but as the military wing of an established movement, one that is politically engaged but believes Israel's decades of conduct resulted in a situation where the movement's objectives cannot be realised without resorting to military action. This may be unpalatable to many – the emergence of guerrilla armies often is – but the evidence of the past almost sixty years would suggest that Hamas is correct in that assessment. There are those who will never accept such a representation and want to believe the reductive profiling of groups like Hamas and Hezbollah as 'terrorists'. This is the consensus in the West, one that attempts to diminish the group's importance and the necessary role it plays in thwarting the real ambition of Zionists that could otherwise see Israel control part of Lebanon and all of Palestine. This Israeli government likes to suggest that Hamas has no mandate and is a terrorist faction that, through its actions, has destroyed the livelihoods of the Gazans it claims to represent.

The claim gets traction; it should not. Hamas has led the government of Israeli-occupied Gaza since 2007, sometimes in an aggressive manner, but criticism of its conduct by Israel feels rich given how it has maintained a blockade on Gaza since 2007 and controls the movements of all its people. The appalling living conditions for Gazans, as well as Palestinians in the West Bank, were as evident on 6 October 2023 as they were for many years before the Hamas attack; and while there were civilian protests against Hamas over the years, Gazans suffered daily oppression at Israel's hands long before any Hamas fighter set foot on Israeli soil on 7 October 2023. This point is critical; any serious analysis of events demands an acceptance that Hamas had due cause on which to base its fight and, for all the inevitable violence that resulted, that legitimacy came from the people of Gaza. Unsurprisingly, as the relentless destruction and killing waged by Israel devastated life in Gaza, the numbers supporting the Hamas attack declined over 2024. Yet, a survey by PCPSR (Palestinian Center for Policy Survey and Research) just weeks before the first anniversary of the Hamas attack showed that, while there had been a drop, 54 per cent of respondents still believed the decision of Hamas to launch the attack had been 'correct'. In the same poll, 78 per cent said at least one of their family members had been killed (57 per cent) or injured by the Israeli offensive. 93 per cent of those interviewed said that they'd had to move more than once over the period of Israel's bombardment. When respondents – in Gaza and the West Bank – were asked who they would want to govern them at the end of Israel's campaign, 58 per cent said Hamas, compared to 20 per cent for the Palestinian Authority. Israel's increasing aggression in the West Bank meant that 73 per cent of respondents there said they supported Hamas, even though it is Fatah that administers the area. Support for Palestinian Authority President Mahmoud Abbas was at only 18 per cent.[66]

◆◆◆

Israel is a coloniser; aided by the West, it has been allowed not just to establish itself as a sovereign state with internationally accepted boundaries, but one that has methodically extended its territory in contravention of multiple UN resolutions and international law. It has been allowed to do so by the passivity of the West and by the active support of some of its most powerful nations. The failure of countless attempts at international diplomacy to find anything approaching a credible and equitable solution is the fault of Israel and those who could have forced its hand but chose not to do so. There was never a point in history where the two sides were given equal weight; the West always felt indebted to Israel, compromised by the past, dazzled by the value of its shekel and convinced by its constant entreaty that it alone in the Middle East could be trusted to guard against the perceived threat of Islam.

By any historical measure, given the status conferred on it by the people whom it represents, Hamas had the right to attack its enemy and to strike at the heart of the Israeli state, which, for decades, has been engaged in the suppression of rights of the Palestinian people as it illegally occupied their land. It is important to recognise it as an enemy of scale – a guerrilla-armed force of an estimated 30,000. There may be an argument about whether Hamas, as a political administrator in Gaza, also functions as a guerrilla army ruling Gaza, but there can be none over whether or not it has a mandate. Over recent decades, Hamas has been the main point of confrontation for Israel, the political and armed force that manifested Palestinian resistance to Israel's refusal to accept even the borders that followed the Six-Day War. While Gaza was its domain, Hamas had come to most powerfully represent the wider Palestinian resolve across the region. It was Hamas that reflected the determination of Palestinians across Gaza, the West Bank and East Jerusalem to say to the state of Israel, 'so far but no further'; it was also Hamas that built a powerbase to protect the rights of the indigenous population.

Israel's behaviour since it was founded in 1948 has been taken from the colonialist textbook; its conduct is what gives rise to the emergence of groups that want to harm its interests. Guerrilla armies do not engage in standard warfare and must strike at any points of weakness that those they are fighting may leave exposed. 7 October was one such rare occasion when, due to a variety of reasons, Israel had left itself open to an attack. Hamas carried out its plan expertly; the damage to Israel was a great deal more profound than the numbers of those killed or taken hostage due to the strategy of its implementation. The date of the attack, just a day after the fiftieth anniversary of the start of the Yom Kippur War and during the Jewish holiday of Simchat Torah that celebrates the conclusion of the annual period of public Torah readings, its location in Sderot and Be'eri on the southern Israel border with Gaza, its scale, and its success contributed to the unified national response in Israel.

While the attack was the work of a guerrilla army, it was logical and not unreasonable that the government of Israel described it as an act of terrorism. The word terrorism, a noun, refers to 'the calculated use of violence to create a general climate of fear in a population and thereby to bring about a particular political objective'.[67] The motivation was clearly political and that particular action did strike fear into the population of Israel – that was a large part of the intention. So even if the attack was a direct result of decades of oppression, even if it could be justified on that account, and irrespective of whether or not the attack was led by trained guerrilla soldiers, it could be argued that the state of Israel was within its rights to profile it as an act of terrorism. The same claim can, as justifiably, be made about the nature of Israel's response. What it unleashed within hours of that attack and pursued throughout 2024 represented a more sustained campaign of terror on civilians than any previously in modern history. Again, referring back to the quoted definition, the intent was to create 'a general climate of fear ... and to bring about a particular political objective'. That this was and, throughout 2024, remained the objective of Israel cannot be questioned. The sheer scale of what Israel has done in Gaza, the massive escalation of its theft of land in the West Bank in parallel with that annihilation and how it widened the theatre of its operations in the late summer of 2024 to Lebanon also meets the definition of state terrorism. The unwritten code, in the West at least, to always profile the violent actions of groups striving to undermine the rule of law as 'terrorism' but never to label those charged with upholding it as 'terrorists' has rarely been so dramatically exposed as Israel's conduct in 2023–24 (and beyond).

In the early months after the attack, there was a weariness in much of the West, a hangover to the regularity with which the different sides were in dispute and, occasionally, at 'war'. The words Gaza and conflict or Israel and Palestine had come to represent a familiar chord of dissension and strife that, to an extent, dulled any sense of alarm at whatever latest incident had occurred. There was also an impenetrability to much of the history, a sense that somehow, without intense study, it was difficult to unravel the rights and wrongs of the conflict, while expressing a pro-Palestine opinion carried the ever-present threat of being labelled an antisemite. The events of 2023 and 2024 were different, as the utter destruction of a tiny strip of land that was home to millions of Palestinians awakened much of Western public opinion as never before, especially among younger generations.

One of the world's most authoritative voices on the Middle East, Robert Fisk, in his last book, *Night of Power*, published posthumously in 2023, wrote about the more recent conflicts: 'The first major "war" lasted for three weeks in the winter of 2008/9 costing the lives of more than 1,300 Palestinians and thirteen Israelis; in the second in November 2014, over 2,000 Palestinians and seventy-two Israelis were killed.'[68] Those statistics, the length of the conflicts and, even more so, the disproportion of numbers killed, put into some perspective what has happened since the attack by Hamas in October 2023. It is important to recognise, as Fisk always did, that while Israel is the aggressor and must carry most of the blame for the huge toll on Palestinian lives and living conditions, Hamas, too, has guilt. Few commentators who want Israel held to account are ignorant of excesses elsewhere. Writing of the conflict of 2008–09, Fisk said, 'Hamas' deliberate rocketing of Sderot and, later, of other Israeli cities and towns, also stains the Palestinian guerrilla force and their allies with crimes against humanity, however pitiful their weapons and despite the grotesque disproportion of Israel's response.'[69] Proportionality, such a commonly used term in most considered analyses of the 2023–24 Nakba, has always been part of what Fisk and other true Middle East experts used to gauge the balance of fault. Interestingly, what Fisk termed a 'grotesquely disproportionate' Israeli response fifteen years ago killed 2,000 Palestinian civilians. While the attack of 7 October would certainly have 'stained' Hamas more than its attacks of 2008–09, it's fair to conclude that even Robert Fisk would have struggled with the scale of the campaign Israel launched in 2023.

Genocidal Intent

In September 2023, just two weeks before the Hamas attack, Israel's prime minister, Benjamin Netanyahu, addressed the United Nations in New York. It was his old stomping ground, having previously served as Israel's ambassador to the UN in the 1980s. Over the years, as prime minister, he had more than once used it to whip up support for whatever political machination Israel was engaged in or planning. This time, just ahead of the Hamas attack that had, by then, already been signalled by Egypt, Netanyahu took one of his most standard approaches, one he'd used frequently at the UN. The prime minister held up a map of the region – one that bore little relationship to reality – and proceeded to give a Netanyahu tutorial on how, with Palestine not shown on his graphic, the Middle East could become a 'corridor of economic prosperity'.[70]

The idea wasn't his but its interpretation was. The 'corridor' would, he said, start in Asia, go 'through the UAE, Saudi Arabia, Jordan, Israel, to Europe'.[71] There was no mention of Palestine's involvement or how the economic corridor could possibly get from Jordan to Europe if it were not to be through Palestine, which did not appear anywhere on his map. Still, his declaration that this development would involve monumental change and would come to be seen as a 'pivotal point' in the history of the Middle East elicited applause. Then, with the map put aside, he told his audience of UN ambassadors and officials that with these developments, a path to peace with Palestine could be achieved. The message was clear: the Palestinians were not going to be involved in the corridor of prosperity but it could, nonetheless, bring them peace. Even that came with a precondition, one that applied exclusively to the Palestinians. The prime minister of Israel, without a hint of irony, wanted to be clear that the Palestinians would need to be truthful: 'there's a caveat, it has to be said here, forcefully, peace can only be achieved if it is based on truth, it cannot be based on lies'.[72]

There followed a diatribe on the ills of war and his own experience as a soldier, preluding a personal statement that he yearned for peace, with a clear message that to gain it, Palestinians would have to recognise the state of Israel as defined by Israel. Netanyahu's map meant peace for Palestinians would involve recognising that the state of Israel would cover the territory from the river Jordan to the Mediterranean. It seemed that peace 'based on truth, not lies' did not apply to Israel; nothing had changed since the first Zionists talked of a homeland that ran from the river to the sea – precisely the original land of Palestine. Netanyahu was portraying himself as a man of peace who wanted the United Nations to understand that not just peace but prosperity was available to everyone, perhaps even the Palestinians, if only, that is, they would recognise Israel's right to all of their homeland.

What the world has witnessed in Gaza since late 2023 is the destruction of a people by repeated war crimes over months on end. That we bore live witness to this was unprecedented and our institutional acceptance of it alarming. We know that Benjamin Netanyahu, as the architect and leader of the campaign, boasted that Gaza would be reduced to rubble.[73] Gaza isn't large – 365 sq. kilometres – but it is one of the more densely populated territories in the world, so reducing it to rubble cannot be done without knowingly killing many tens of thousands. It cannot be done without knowingly destroying villages, towns, cities in a wanton, relentless and unforgiving military campaign that means those whom you do not manage to kill have no choice but to flee. Their flight is that of a dazed bird, disoriented, flying from here to there within Gaza as Israel instructs them to move north, then south, then north again, before there's nowhere to go but to leave. That might be the objective; what else do you do as a civilian fleeing war if staying means you will, most likely, die? But what if you cannot leave? You are trapped in a warzone, so you constantly take flight from wherever the danger is most acute.

It's not just the government of Israel that pursued this knowingly; those sponsoring the onslaught were every bit as aware of the facts yet provided the Israelis with the arms and money to execute their plan, knowing full well the intent was to destroy Gaza and, in the process, its people. Israel's objective cannot be realised without destroying the surroundings and, most critically, the capacity of the Palestinians to support themselves and feed themselves. Even one of Netanyahu's less compliant cabinet ministers, Yoav Gallant, struck continually aggressive chords in his resolve as the man leading the military campaign, describing Palestinians as 'human animals' and warning that Gaza would never return to what it was: 'We will eliminate everything.'[74]

Critical to Israel's long-term mission is to make everywhere Palestinians live uninhabitable so that if they survive, they leave with nothing to return to. It's why refusing to acknowledge Palestinians as refugees is important; for Israel, the denial of that status is critical as it is inherent in international law that all refugees have a 'right to return'. It helps Israel realise that objective if, as part of its campaign of terror, it destroys the sense of place that could provide motivation for those who leave to even want to return. An important part of a truly genocidal campaign is to remove evidence of a civilisation.

In February 2024, Israeli Minister of Settlement and National Missions Orit Strook, who herself lives in an illegal settlement in the occupied West Bank, echoed words used by Golda Meir, Israel's prime minister in the 1970s when she said, 'every cultured person in the world knows that this land is ours, for the Israeli people, and for us only … and for that reason, there will never be a Palestinian land in the land of Israel. Because there is no such thing as Palestinian people'.[75] Netanyahu's minister of finance, Bezalel Smotrich, and minister of foreign affairs, Israel Katz, expressed similarly chilling remarks that, in some respects, did the Palestinians some service. When Smotrich suggested that it might 'be justified and moral'[76] to deliberately starve the people of Gaza, governments in the West called for Prime Minister Netanyahu to distance his government from the remarks. He did not, and nor did the governments of Germany, Britain and the US make any changes to their provision of arms to Israel, though each of them had, to varying degrees, been vocal in their criticism.

These members of Israel's thirty-seventh government represent how certain Israel is of the rightness of its position. With the multiple declarations of members of the Knesset as stark as these and the commentary of many opposition figures, there can be no denying what Israel intends for Palestine, no denying that its people in Gaza are the subject of a genocidal campaign. The relentlessness of Nakba II should have helped awaken some of Israel's most important and influential backers to the fundamentalism at the heart of its politics, its mission and its genocidal intent. In some respects, the ludicrous nature of the state of Israel's belief – the notion of the Jews being a people without a land and Palestine a land without a people – makes it harder to defeat, but what events since 7 October 2023 have shown is that the West's major powers are not, in any event, disposed to giving Tel Aviv a history lesson.

The brazenness with which Israel has conducted its campaign to seize land to which it has no right, killing people and destroying infrastructure in the process, all without sanction, is itself shocking. That its genocidal campaign is being sponsored by the United States, Britain, Germany, France and others means it is unprecedented in modern history. The strategy that Benjamin Netanyahu and his government have implemented is in line with what Theodor Herzl, had suggested. At the dawn of the twentieth century, he believed it would be difficult to achieve colonisation by anything other than stealth, such would be the reaction from the rest of the world to openly annexing a land that belonged to others.

We like to imagine ourselves as considerably more civilised now than over a century ago, yet the very originator of the Zionist plan to annex Palestine understood its inherent wickedness so well that, advocating it as the nineteenth century ended, he urged caution in how it would be pursued! What would Herzl make of Israel in 2024 and its audaciousness? What would he make of how – under the cover of an attack on its soil by those determined to protect Palestinian interests – Israel has not just been able to do what he proposed but to do it in full public glare of every country in the world? What would he make of countries among the wealthiest and most powerful in the world actively supporting and funding the genocide against the people of Palestine so that the Zionist dream could be realised? What would he make of the country that likes to see itself as the 'leader of the free world', the United States, supplying the arms and ammunition necessary to further the Zionist ambition?

Four

Oppression

Detention

To fully understand the extent to which Israel is and has been, for decades, committed to policies of oppression against the Palestinian people, it's essential to understand that it not only steals their land but also terrorises them in the process. One of Israel's most successful means of doing this is the abuse of its own laws and those of the international community in the incarceration of Palestinians and in how they are managed when in detention. This has long been a critical foundation stone of its policy of oppression. We know the scale on account of international and Israeli NGOs that have, for decades, provided independent accounts.

B'Tselem, one of Israel's most respected human rights organisations, addresses how oppression has been a constant trauma for Palestinians for many years. It warns that its impact should never be underestimated.

> The current situation, horrifying as it is, cannot be fully understood without examining the key role of this project in the social and political oppression of the Palestinian collective over the years. The prison system is one of the most violent and oppressive state mechanisms that the Israeli regime uses to uphold Jewish supremacy between the Jordan River and the Mediterranean Sea. Israel has incarcerated hundreds of thousands of Palestinians from all walks of life over decades, as a way of undermining and unravelling the social and political fabric of the Palestinian population.[77]

Just before 7 October 2023, the overall number of Palestinians incarcerated by Israel and classified as 'security prisoners' was just over 5,000, about 1,300 of whom were being held without trial as, to use the official term, 'administrative detainees'. By July 2024, the number of Palestinians held almost doubled to just under 10,000, and nearly half of them (6,162)[78] were being held without trial, with no effort ever being made to present them with the nature of the allegations made against them. It follows that they had no access to any basis for or any means to a defence.

The roll call of detainees included physicians, academics, lawyers, students and political leaders, and the circumstances of the arrests varied greatly. According to the NGOs, the list also included children, with frightening numbers – 'at least 880 detained by the IDF'[79] in the year before the Hamas attack. The only thing all the detainees had in common was being Palestinian, which was sufficient grounds for them to be 'lifted' and taken into detention, where most were handcuffed and blindfolded, often for a considerable period of time. There is compelling evidence of the widespread use of physical, mental and sexual abuse of minors in detention. The international NGO Save the Children found that 86 per cent of detained Palestinian children were beaten, 69 per cent were strip-searched, 68 per cent were denied healthcare and 60 per cent spent time in solitary confinement. Its country director in occupied Palestine, Jason Lee, said that 'Palestinian children are the only ones in the world to experience systematic prosecution in military courts'.[80] The children surveyed were from across the West Bank and had been detained from anywhere between one and eighteen months, most of them on charges of stone-throwing, which can carry a twenty-year prison sentence. Over the years, Western media has regularly focused attention on just such policies in Russia, China and Iran but, in marked contrast, has largely ignored the use of unlawful imprisonment in Israel as a means of striking fear into the people of Palestine.

In the social climate that prevails in Israel, the default treatment of Palestinians in Gaza, the West Bank or East Jerusalem is generally abusive, certainly in how they are deprived of their basic human rights. It is unsurprising, therefore, that there is no public interest in how those who are detained are treated by the prison system. Without the work of exceptional Israeli human rights NGOs like HaMoked, B'Tselem and others, the international community would not know just how distorted Israel's system of justice has become. However, despite their regular detailed reporting of appalling abuse, little or no attention is paid to their testimony on the institutionalised mistreatment of the Palestinian people. The work of these agencies has established beyond any doubt that the management of the courts, the use of the prison system and the extensive use of detention without trial is a carefully managed part of government policy in Israel.

Detention without trial and the impossibility of detainees getting access to information have been part of Israeli policy for decades. The conditions in which detainees are held have never been of the standard demanded by the UN but, however poorly Palestinian prisoners were treated before 7 October 2023, their treatment since has disimproved markedly. Israel is so certain of the rightness of its Zionist mission that the state has made no effort to hide how it uses the prison system as part of its strategy. This was acknowledged by Minister of National Security Itamar Ben-Gvir, who, even before the infamous Hamas attack, had tasked the IPS (Israel Prison Service) with making changes so it could play its part in the destruction of the Palestinian cause.

Ben-Gvir issued a series of directives that included limiting family visits, cancelling the option of early release, reducing the time allocated for showers and cancelling prisoners' option of preparing their own food. More serious moves came after the Hamas attack, with severe restrictions on time spent outside their cells and with senior members of the IPS outdoing each other in the claims they made about how the detainees would be treated. Negev Prison Commander Brigadier General Yosef Knipes boasted, 'Most of the day they are actually inside the cells, 23 out of 24 hours ... The cells are currently crowded because we are in an emergency situation. They have a mattress and a blanket, with the minimum conditions required by law.'[81]

While there's overwhelming evidence that, for decades, Israel has been deliberately using the prison system as a means of oppressing the Palestinians, the number of civilians exposed to this militaristic approach to the detention and treatment of detainees has increased dramatically since the Hamas attack. One of HaMoked's legal team told me that, however malevolent the state's policy toward detainees, including those held without charge, it got considerably worse after 7 October 2023. 'The food given to them dropped dramatically. We started to visit them two months into the war and we saw that everybody had lost between 15 to 25 kilos [2.4 to 4 stone]. People in these prisons were starving, there were harrowing stories so we filed principled petitions.'[82]

The NGOs working in the area say the government used starvation policies and deprived inmates of the most basic hygiene protocols. Their evidence included that people hadn't been allowed to shower for weeks or to see daylight for months. Their personal belongings had been taken, so all they had were the clothes they wore. They were held in cells that were only built for six or seven detainees but were holding a dozen or even up to fifteen. In 2017, Israel's High Court had ruled that the cells were too small for even half a dozen detainees but the policy in 2024 was to fill them with at least twice that number and more if possible. Many of those detained were held without charge. As one senior leading advocate put it, 'Israel routinely uses administrative detention and has, over the years, placed thousands of Palestinians behind bars for periods ranging from several months to several years, without charging them, without telling them what they are accused of, and without disclosing the alleged evidence to them or to their lawyers.'[83]

The 'Troubles'

Over the course of the Northern Ireland 'troubles' in the 1970s and 1980s, Paddy McGrory was an esteemed Belfast solicitor who acted for many in the city who were arrested and charged with public order offences, as well as those who had been wrongfully arrested and detained. Most but not all were on the Catholic or nationalist side. McGory was one of the most erudite critics of a system of law and order that was, at its heart, discriminatory. In one interview I did with him, he likened the society he lived in to a piece of fabric that was being stretched, often as much by the actions of those governing it as those fighting against the establishment.

One of the early titans of human rights advocacy in modern Ireland, McGrory regularly warned the British government and its agencies of its absolute obligation to stay within the law in the exercise of its powers. There could be no exceptions in his book. Even if those elements that the government wanted to constrain chose to act criminally, this could not grant any government of a democratic nation the right to do likewise, and he was contemptuous of those who argued otherwise.

The 'war' that prevailed in Northern Ireland in the 1970s and much of the 1980s involved paramilitary groups on both sides of a sectarian divide, all of which operated outside the law. They were widely described as 'terrorists'. The institutions of the state that were tasked with maintaining law and order and protecting the interests of the state (meaning Britain) were, in contrast, supposed to do their job within the laws of the land. Throughout the 'troubles', however, that isn't always what happened; often, various agencies of the British state operated outside the rule of law.

In 2024, a group of international human rights experts working with former police officers reported that during the conflict, the British government had operated a 'systematic' practice of impunity to protect the army and police from sanction. The report found that what it termed 'state actors' had killed at least 374 people over the thirty years involved, the vast majority of whom were civilians. 'Over 70 per cent of those killed were indisputably unarmed at the time of their deaths and the victims were disproportionately Catholic [nationalist].'[84]

The report also highlighted that prosecutorial decisions were compromised: 'the Attorney General, an official of the British government from 1972 onwards, controlled the DPP's [Public Prosecutor] decision-making and the DPP didn't provide reasons for decisions not to prosecute.'[85]

In a democracy, the government needs moral authority and nothing puts that more at risk than for it to abandon the rule of law; neither can it sanction the execution on sight of terrorist suspects. With such a rogue approach, real authority is lost. With such tactics, the credibility of a state lecturing on the evils of paramilitarism or violence is eroded. When a state behaves with impunity, it is further fuelling the sense of injustice of those – no matter the threat they may pose – whose rights it chooses to ignore. Throughout Northern Ireland's 'troubles', there were independent voices who warned the authorities that state breaches of human rights forced more citizens to take up arms.

Even decades after its withdrawal from most of the island of Ireland and the establishment of the Republic as an independent state, the British government's behaviour toward those stranded by the act of partition was discriminatory. This included but went beyond socio-economic factors at one level and its capacity to order the killing of those it considered 'undesirable' on the other. In times of conflict, the approach of any state toward those it arrests or imprisons should be lawful and the application of the law should be even-handed.

In 1971, the Westminster government introduced a policy of internment or imprisonment without trial. It was to last four years, over which time about 2,000 people were detained, all but seven of whom were nationalists. The European Commission on Human Rights found, in 1976, that the interrogation techniques used on some detainees amounted to torture, a finding that was supported by a review conducted by the UK's Supreme Court almost 50 years later. The same report by the human rights body that looked at government-sponsored killings concurred with the findings of the European Commission on British government-sanctioned torture of detainees in Northern Ireland. It found that the abuse and torture of prisoners, including waterboarding, electric shock treatment, mock execution, sexual abuse and sexual degradation, was widespread and that it involved the British Army, the RUC (Royal Ulster Constabulary, Northern Ireland's police force) and prison officers. It found that 'Torture mostly took place within formal detention contexts, but also occurred outside of it, for example, when people were subjected to ad hoc beatings during everyday street and house searches.'[86]

In 1980s Northern Ireland, one of the British government's most vocal critics, who somehow also managed to be detested by the Provisional IRA, Fr Denis Faul, a priest from Dungannon, argued that its policy on prisoners was self-defeating. He contended that every single person who was held without trial represented a threat to law and order in the community because the impact of their detention on family or friends was so ruinous. Faul always said that by rounding up 'suspects', the state only deepened the pool of those who felt discriminated against.

Project Incarceration

Those at the human rights or social support coalface in Israel argue the same point. A UN report released in July 2023, never challenged by Israel, suggests that, from the time of the Six-Day War in 1967 to the summer before the Hamas attack, Israel has incarcerated more than 800,000 Palestinian men and women and children from the West Bank (including East Jerusalem) and the Gaza Strip.[87] It is a staggering number; the sheer scale of Israel's approach means there can hardly be a Palestinian family unaffected by its determination to pervert international law into a tool of oppression. According to Francesca Albanese, the UN Special Rapporteur on Palestine, there are a number of particularly notable features to how it goes about this policy: 'I found that widespread systematic arbitrary deprivation of liberty of Palestinians is a structural component of the regime that Israel has imposed upon them.'[88]

In Israel, administrative detention is used to hold a person without trial, without having committed an offence, on the grounds that the state believes he or she plans to break the law in the future. The arrest is made by order of the regional military commander based on evidence not revealed to the detainee. This leaves detainees helpless, facing unknown allegations with absolutely no way to disprove them, not knowing when they will be released, and all without being charged, tried or convicted.

In the West Bank, individuals can be held in this way for up to six months at a time if the local commander has 'reasonable grounds' to do so for security reasons. All hearings are held in private; the judges can set aside ordinary evidence law and accept evidence in the absence of the detainee or their counsel or without ever disclosing it to them. On the local IDF commander's own judgement alone, the detention can be extended for a further six months. In fact, there's no time limit on such extensions, so without even a civil court appearance, Israel, which is the occupying force, can hold Palestinians in jail for years. And it does. Under international law, Israel is meant to use administrative detention only in exceptional circumstances but it has chosen to use it routinely. It is documented by HaMoked and B'Tselem that it has imprisoned thousands of Palestinians, some under 18 years old, for periods ranging from a few months to several years without ever charging them.

Israel uses the measure to detain Palestinians for their political opinions and for engaging in non-violent political activity. The secrecy around any evidence that might exist means that counsel for detainees, normally provided by NGOs, cannot review any information being used to put their clients in prison. Sometimes, ridiculous as it is, the military judges argue that, given the confidentiality involved, they can offer legal guidance to defend the detainee. In practice, judges don't ask to see the evidence or examine the information on which the administrative detention is being sought.

The power to incarcerate people who have not been convicted or even charged with anything for lengthy periods of time, based on secret 'evidence' that the defendant cannot challenge, is an extreme abuse of human rights. Israel uses it continuously and extensively, routinely holding hundreds of Palestinians at any given moment.

Another important but under-reported feature of Israel's management of detainees is that it routinely 'disappears' prisoners, something B'Tselem reported as happening on a new scale after 7 October 2023. It said the practice of enforced disappearance has been used for some time but that, over 2024, 'The testimonies we collected describe how prisoners seem to vanish off the face of the earth once taken into custody. Their families have no way of finding out where they are or what state of health they are in … Exposed to the harrowing accounts of released prisoners, the families live in constant uncertainty and fear for their loved ones.'[89]

HaMoked put it this way: 'Israel has been holding hundreds of Gazans in incommunicado detention in unknown locations, under conditions that are far from meeting the obligatory minimal standards, with no access to attorneys or the ICRC [Red Cross] and without informing their families of their whereabouts.'[90] HaMoked argued that under all relevant laws, Israel was obliged to communicate without delay the whereabouts of detainees, including those suspected of taking part in hostilities. Israel does not do so. HaMoked has handled more than 100,000 cases since its foundation in 1988 and considers the current approach to prisoners as representative of the most hardline Israeli policy on Palestine in at least a generation. HaMoked's legal team believes there's more than the numbers being detained and the conditions of their detention to be concerned about.

> Put the actual war crimes in Gaza aside to look just at things Israel has done to Palestinian detainees in Israeli prisons and it's almost impossible to be surprised by its actions. We know from those who've been in prison for many years – from the West Bank or Jerusalem – the conditions they were held in were awful but now it's completely inhumane and this has been done openly as a bargaining tool vis a vis Hamas. That's illegal; there's no legal basis for such an action by the state so it's brazenly breaking the law by holding people in these kinds of conditions.[91]

In common with all the Israeli NGOs involved in monitoring the treatment of prisoners, B'Tselem believes abuse and torture are a routine part of prison policy and at levels that suggest an institutionalised management of Palestinians that is about their humiliation. The dehumanising of Palestinian prisoners begins the moment they're detained. The approach is consistent:

> All are deemed 'human animals' and 'terrorists' simply because they are behind bars, whether their detention was justified or

> arbitrary, lawful or not. This is how abuse, degradation, and the violation of rights become permissible. Arbitrary and extreme violence, withholding medical care from the injured or ill, denying food and water in overcrowded cells – none of these would have been possible if the guards saw Palestinians as human.[92]

Once Israel began its offensive in Gaza, the situation in the prison system escalated. Israel's obligations as a member of the United Nations should mean that it does not break the rule of law, yet it has been doing so for years. It behaves as those it would describe as 'terrorists' might do. It has lost any sense of principle attached to being the state – it had long ago stretched the fabric that Belfast lawyer Paddy McGrory used to speak of in the 1980s to a point where it had to rip.

The NGOs knew that the depraved violence of the IDF in its pursuit of Hamas across Gaza would be matched by the IPS; that, as the prisons and detention centres became ever more crowded, those in charge would become more brutal in their treatment of all those detained. The earliest moves to the courts had proven so unsuccessful it was impossible to see how the government's largely unlawful use of detention could be curbed.

Sourcing legal remedy has always been difficult for Palestinians and those Israelis who choose to fight their corner. The events of 7 October made it considerably more so, but after the ICC (International Criminal Court) announced its intention to issue arrest warrants and the ICJ (International Court of Justice) heard the proceedings taken by South Africa, there was some change. Until then, HaMoked, B'Tselem and others were, fingers in the legal dike, monitoring the state's behaviour, making petitions on an ongoing basis in an attempt to hold Israel's justice system to some form of account. They got little traction.

While the mistreatment and abuse of prisoners in the standard civilian prison system breached human rights principles, what those actively looking to help Palestinian detainees knew was that conditions in the military installations where thousands were detained after 7 October were even worse. The largest facility, Sde Teiman, located in the Negev Desert not far from Gaza, gained notoriety for its mistreatment of detainees. The testimony of countless Palestinians was of a particularly brutal regimen that earned it the name of Israel's Guantanamo. It was like an open-air cage where hundreds of detainees were held handcuffed and blindfolded all day, and they had to sit on their knees on the floor for most of the day. They were not allowed to move or to speak and could lie down only at night. They were given very little food and were subjected to all forms of corporal punishment for even minor breaches of the rules.

The Association for Civil Rights in Israel worked with Physicians for Human Rights, the Public Committee Against Torture and HaMoked to petition the High Court to have Sde Teiman closed. The group's submission said, 'more than 1,000 detainees are held in cage-like facilities ... in painful positions and such severe handcuffing that [it] led to amputation.'[93] The account of HaMoked's legal team was no less distressing: 'The situation had deteriorated rapidly; both the general physical situation of the detainees and the medical treatment people got there was utterly inhumane, including detainees having limbs amputated but with no anaesthesia. People were held there for weeks without knowing why. They were blindfolded, handcuffed with their legs tied and they were given diapers.'[94] The law was changed so detainees could be held for 90 days instead of 14 before any judicial review would be required and detainees could be held for 120 days without being allowed to see a lawyer. The intent was clear: the authorities had four months when they could do as they wished with the Palestinians they detained without there being any legal recourse open to the prisoners, many of whom are being held without charge.

Arguably, death, even at the levels of Gaza over the course of Nakba II, is not what most represents the decades-long horror of Israel's behaviour toward Palestinians. The fatality statistics are shocking, but what also needs to be factored into a real attempt to understand Israel's intent is how it treats those Palestinians it doesn't kill. For generations, most Palestinians in the occupied territories have experienced 'exclusion, discrimination, belittlement, obstruction, destruction of their fields and houses, subjection to the violence and arbitrariness of authority. To use an evocative word, they are disposable.'[95]

This is meant literally. Palestinians can either be killed by Israel with practically zero risk of any consequences for their killers or they can be arrested, at any time, without any reason, imprisoned without charge, detained for indeterminate lengths of time and subjected to starvation and violence while in state custody. Nakba II, the freedom granted to Israel to conduct its genocide, has to be seen in this context, with the question of how the decades-long independent and verifiable reporting of Israel's wilful oppression of the indigenous people whose land it occupies has escaped censure. When, for decades, much of the investigating has been done by reputable Israeli NGOs, some of whom receive grants from Western governments, it is even more concerning that the institutional West has paid little or no attention to their reports.

With Gaza as the backdrop, the government closed off the prisons from the outside world. There were no family visits, phone calls were banned and lawyers were denied visiting rights. Information was hard to access but, as some detainees were released, the NGOs heard harrowing stories of abuse. HaMoked hastily filed a petition encompassing the whole range of issues from food and hygiene to torture. The High Court dismissed it summarily on a technical point that it could consider only individual petitions in the name of individual detainees. The lawyers countered that, as all access was denied, it would be impossible to file petitions on that basis but the Court said in a time of war the state cannot be expected to uphold the rules as it would in normal times. Legally, this is groundless. For this to apply, the state must declare a state of emergency, but even then there would be basic minimum standards that apply, like the provision of food, the maintenance of standards of hygiene and other basic rights even of those taken captive in the course of war.

HaMoked's legal team quickly understood the scale of the challenge. 'As human rights defenders in Israel, we couldn't sit back and do nothing when those detained, most without charge, were starving and suffering other forms of abuse. The outcome was as expected, within hours of our filing, the court dismissed it without even a hearing.' The Israeli justice system paid little or no attention to the appeal of human rights. The petitions were just dismissed out of hand by the court. 'It was as good an insight as any into how Israel wages war – completely outside the international ecosystem. With prisoners, as with many other considerations, Israel is unconcerned about how its actions are perceived internationally.'[96]

While NGOs pursued legal challenges, the conditions of detention remained unchanged. No ICRC (Red Cross) visits were allowed even though HaMoked petitioned the court because it is an international legal obligation to give the ICRC access to detainees. The government stopped them completely so that there could be no international supervision of what goes on in Israeli prisons as it continued to use the taking of hostages by Hamas as just cause for it to manage things according to its own determination.

In the summer of 2024, evidence emerged that the IPS had used outbreaks of scabies in some prisons (Naqab, Megiddo, Nafha and Rimon) as a means by which they could harm the prisoner population. Prisoner rights organisations claimed that as well as the torture and abuse of prisoners, the prison service had effectively 'weaponised' the scabies outbreak to impose even more hardship on the detainees. 'The IPS has actually turned the disease into a tool of torture and abuse by deliberately committing medical crimes against them, by depriving them of treatment, and not taking any of the necessary measures as a prison authority to prevent the spread of the disease.'[97] They made a further, even more serious charge: 'the deliberate transfer of those infected with contagious diseases from one section to another, which contributed to the increase in the number of infections', noting that children were among the infected prisoners.[98]

What the NGOs describe as the 'incarceration project' is one of the most toxic elements in the pursuit of the Zionist mission by the government of Benjamin Netanyahu and the state of Israel. In the summer of 2024, B'Tselem said the detainee witness statements it had gathered were 'a window into a much broader reality of an increased dehumanising of Palestinians in Israeli discourse, a radically right-wing government, a weak judicial system swept up in public sentiment and a minister [Itamar Ben-Gvir] who takes pride in violating human rights; this system has become an instrument for the widespread, systematic and arbitrary oppression of Palestinians through torture'.[99]

Destruction of All Life

Well before Israel's October 2023 onslaught began, Gaza had experienced its constant aggression involving similar tactics to those its 'settlers' have continued to use under the supervision of its security services in the West Bank. The military-occupied buffer zone, which consists of heavily fortified fencing with heavy surveillance by the IDF, has long been used by Israel as a basis to restrict farming in Gaza. The occupying army had for years insisted that nothing above one metre high could be cultivated, arguing that as those Palestinian lands neighboured the buffer zone, any cover above that level could represent a security threat. Whenever Palestinians ignored those warnings, they would find army bulldozers on their land, destroying their crops and orchards. Around half of Gaza is agricultural land, which, left to its farmers to cultivate, would be more than sufficient to feed and nourish the whole population. Strangling that capacity has been part of Israel's strategy since before it launched its offensive in Gaza in October 2023; it has scaled it up markedly since.

Much of it has been destroyed now but, then, close to 50 per cent of the total land area of Gaza – about 150 sq. kilometres – was productive agricultural land, either fields of crops or fruit or olive orchards. Gaza also had 8,000 greenhouse structures, so this agricultural base was the primary source of food security and income for the long-besieged population. This was always anathema to the Zionists, and for decades, the Israeli army had been using the blockade and its presence along the border to limit Gaza's agricultural capacity. But bulldozing wasn't all it did to affect that outcome. Using satellites and other technology, London-based Forensic Architecture, which brands Israel's destruction of Gazans' agricultural lands as 'ecocide', has closely monitored its activities for years. It reported that since 2014, 'Palestinian farmers along Gaza's perimeter have seen their crops sprayed by airborne herbicides and regularly bulldozed, and have themselves faced sniper fire by the Israeli occupation forces.'[100]

While Israel's determination to make life as hard as possible for the people of Gaza is long established, with the ground invasion in late October 2023, any pretence of needing local farmers to keep their crops below a metre in height for security reasons was moot. Since the full-scale invasion, huge tracts of farmland and orchards were destroyed, with much of the land levelled and then fortified for the building of military bases and roads. Together, these earthworks transformed a previously productive Palestinian agricultural area into a colonial military outpost. In spring 2024, Forensic Architecture reported that, among the more than 2,000 agriculture sites that the IDF had destroyed since the previous October, almost half of Gaza's greenhouses, a critically important source of food for its people, had been demolished. The approach was strategic. The military precision with which farms and greenhouses were targeted within the overall military campaign revealed the extent to which Israel had planned the exercise. The rollout of such a sophisticated approach to disabling local food producers to cater for a population already under a decades-long siege confirms Forensic Architecture's assessment of ecocide:

> We used remote sensing to measure the scale of agricultural destruction resulting from this military activity, by comparing the region's 'vegetation index' (an indicator of the health and robustness of plant life, measured by analysing satellite imagery) before and after the invasion. This comparison reveals that as of March 2024, of the agricultural areas targeted, approximately 40 per cent of the land in Gaza previously used for food production has been destroyed.[101]

The impact of Israel's devastating military assault on Gaza's potential to feed itself may already have been clearly emerging by early spring 2024, but by mid-summer, the situation was catastrophic. One part of the IDF's campaign was to augment the direct killing of Palestinians with the planned destruction of its agricultural capacity and the gradual restriction – citing military considerations – of aid. Forensic Architecture monitored this and reported that, by the end of June 2024, 'about 83 per cent of all plant life in Gaza had been destroyed … more than 104 sq. kilometres of the 150 were destroyed as were 45 per cent (3,700) of its productive greenhouses.'[102] More than 47 per cent of Gaza's groundwater wells and 65 per cent of water tanks were destroyed or damaged over the same period and not one of the region's wastewater treatment facilities in Gaza remained intact or functional. Forensic Architecture reported that its month-by-month analysis, which included detailed consideration of satellite imagery, eyewitness accounts and even material made public by the IDF, showed 'a correlation between the destruction of agricultural lands and infrastructure, and the Israeli military's ground position. The destruction of agricultural lands and infrastructure was cumulative and repeated. Agriculture and water resources were destroyed using military equipment and weapons'.[103]

Israel's policy of denial extended to this destructive element of its campaign as it did most others. Just as throughout the bombardment of Gaza, it had insisted there was no risk of starvation of the local people, it accused others of being responsible for any harm to their welfare. All reputable international sources, including agencies working on the ground in Gaza, were clear that Israel was directly responsible for preventing aid from getting through to the Gazans. In March 2024, the FRC (Famine Review Committee) reported, 'The Famine threshold for acute food insecurity has already been far exceeded … The FRC expects the upward trend in non-trauma mortality to accelerate and for all Famine thresholds to be passed imminently.'[104]

In April 2024, the global NGO Oxfam reported that, since the start of the year, people in Gaza were surviving on an average of 245 calories a day. This was a direct result of the level of bombing, which forced people to be on the move, but it was also an early signal of just how destructive the Israeli military campaign was to the agricultural infrastructure that had, with whatever degree of fragility, allowed the Palestinians to feed themselves. The average calorific intake was 11 per cent of the recommended minimum requirement set by the Israeli government itself for Gaza. In its 2007 report, *Food Consumption in the Gaza Strip: Red Lines*, made public by the Israeli rights group Gisha in 2012, the Israeli government determined, considering factors like age and gender, that an average of 2,279 calories per person per day was required for survival.[105]

In a predictably self-serving address to the United Nations General Assembly in late September 2024, where a year before he'd prophesied his new economic corridor through the Middle East, Benjamin Netanyahu accused Hamas of being responsible for the food shortages in Gaza. In his standard manner of addressing world leaders, as though he was giving a tutorial to a group of postgraduate students, he admonished Hamas, claiming that it had taken the food sent by aid agencies to feed themselves before selling what remains to the people of Gaza 'at exorbitant prices'.[106] It was a lie; the reason famine conditions prevailed was twofold: Israel had purposefully disabled Gaza's agricultural capacity and it had very deliberately limited the supply of the emergency aid necessary on that account.

In May 2024, USAID (US Agency for International Development) said in a memo to Secretary of State Anthony Blinken that the looming famine in Gaza was the result of Israel's 'arbitrary denial, restriction, and impediments of U.S. humanitarian assistance'.[107] The seventeen-page memorandum came from the head of USAID, Samantha Power, a respected former international diplomat who would have understood the full political implications of what was being brought to the attention of the US administration. In Barack

Obama's second term in the White House, Power had spent four years as US ambassador to the United Nations so she was wise to Israel. The damming memorandum delivered to Biden was sent in her name.

With overwhelming independent evidence to the contrary, Israel has long promoted the narrative that it transformed a barren Palestine into some kind of agrarian miracle. Power and her experienced colleagues in the aid and development business knew otherwise but, shamefully, there were others in the West who chose to promulgate that Israeli myth, among them EU Commission President Ursula von der Leyen.

In words addressed to Israeli President Herzog on the state's seventy-fifth anniversary, von der Leyen said, 'Seventy-five years ago, a dream was realised with Israel's Independence Day … You [Israel] have literally made the desert bloom',[108] and she referenced how she had seen this miracle with her own eyes. It was, firstly, a mirage of her imagination, but, secondly, her remarks were racist in tone, displaying a capacity for blind indifference to Israel's colonising of Palestine – an approach this leading European politician would repeat months later when she travelled to Israel days after the Hamas attack. It could be that von der Leyen's pro-Israel imagination wasn't playing tricks on her but that her speechwriters had copied words used by US Vice President Kamala Harris years previously. In 2017, then a Democratic senator for California, Harris had addressed an AIPAC (American Israel Public Affairs Committee) meeting as follows: 'having grown up in the Bay Area, I fondly remember those Jewish national fund boxes that we would use to collect donations to plant trees for Israel. Years later when I visited Israel for the first time, I saw the fruits of that effort and the Israeli ingenuity that has truly made a desert bloom'.[109]

In choosing to misrepresent history by implying that the Palestinians had shown neither the resolve nor the capacity to cultivate their homeland, these political leaders were lazily racist and politically motivated. They used their public status to present a fictitious framework of Arab indolence, one where, before the Nakba, Palestine was a desert wasteland that only fulfilled its agrarian potential through the work of Zionist settlers. The records prove otherwise; in 1948 about 3 million dunams or c. 330 sq. kilometres of Palestine was cultivated land. Seventy-seven years on, the vast majority of the cultivated land (150 sq. kilometres) left after decades of Israeli aggression was still cultivated by the indigenous Palestinians, as it had been since well before the 1948 Nakba.

The complete misrepresentation of the facts around land and the interest and capacity of the Palestinians to cultivate it and to provide for themselves is another strand of a generally uninformed, predetermined narrative of those in the West who could, if they wished, put the brakes on Israel's colonial intent. There was a point at which any interest in protecting the rights of the Palestinians became lost in an all-consuming need to serve Israel, a belief in its assumed status as the West's only friend in the region and a misplaced guilt over the calamity that had been allowed to befall Europe's Jews many decades ago. Whatever about the arming and funding of its massively destructive military campaign on the innocent people of Gaza, it can be argued that the wilful strategy of destroying the Palestinians' capacity to feed themselves while also allowing only very limited food aid into the region represented the point at which Israel's legislators lost any and all sense of a moral compass. The objective of its government's campaign was to destroy Palestine and to kill its people, if not with bombs and bullets, then by starvation. The West's main political powers knew about and did nothing to stop the unfolding Nakba; instead, the usual suspects were aligned in their support of a state that was committed to the eradication of another.

It didn't seem to matter how many millions marched on Europe's streets or how many students campaigned on campuses across the West. Those with the power to do something about the untrammelled ambition of Israel's Zionist government refused to budge. What's telling about the idea of shared complicity in this genocide is that no nation can credibly argue that it was unaware of how it was being conducted. No leader of any country that supplied Israel with arms can make that claim. The complicity of the United States is particularly marked; in fact, in its case, the word 'sponsorship' of the genocide is a more accurate one.

FIVE

Erasing The Past

Leaving No Trace

At its most extreme, the Zionist intent would see Palestine erased from history. In the literal sense, in today's world, any such aspiration is impossible but the ambition is no less egregious; not only does Israel want to expand its territory to absorb the lands it has occupied illegally for at least fifty-seven years, it wants to destroy the cultural heritage of the land's rightful owners. Israel believes wiping out the heritage of the people of Palestine would make the idea of 'return' – something it has always refused to countenance for Palestinians – less compelling.

It is estimated that over the course of its military annihilation of Gaza and killing of as many of its people as possible, Israel had, in the first year of its onslaught, destroyed about 70 per cent of its cultural heritage sites, including a Bronze Age settlement, a Christian monastery of about 300 AD and Pasha's Palace, which was built in the thirteenth century. Cultural heritage includes sites, historical monuments, artefacts, archives, works of literature or art and museums, and anything that provides a link to past peoples. Mosques appeared to come in for special treatment. In October 2024, it was reported that over 800 out of the 1,200 mosques in Gaza had been destroyed,[110] among them the Great Omari Mosque, originally the Cathedral of Saint John the Baptist, which was built by the Crusaders in the twelfth century and converted into a mosque by Salah al-Din in 1187. The Ibn Uthman Mosque, which is 2,000 sq. metres in size, was targeted by Israel as it had been in previous conflicts, it 'was considered a centre of confrontations with the Israeli occupation forces during the First Intifada'.[111]

Salah Al-Houdalieh, secretary general of the International Council on Monuments and Sites – Palestine and of the Society for Palestinian Archaeology, believes, 'The losses unfolding now in Palestine … are unprecedented in scale and speed. International agreements enshrine the protection of cultural heritage and recognize its destruction as a war crime. But agencies responsible for policing these agreements have been conspicuously and inexcusably absent from the current conflict.'[112]

Across the occupied territories, Israel has wrested control of planning, zoning, and the mapping and surveying of archaeological sites from the Palestinians and placed this under the control of the IDF. Generally, the army commanders liaise with the Israel Antiquities Authority about sites as well as any Palestinian antiquities that are uncovered, thereby placing the indigenous population's cultural heritage in the hands of those whose task is the protection of Israel's cultural interests.

When tens, if not hundreds, of thousands of Palestinian civilians are being killed by Israel, paying attention to the damage or even appropriation of features of Palestine's cultural heritage may seem relatively unimportant. However, Israel's great interest in attacking this part of Palestinian life is an important part of its intent: to remove Palestine from existence. In order to advance the Zionist plan and to progress the objective of settler-colonialism, erasing Palestinian culture is critical.

The Nazis wanted to do the same with the Jews; to somehow try and downplay the importance of their intent of ethnic cleansing, they wanted to remove evidence of anything that could suggest a whole people had been removed. The language of generations of Zionists, arrogantly repeated ad nauseam by members of Netanyahu's cabal, portrays the Palestinians as somehow lesser beings, suggesting, somehow, that when it comes to cultural heritage, there is 'nothing to see here'.

The ICC believes that crimes that affect cultural heritage can 'touch upon the very notion of what it means to be human, sometimes eroding entire swaths of human history, ingenuity, and artistic creation'.[113] UNESCO describes cultural heritage as 'the product and witness of the different traditions and of the spiritual achievements of the past and thus … an essential element in the personality of the [different] peoples of the world'.[114]

This cultural heritage is protected by a range of internationally established legal instruments. The Hague Regulations prohibit the destruction, pillage and theft of cultural property, while the Fourth Geneva Convention prescribes the respect and safeguarding of cultural objects of war. It is also covered in Article 22 of the Universal

Declaration of Human Rights, which says that every person is entitled to 'social and cultural rights indispensable for his dignity and the free development of his personality'.[115]

Israel, which ratified the relevant 1954 and 1972 UNESCO conventions for the protection of cultural property in wartime, refused to ratify the 1970 UNESCO Convention on the Means of Prohibiting and Preventing the Illicit Import, Export and Transfer of Ownership of Cultural Property in time of conflict. Ever since Israel's occupation of Palestine began in 1967, its policy of settler-colonialism has included a considered and consistent policy of wiping out the heritage of the indigenous Palestinian people. It has targeted cultural sites, removed artefacts, undertaken illegal archaeological works, all with the intent of carefully building a narrative about the territory that would fit with the Zionist mission rather than a representation of its Palestinian or Arab history and culture.

UN Resolution 242, passed in 1967, states that the Palestinian territories were under occupation and that, as the occupying power, Israel, was responsible for the safeguarding and protection of the cultural and natural heritage of the Palestinian people. Over the course of its 2023–24 assault on Gaza and the continued targeting of communities in the West Bank, Israel has done the opposite. Worse still, the history of its actions since the end of the war in 1967 means this behaviour represents nothing more than a serious increase in its ambition to destroy Palestine's cultural heritage systematically.

London agency Forensic Architecture pays particular attention to the heritage of the Gaza coastline, which it believes is of major archaeological significance. The known treasures of the area include a Roman-era city wall with adjacent streets and buildings; ramparts from the Iron Age; ruins of houses dating from the Achaemenid period (539–332 BC); an emporium and a villa from the Greco-Roman City of Anthedon during the Hellenistic and Roman periods (334–25 AD) and a church and cemetery from Byzantine times (324–638 AD).

Apart from the natural hazards all such sites face, Israel's blockade of Gaza has made it impossible for archaeologists to do their work for more than a decade and its bombing campaigns have done considerable damage to the sites. This had started well before the current conflict. Over a ten-day military assault on Gaza in May 2021, a number of special antiquities and cultural heritage sites were damaged among the wider list of 124 places of worship. One market and thirty-seven tourism facilities were either completely destroyed or sustained serious damage. There is a pattern to this utter disregard of its responsibility, as the 2021 offensive replicated a longer military offensive in July and August 2014 when 61 mosques were completely destroyed and a further 120 suffered serious damage.

Despite its history of deliberate destruction, its determination to annul Palestine's cultural heritage reached new levels over the course of 2023 and 2024. In line with its unprecedented savagery in killing Palestinians, its destruction of the rich cultural heritage of those people was at levels not previously seen. The Palestinian Ministry of Culture reported that, as the first anniversary of Israel's offensive on Gaza approached, well over 200 archaeological sites and buildings of cultural and historical significance in the Gaza Strip had been damaged or destroyed. This included the seventh-century Grand Mosque in Gaza City, with its minaret that dominated the skyline, and the 1,600-year-old Church of St Porphyrius, which was bombed, killing at least nineteen people inside. The IDF bombed and bulldozed part of an archaeological site at what was Gaza's port from 800 BC to 1100 AD. Archaeological objects from the site were among some 4,000 artefacts in a warehouse that Israeli soldiers seized.

This approach and its sustained callous determination should not surprise us. What else should we expect of Israel once we appreciate that completing its settler-colonialism task demands the replacement of one heritage (those they want rid of) by another (their own)? Their new narrative must support the lie that the land wasn't stolen, that it had always belonged to them. Israel has committed considerable thought and resources to this important dimension of its replacement strategy.

The state of Israel is fully aware of the cultural importance of these lands and that its campaigns represent a violation of international statutes but it continues to do whatever is necessary to try to erase the history of those territories it has illegally occupied for more than half a century. Al-Haq, a respected Palestinian NGO based in Ramallah, argues it this way: 'through its policies and practices, Israel is targeting cultural heritage sites with the sole objective to entrench its cultural hegemony over Palestinian lands, without the Palestinian people'.[116]

In the West Bank, Israel's aggressive settlement expansion, construction of bypass roads for the exclusive use of Israelis and its establishment of boundaries with walls and fences all represent a concerted effort to do more than control the lives and behaviours of the people. Over time, these actions help to erase the social history and traditions of the indigenous people. Al-Haq suggests that Israel's approach is considered:

> Israel sets up two distinct standards tailored upon their added value to the entrenchment of the Zionist narrative over Palestinian lands. On one hand, cultural heritage sites that serve this narrative and are directly controllable by the Israeli Occupying Forces are appropriated and exploited to reinforce this narrative. On the other hand, cultural heritage sites that conflict with this narrative are, straightforwardly or not, targeted, damaged and destroyed, in an attempt to erase them from memory.[117]

It is important to acknowledge that Palestinian archaeologists confirm that some of the sites have also been plundered by Palestinians, civilians who have taken advantage of the chaos all around them to gain some kind of profit from the prevailing lawlessness. Whether it's an act of theft by a Palestinian or the far more common plunder of the occupying force, antiquities lost to the black market diminish, to whatever small degree, Palestine's cultural heritage. For the occupier, for Israel, it is not about money; the more valuable prize is to turn the cultural part of Palestine's history to dust.

One of the most sobering examples of Israel's determination to destroy even the idea that there ever was a Palestinian, an Arab, a Muslim culture in this land is its desecration of the Mamilla (Ma'man Allah) Cemetery in Jerusalem. It was used until 1927 and is considered by the people to be the most important cemetery in Palestine. In *Forgotten*, Raja Shehadeh and Penny Johnson write,

> Criss-crossed by paths that pedestrians used as shortcuts, the cemetery was divided into various plots, some of which had

> been tarmacked and used as a parking area. Other sections had residential homes built on them ... while elsewhere construction was ongoing for some housing projects. It was altogether a sorry site [*sic*], indicating a total lack of respect and redolent of an absolute absence of tolerance for the Muslim dead.[118]

So it is that even sacred burial sites that go back millennia only have real estate value to the state that occupies the land of Palestine. This targeting of Palestinian cultural heritage impacts the fundamentals of their identity, the very reason why the ICC gives it such importance, recognising that within the context of its focus on crimes against humanity, the destruction of cultural heritage is of great relevance. Its provisions stress this and state that criminal intent is marked if and when the theft or destruction of a people's cultural inventory is part of the aggressor's (or occupier's) state policy and is carried out in a widespread or systematic manner. Al-Haq says that, over the last decade, Israel's policing of most known archaeological sites on the West Bank threatens their survival as a part of Palestine's cultural legacy.

Fuelling the Zionist Flame

Education in Israel is compulsory and free, from the age of three to the end of secondary school, with the Jewish and Arab school sectors largely separate. In Israel, a school is considered 'mixed' if the minority of students (Jewish or Arab) is more than 1 per cent of the total number. The most complete study of those mixed schools attended by Jewish and Arab pupils is a decade old but it is comprehensive. The study found that of the 1.6 million attending primary and secondary education, 870,000 attended schools without even a single Arab student and 330,000 attended a school with no Jewish student. What is noteworthy is that of the balance of 390,000, only 5,600 Arab pupils attended Jewish schools and 360 Jewish children attended an Arab school.[119]

The segregated nature of how both groups live is manifest in the educational system, where the impact of high levels of economic inequality is evident in the contrasting levels of educational achievement. 'The public educational system is centralized and curricula are standardized, but religious Jewish groups enjoy considerable organizational and curricular autonomy. Arab state schools, in contrast, do not enjoy similar autonomy. Rapid expansion of higher education has contributed to a dramatic increase in graduation rates in all social categories but large gaps remain, especially along ethnoreligious lines.'[120] While this socio-economic element is not unique to Israel, researchers see wider trends of concern.

> In addition to systemic differentiation between Arab and Jewish schools and to the differentiation by religion and religiosity, there is some de facto segregation, as in many other countries, between students of the [*sic*] different socioeconomic strata and ethnic groups. Inequalities in scholastic achievements between socioeconomic strata and ethnic groups have been a major concern for both educational policymakers and researchers in Israel. International large-scale student assessments indicate that achievement gaps in Israel are among the widest in the world.[121]

Apart from the independent ultra-Orthodox education system, much of the curriculum is uniform across the Jewish-religious, Jewish-secular and Arab education sectors, and is under the control of the state advisory council. The Arab population does not have the autonomy to influence curriculum design in its schools, meaning that teachers have to accept an approach that expresses the position of the Jewish majority, rather than that of the Arab minority. This peculiarity became considerably more marked in 2019 when the nation-state law became part of the state curriculum.

In the summer of 2024, the Knesset adopted the Basic Law of the Jewish Nation-State, the purpose of which was to institutionalise statutory inequality by granting national self-determination to Jewish citizens only. The law codifying Jewish supremacy in the country became a mandatory topic in schools in September 2019. There was considerable opposition to it becoming a mandatory subject as teaching it would drive home discrimination and the legal basis for considering the state of Israel as the nation-state of the Jewish people. After the legislation was passed, the Department of Education announced, 'students will internalize the vision for the country, which includes Israel being the state of the Jewish people'.[122] The consequence was that Arab children – and those in the Druze community – would come to understand that their rights, those of the 20 per cent of the non-Jewish population, were 'secondary'.

The law and its direct influence on the education of young people was about normalising the apartheid nature of the state. The segregated nature of the education system was one thing, but this new law enshrined into law and into the curriculum the supremacy of the Jewish citizens. The human rights lawyer, Jihad Abu Rayya recognised the long-term humiliation behind the move: 'They want to teach our children that Jews are the rightful owners of this land, and that we are here as guests, that as Arabs they do not have the right to live in equality with Jews.'[123]

The significance was that the history of Zionism became a formal part of the curriculum that children would have to learn in order to be able to attend university; Arab students had to learn this information to pass their High School exams. It was another important plank in the long-term nationalising of how children were to be educated; understanding and knowing the law that enshrined Jewish supremacy in the constitution but also referenced how Jewish 'settlement' was a national value that would be encouraged and promoted. The law went further. Arabic was downgraded from being an official language of the state to having 'special status', reiterating that only Jews could immigrate and receive automatic citizenship. Furthermore, it meant that, as part of their curriculum, Arab students, for whom the city of Jerusalem had a particular historical importance, would have it drummed into them that 'The complete and united Jerusalem is the capital of Israel', as per the so-called Jerusalem Law passed by the Knesset in 1980.[124]

This move by those in charge of educating Israel's children reinforced a key part of its apartheid approach to governance. For many Palestinians, it was no more than a formalisation of the established apartheid policies but its effect could be a great deal more profound. Not only did it force Arab students to answer questions that were racist against them in order to be able to matriculate (students were tested on material that explicitly outlined the supremacy of Jews over non-Jews), but it strengthened a sense of superiority in the minds of young Jewish students. Internationally, the Jerusalem Law had been declared null and void by Resolution 478 of the UN Security Council as the move violated international law that an occupying power cannot have sovereignty over the territory that it occupies.

Today's Palestinians in Israel are descendants of those who remained during the Nakba – the ethnic cleansing campaign to establish the state of Israel by force – in 1948. Ever since, many of Israel's Palestinians, despite their Israeli passports, have faced continuous policies of discrimination, but inserting the nation-state law into the educational curriculum in 2019 was a marked escalation. It shifted the policy of apartheid directly into the education system in a way that trapped Arabs into either repeating the institutionalised discrimination or self-excluding themselves from being able to attend university. What was most shocking about this, both its intent and the general acceptance of the change, was its supremacist nature; the very tactics deployed by the Third Reich were being used to influence the youth of the state: that a Jew has national supremacy over others and that the land, including 'settled' land is for the Jewish people alone. The idea of settler-colonialism was being embedded into the education of young Israelis – being normalised. It is also how this move is 'policed'. While the monitoring of staff at Arab schools was supposed to have ended in 2005, it is generally understood that Shin Bet, the state's internal security service, works alongside the Department of Education to supervise the appointment of teachers and to monitor the strict implementation of the curriculum in the Arab schools.

Israeli Arabs working in education believe that for the past two decades, the state has worked hard to promote the Zionist narrative through the curriculum across civics, history and geography, eliminating Palestinian history or anything linked to it, including the Nakba. The challenge for Arab families and Arab teachers is stark: do you put the truth, your pride in Palestine and your heritage to one side in order that the matriculating Palestinian gets through the process? The sad reality is that most do.

Jewish families and Jewish teachers do not face such an alarming choice, but they do need to make one regardless, because if they want their kids – their own children or their students – to mature into balanced, civically-minded young adults, then they need to find ways of addressing with them that apartheid is part of Israel's Basic Laws. The failure to do this, by whatever means, can only stimulate a notion of supremacy or superiority, one that some observers believed was diminishing twenty years ago. The Knesset's passing of the nation-state law in 2018 may have reversed this but the events of 7 October 2023 and Nakba II unleashed by Israel made almost impossible any hope that education could provide a basis for a counter-narrative to emerge. In September 2024, the Middle East TV channel Al Jazeera, whose offices and studios in the West Bank were shut down by order of the Israeli courts only a week before, published a video taken in a mixed school in Israel. It was of scores of children in their early teens harassing and intimidating an Arab classmate who had suggested that the IDF was involved in the murder of Palestinian civilians. For those who know the school environment in Israel over the last decade, it was surprising that any Arab child would have the courage to make such a charge.

The increasing challenge within the education sector has been exacerbated by legislation governing the behaviour of school teachers, prohibiting them from speaking about anything that could be deemed as 'incitement'. In the summer of 2024, Aaron, in his late thirties, left his position in a state school outside Tel Aviv and moved his family of two small children to Europe. Aaron is a secular Jew who felt he had to break ranks with the approach being taken in the school as the scale of Israel's assault on Gaza became more visible to him. '*Haaretz* apart, the Israeli media is hopeless but I've a brother and friends overseas so I've been fully aware of what Prime Minister Netanyahu and his people are doing in our name.'[125]

Aaron and his wife believed they had to leave Israel or else their two boys would be sucked into an education system that, no matter how hard they might try to balance things at home, threatened what they would want for them. 'I couldn't take it anymore, the idea of being an educator in the Israeli public education system without being able to speak my mind without telling some basic truths about humanity, about equality and respect for all.'[126] What happened in spring 2024 meant that the nuclear option he and his wife had been discussing for some months, leaving Israel – perhaps for good – leaving parents, siblings and friends behind, was no longer an option; it was a must.

> I had tried a few months into the Gazan campaign to suggest that as teachers we should prompt some discussions in civics classes about the need for Israel to let humanitarian aid in but there were no takers; I was met with silence. Anyway, one day in the classroom, without any particular plan or thought as to what I was doing, I raised it in a limited, careful, almost timid fashion.[127]

However, the students had no interest in discussing it. Aaron described how he was met with a wall of silence. It was the next day when he realised that in raising the issue, he had turned the attention onto himself. The school was alive with whispers that he was a Hamas supporter, a traitor, and there were even pupils who walked around him saying, 'traitors and backstabbers should be killed'. When Aaron went to the principal to see about reporting this to the police, the principal immediately asked the school's lawyer if Aaron's actions had put the school at risk. The concern was not the welfare of the teacher but the risk that his actions could lead to the school facing official sanctions.

The principal may have sensed the level of scrutiny the school was under, an intensity that was to become more acute. Months later, in November 2024, the Netanyahu government proposed strengthening further the powers of the Department of Education, including vesting it with 'the authority to fire, without prior notice, teachers who have either been convicted of a security or terror offense, or have "published a direct call to carry out an act of terrorism or published words of praise, sympathy or encouragement for an act of terrorism [or] support for or identification with it"'.[128] The law also allowed the ministry to cut or reduce funding for schools if it could be established that school management knew or should have known about their existence. The events involving Aaron and his students predated the further legislative tightening of the government's grip on the oxygen supply that education should offer to debate.

What Aaron and his wife had been considering in principle for some time, even before 7 October, was suddenly urgent. They felt the mood becoming darker, sensed an erosion of the basic democratic principles essential to them in rearing their young family and, absent any great optimism that things would change in their lifetime, they thought it was time to leave Israel. In some respects, this one small family's experience might seem relatable to that of millions of Palestinians since the end of the Nakba – the ethnic cleansing by Israel of Palestinians – in 1948. The story of a young couple with children feeling obliged to leave home and seek refuge elsewhere, to take their chances and forge a new beginning in a strange land, is historically resonant. They were beginning to feel unsafe, threatened by what was happening to and around them, and so, with little or no notice to their wider family, they left. Even though they were well-off citizens of a self-declared democracy, they too had felt threatened, because, to quote the poet, Warsan Shire, 'home is the mouth of the shark'.[129] The civic distortion within their society was gradually stifling them and threatening their wish to rear their children as liberal, moral, upright citizens of the world.

Yet, in the most important respect of all, this story of emigration from Israel is totally different to that of the Palestinians; the very idea of Palestinians having a homeland to return to is denied by the state of Israel. The seeds of this great travesty lie in the ineptitude and indifference of the West and most other Arab nations in the aftermath of the Nakba. In December 1948, the UN passed Resolution 194, which included the idea of Jerusalem as an independent international city – whatever that was supposed to mean – that a two-state solution would be negotiated and, most importantly, that Palestinian refugees would have the right to return.

In the decades since, not only has Israel's accretion of more and more land continued, but it has steadfastly refused to acknowledge

Palestinians. This is not about semantics; it has very real material consequences. To acknowledge Palestinians anywhere as refugees implies they have a land to return to, something Israel does not accept.

Others are equally disturbed by what they see happening in their society, by the trends that represent a hardening of attitudes against Palestinians, even among younger and well-educated Israelis. Ben, a human rights lawyer, explained that the system is so controlled and so warped that were he to go to a school to give a talk about his work, he could be charged with incitement to hatred. 'I cannot go to a public school and speak about my work; it's prohibited. That says something about our society and, increasingly, people are afraid to publish stories about this kind of thing so people don't know, but also a considerable percentage of the population has "tuned out", don't want to know; it is us against them!'[130]

Smothering Thought – Inside and Outside Israel

Genocide goes beyond ethnic cleansing. It means more than permanently displacing the people whose land you have taken; it means that your intent is their complete destruction. Israel has no interest in pursuing the estimated five million Palestinian diaspora scattered around the world, but it is determined to rid what they see as their world, their immediate environs, of Palestinians and that means killing all those it can and driving the remainder away forever. This is the reason they refuse to allow them to be described as refugees. Genocide means erasing them and everything about them.

While Israel's goal goes beyond ethnic cleansing, the 'cleansing' idea is helpful in any understanding of Israel's evil intent. What Israel intends for the Palestinians isn't a good 'hosing-down' in order to wash away unsavoury elements, nor is it even about a whole society going through some elaborate detox to rid it of toxins that are doing it harm. 'Cleansing', in this case, means an obliteration for all time. It is absolutely axiomatic that any prospect of a return by those being forced out is removed.

The shift in the approach to education is deeply embedded across all areas. In early summer 2024, Israel's minister of education introduced new legislation that would give a government-appointed committee the power to order the firing of academic staff who it decides have expressed 'support for terror'. The legislation is prescriptive; any universities that refuse to comply will have their funding cut. Earlier in the year, Jerusalem's Hebrew University had suspended one of its internationally best-known professors, Nadera Shalhoub-Kevorkian, for saying Israel was committing a genocide in Gaza. Shalhoub-Kevorkian, a dual Israeli and American citizen, was later arrested and detained for twenty-four hours. The intervention of the courts to have her released was believed to be a factor that influenced the government to introduce the tough new legislation.

While leading figures in academia, including the president of Israel's globally respected Institute of Technology, Uri Sivan, attacked the legislation, remarkably, the country's national union of students supported the proposals. As the head of one of Israel's best-known third-level institutions, Sivan described it as 'a form of McCarthyism, a very violent form, because it is meant to threaten people not to express their mind, in a system that should be free of any intimidation, encouraging free speech, encouraging criticism.'[131] Yet the Israeli students' union supported the legislation, meaning third-level students – normally a rich source of anti-establishment thinking – lobbied for the new law and the official union body spent more than $120,000 on an advertising campaign backing the need for greater control over the freedom of expression of the country's academics. It would appear the changes enshrined in law less than a decade ago are already bearing political fruit for the Zionist influence; otherwise, the acquiescence of university students would seem particularly hard to comprehend.

Across many places in the world, huge numbers of university students held campus protests in support of the rights of Palestinians and yet, in the one place where you would most hope and expect to see resistance to the government narrative, it was absent. Worse, the union representing third-level students was actively campaigning for restrictions on the freedom of university professors and teachers to speak their minds on the conduct of the state. Outside of Israel, in many universities in the US, Britain and Europe, faculty staff had taken the side of their students and often risked their career in doing so, especially in the US where many top universities, threatened by the potential withdrawal of funding by Jewish mega-donors, had put them on notice that protests would not be allowed. Many academics were arrested as a result. To oppose Israel's genocide was to be branded antisemitic.

It is important to recognise antisemitism for the evil that it is and not to ignore its inherent ugliness just because the state of Israel has, for decades, used it mischievously to sabotage all those who want to call it to account for its gross misdeeds. There have been critics of Israel who are Jew-haters and they should be denounced as racists whose intention is to spread distrust and dislike of Jews. The genocide, Nakba II, is not the fault of Jews: it is not their work, it is the responsibility of a sovereign country, a member state of the United Nations, that believes it has the right to destroy the right to nationhood of another people.

All those who choose to defend Palestine by targeting Jewish people are misguided and are not representative of those who see Israel as the problem – those for whom Israel is a rogue state that has deliberately oppressed the people of Palestine for generations. It suits Israel to suggest all its critics are antisemites, including anti-racist activists. As Dave Rich, who has written extensively about antisemitism, puts it, 'our basic understanding of racism and all anti-racist campaigns, initiatives and education that flow from it includes antisemitism'.[132]

In the United States, over a period of several months, in spring 2024, before the summer recess, the internet was alive with coverage of academics of all ages being treated roughly and arrested by police, called in by university presidents who chose to put the dollar before the welfare of millions of Palestinians. There were similar scenes elsewhere in the West but the aggression toward protesters was particularly marked in Germany and the US. Some in academia resigned, while others were forced out for failing to act decisively to curb the protests; the typical, if morally bankrupt, accusation of antisemitism was levelled at, among others, the presidents of Harvard, Pennsylvania and Columbia.

In May 2024, the University of Massachusetts academic and author Christian G. Appy wrote about his decision to join a handful of faculty members in protesting with students over the genocide in Gaza. Appy, who was in his seventieth year, and his staff colleagues were the first to be arrested after the decision of the university to call in state troopers. As with protests everywhere, the accusations of antisemitism dominated criticism of the actions of academics and students alike. The Jerusalem Declaration on Antisemitism, signed in 2020 by 350 international academics in Jewish studies, referenced 'supporting the Palestinian demand for justice and the full grant of their political, national, civil and human rights'[133] as one of the claims that did not qualify as antisemitic. Appy recounted his and some of his students' arrest:

> We were treated with reasonable restraint. However, as many videos and personal testimonies demonstrate, there was widespread use of excessive force against students. One of my graduate students was thrown face down to the ground, with a knee pressed so hard in his back he struggled to breathe. He was zip-cuffed so tightly his hands soon began to swell. He was then put in the back of a small windowless police van for several hours before being driven to the Mullins Center arena to join many of the 134 arrested protestors. His experience was not exceptional; some arrestees were subjected to greater violence. At the arena, many were held all night (still zip-cuffed), denied food or water, and were only allowed to use the bathroom after hours of pleading, if at all.[134]

There is a striking contrast between the awareness and fearlessness shown by young students around the world and the slavish endorsement by the Israeli university students' representative body of its government's determination to wipe out the Palestinian people; it is one of the more concerning features of Israeli society today. It's alarming that in a state claiming to be democratic, one that even uses the moniker 'Western democracy' as though that offers it some special status, most students attending higher education appear to support its determination to manacle academics, to prevent them from speaking freely.

The Israeli student union's support of its government's plans to introduce such draconian measures is antithetical to the place of university students in an open society. It's in stark contrast to the solidarity shown by students toward Palestine in most places across the world. It's easier for people elsewhere to protest but the subjugation of the union representing students in Israel shows the impact of the state's vice-like hold on education. With the steps it has taken over the last decade to control the narrative, Israeli youth appears increasingly in line with its government.

When young minds are being educated in a system where the supremacy of the students' ethnicity is being promoted and where issues like citizenship, democracy, and human rights are not discussed, never mind taught, there can be only one outcome. When this approach is being driven by a political leadership fixated on the realisation of its colonial ambition to commit a genocide against Palestinians, the embedment of superiority runs deep. It means Israel is on course to establish cross-generational support for the Zionist mission.

Some days after the assassination of Hezbollah leader Hassan Nasrallah, Israel's Education Ministry wrote to the heads of all state-run religious schools suggesting that they should organise celebrations to mark his killing by the Israeli armed forces. The ministry even suggested different formats for the celebrations, like dancing, distributing food, or toasting in the teachers' room. There was some criticism of this, not on the grounds that encouraging children to celebrate such events, no matter the nature of the person assassinated, was unhealthy, but because there were still Israeli hostages in Gaza and others had been forced to leave their homes on the Lebanese border. It was for that reason alone that some officials in the department were unhappy with the move.

Six

UNRWA

An Agency for One People

It may be impossible to erase the history of a people completely but this does not deter Israel from its efforts to destroy the most valued of Palestine's cultural sites, its most treasured places of worship and its historical heritage. Thankfully, its social history is being catalogued by countless individuals and groups across the world. One of the richest sources of that social fabric is the agency UNRWA (United Nations Relief and Works Agency), which was established by the United Nations at the moment when the state of Israel was founded. It is effectively Palestine's defender-in-chief, the body without which it would long ago have lost any capacity to survive.

UNRWA was established in 1949 specifically to provide vital services and human development programmes for Palestinian refugees. It is unique in two important respects: it's the only UN agency that caters to the refugees of just one nation and it's the only one that delivers its services directly to the beneficiaries.

The headquarters of the agency is in the Jordanian capital, Amman, a city that hosts about 400,000 Palestinian refugees in UNRWA camps. Amman sits on the eastern side of the river Jordan, across from the West Bank, and is just over 100 kilometres from Ramallah, the administrative capital of Palestine.

The Israeli-Palestinian conflict is a constant drumbeat in Jordan, a country that had once formally annexed the West Bank. Jordan is home to approximately 2.5 million Palestinian refugees, and its queen, Raina, is of Palestinian origin. It is one of the more Westernised Arab nations with quite an open and liberal outlook. Its relationship with Israel was close for periods under King Hussein, who died in 1999, and the peace treaty, signed in 1994, is still in place. That treaty, known as the Washington Declaration, followed increased tensions over the West Bank, which Jordan had at one point claimed as part of its sovereign territory. With the treaty, border crossings were opened, resulting in trade and tourism initiatives and, ever since, Jordan has sought to promote peace between Israel and Palestine.

Jordan's relationship with Israel has gradually become more fraught. King Abdullah II had invited President Herzog to Amman in March 2022, the first visit ever by an Israeli head of state. However, later that year, on the appointment of the Netanyahu government, the King, unusually choosing to dispense with the language of diplomacy, publicly warned Israel against changing the status of Muslim and Christian holy sites: 'If people want to get into a conflict with us, we're quite prepared.'[135] Following 7 October 2023, the King's position became more hardline, never more so than when he addressed the UN General Assembly in September 2024. With a finger pointing at the camera, he said, 'This Israeli government has killed more children, more journalists, more aid workers and more medical personnel than [in] any other war (sic) in recent memory.' There was a message, too, for those in diplomatic circles foolish enough to suggest Jordan as an alternative home for the Palestinians. Supporters of Israel have peddled that idea for decades. King Abdullah was happy to disabuse them of any such notion, declaring to 'those who continue to propagate the idea of Jordan as an alternative homeland … let me be very, very clear – that will never happen. We will never accept the forced displacement of Palestinians, which is a war crime.'[136] The King's emphasis was not on the enormous economic burden that such an arrangement would place on his country but on the immorality of Jordan helping Israel realise its criminal intent. For the Palestinians, arguably, the most important role Jordan plays in its support of their cause is as host of UNRWA's headquarters, the UN organisation that offers such hope to the people of Palestine, the oppressed in Gaza and the occupied territories on the western side of the river and the millions of refugees in Jordan and Lebanon. Without the agency in their corner, most Palestinians would have none.

It is precisely because of that critical sense of hope that UNRWA is uniquely disliked and distrusted by Israel. In the summer of 2024, Israel's determination to undermine its status reached new levels when the Knesset introduced legislation to ban UNRWA from East Jerusalem, revoke its privileges and designate it a terrorist organisation. This denigration went to the heart of the story of Palestine and Israel. It's a story of the theft of land, the killing of people and the creation, through Israel's determination that no state of Palestine can ever exist, of an idea that, consequently, those whom it fails to kill cannot be considered refugees.

Under the Universal Declaration of Human Rights, if the Palestinians who managed to survive the Nakba were called refugees, they would have had the right to return to their land, so the denial of any state of Palestine was and remains critical to the Zionist ambition. To reinforce Israel's control over that land, its assumed ownership, it must drive away the indigenous people or kill them.

When the state of Israel was formed, Jewish people from all over the world, but primarily Europe, came to Palestine to claim land that they considered to be theirs. More correctly, they chose to use and interpret the Bible as granting moral as well as legal rights to the land of Palestine. The native population would have to be removed. This was how the Nakba, the ethnic cleansing of Palestine, started, and with it, Israel's determination to realise the Zionist ambition, which would mean the complete removal of non-Jews from Palestine. The Nakba of 1948 was conducted with brutality by the Zionists, especially under the leadership of David Ben-Gurion with his notorious Plan Dalet, or Plan D. Its impact was captured by the Palestinian scholar and founder of the Palestine Land Society, Salman Abu Sitta, in his remarkable book, *Mapping My Return*:

> There are Palestinians who saw loved ones machine-gunned down before their eyes, others who fled into darkness under the thud of bombs from tanks and planes, families who were decimated by explosions while having dinner, mothers who left in a hurry carrying with them a pillow instead of an infant and

> children who were lost in the long marches of people seeking safety, crying for their mothers.[137]

The Zionist mission was simply to build their nation, 'an Israeli Jewish nation in a land that had in large part belonged to another people, the Palestinian Arabs'.[138] The intent was to completely eradicate the past, exemplified by the establishment of a National Naming Committee that would replace Arabic names of towns and villages with Hebrew ones as the great majority of Palestinians were forced off their land. A minority remained; the majority became refugees, as most Palestinians are today. The success was the realisation of a programme of displacement, the realisation of what Zionists considered their destiny. It involved theft, as Israel's then minister of foreign affairs, Moshe Dayan, acknowledged in comments he made in 1969: 'We came to this country, which was already populated by Arabs, and we are establishing a Hebrew, that is a Jewish state here.'[139]

Reputational Target

UNRWA has had to deal with many difficulties and been embroiled in different controversies since its establishment, but nothing it has faced was as existential as that which followed the accusations that a dozen of its staff had been involved in the Hamas attack of 7 October. Once the allegations were made – in a short dossier produced by the Israeli government – funding was withdrawn by, among others, Japan, Germany, France, the UK and the USA.

The impact of such drastic and ill-considered action by many of its larger donors was catastrophic, with an immediate shock to its capacity to serve the needs of all Palestinians across the occupied territories but also in the large number of camps it had in Lebanon and Jordan.

Independent journalists who reviewed the Israeli briefing document said it failed to provide evidence to support Israel's claims but it was only after an independent review by former French Minister of Foreign Affairs Catherine Colonna that most countries chose to restore funding, though the US was not among them. In a further sign of its abandonment of the oppressed Palestinians, the US deferred a decision about funding until October 2024. It was as dramatic a signal as any that the Biden administration had chosen, in this case, to mould its foreign policy toward supporting the oppressor, not the oppressed. The loss of financial support over a six-month period was bad enough but even more serious was the damage to the credibility of the agency, whose 13,000 employees in Gaza run its schools, health and social services.

The West's acceptance of the Israeli narrative on UNRWA betrayed as much a failure of understanding as it did a predetermination to believe whatever Israel tells it. How could UNRWA do what it does and what the world wants it to do in Gaza without liaising with Hamas, which administers the area? Israel's allegations were placed into a Western institutional mindset that is unprepared to do anything that could cause Israel upset, knowing that linking the essential work of the agency with Hamas, which is routinely and simplistically branded a 'terrorist' group, would undermine UNRWA's position overnight. There are those in the Middle East who believe that, without UNRWA, without its establishment by the international community coinciding with the foundation of Israel, the Palestinians' cause might already be lost.

Israel's propaganda against UNRWA in the aftermath of 7 October did work. The success for Israel went well beyond sovereign donors shutting down funding; if it could damage UNRWA's global standing, that would help it achieve the core of the Zionist ambition – the denial of any right of return. Israel wants the world to forget Palestine. Israel believes its cause – its need for nationhood – can be realised only with the removal of any notion of a conflicting narrative. The Zionist mission cares little about how its realisation, even its pursuit, would leave the standing of Jews across the world. To pursue what Theodor Herzl had charted at the turn of the nineteenth century meant acting in a manner that would mean the land of Palestine must be theirs: 'Oppression and persecution cannot exterminate us. No nation on earth has survived such struggles and sufferings as we have … Palestine is our ever-memorable historic home.'[140]

In his writings at the end of the nineteenth century, Herzl promoted the idea that Zionism would right a historic wrong and correct the world's failure to recognise the Jewish people as 'special', one that carried a status that was not about religion but about nationhood. 'We are a people – one people … In our native lands where we have lived for centuries we are still decried as aliens.'[141] The direction and tone of most of what he wrote is not unlike that of other messianic leaders in history who believed they were part of a special race, but the passage of time has never diluted Herzl's importance to Israel. Even though he has been dead for over a century, his doctrine remains fundamental to the state of Israel. When David Ben-Gurion declared its establishment on 14 May 1948, he did so beneath a large portrait of Herzl. Israel has an annual national holiday, Herzl Day, to commemorate his life and vision. The Nakba was Israel's first attempt at the realisation of Herzl's ideal, though more aggressively and certainly more openly than he'd espoused. Salman Abu Sitta wrote about that time:

> I became a refugee at the age of ten. I vaguely heard talk about Jews ... they started to attack villages near Jaffa, far away in the north. I had never seen a Jew before, let alone a Jewish soldier with a gun. My life's mission became to try and put a face to this invisible enemy, in particular, the Zionist soldiers who attacked and burned down my home. I wanted to find their names, photographs of them. I wanted to understand their hatred of us, their desire to make us refugees and to destroy our country, Palestine.[142]

To Zionists, taking the land is the critical first step toward a denial of the existence of a state of Palestine, with, consequently, an inherent denial that Palestinians can be refugees. The theft of their land, turning their communities into Israeli villages and towns, and bringing Jewish people, living all over the world, back to the land that the Zionists believed should always have been theirs would mean that the Palestinians would have no place to return to; they would become someone else's problem, not Israel's concern. The justification was clear. Herzl, the revered founder of Zionism, had written about the oppression of Jews being unprecedented, and that was forty years before the horrors inflicted on the Jewish people by Hitler's Germany added grim weight to his words.

UNRWA's very origins hint at the West's desperation to facilitate Israel: the acronym of the agency that looks after the needs of Palestinian refugees makes no reference to them as such. Unlike UNHCR (United Nations High Commissioner for Refugees), the 'R' in UNRWA is for 'relief' not 'refugees', and yet, for Palestinians, 'no one ever questioned the idea of returning home. The refugees discussed only "when?"'[143] In the world of global diplomacy, the sensibilities of the time meant it was important not to acknowledge that essential ingredient, 'the right to return', when the agency was formed. So soon after World War II, the manner in which UNRWA was established signalled the West's determination to somehow offer some level of protection for Palestinians but without upsetting Israel. Whatever steps it needed to take for Palestinians, the sensibilities of the Jewish people had to take precedence. In many respects, the manner in which UNRWA was established betrayed the West's predisposition, one that continues to this day.

In Gaza, UNRWA has been providing education to more than half a million children across 700 schools, hundreds of millions of dollars in loans for small businesses and job creation, and healthcare support covering more than seven million visits by patients every year. Quite how it could be expected to do this essential work without liaising with the Gazan elected administration led by Hamas is hard to understand but the military capacity of Hamas – conveniently branded 'terrorist' – always made criticising UNRWA relatively easy. When Hamas guerrillas led the attack on Israeli soil on 7 October 2023, targeting UNRWA became easier still.

Yet, despite the fact that it employs a staff of 13,000 in Gaza alone, no evidence was produced that showed anything approaching a fundamental or systemic problem in UNRWA maintaining its independence from Hamas.

Most of the criticism directed at UNRWA is predictable and usually originates, however indirectly, in Israel. In spite of its inherent lack of balance, much of the bad press gets traction, especially in America. The Washington Institute, a pro-Israel think-tank, has promoted analysis by former General Counsel to UNRWA James Lindsay, who has consistently worked to undermine the agency. In an analysis of the Catherine Colonna report he wrote for the Washington think-tank, Lindsay concluded it was 'unlikely to prompt significant changes so long as the agency is operating in an environment like Gaza, where the de facto authority is a terrorist group'. This kind of analysis, its partiality, reinforces the Western view of Israel as a 'victim', which in turn reinforces institutionalised prejudice. 'UNRWA can train its staff on neutrality, proper procedures, educational curriculums, and the like, but when it comes to actions – e.g., teaching anti-Israel or antisemitic material – staff members do what Hamas or like-minded actors tell them to do, whether out of conviction or intimidation.'[144] What organisations like the Institute produce is used to brief politicians, influencers and media, spreading disinformation and lies in the process. Lindsay's history of criticising UNRWA goes back as far as 2009, when he published a paper that criticised it for failing to match UNHCR's success in resettling refugees, which, he argued, betrayed a political choice by the agency that 'seems to favor the strain of Palestinian political thought espoused by those who are intent on a "return" to the land that is now Israel'.[145]

The Israeli political machine in the West is about more than the direct funding of politicians; much of its advocacy is bound up with groups that it finances to do analysis and promote narratives that are based on a twisted interpretation of events. US institutional commentary on the Middle East is riddled with such bias. Only that could explain a report that questions the very idea of 'return' as if it is not a fundamental right of all refugees or that refers to the land of return as 'the land that is now Israel'.

Like most UN agencies, UNRWA's work is complex and while it alone is focused on the needs of just one people – the Palestinians – the circumstances surrounding its establishment and the determination of Israel to always find a means of suppressing Palestine's interests makes that work even more complex. While the agency's task is to protect the interests of a nation that is homeless, managing the interests of a people under constant threat of another state that steals their land with the tacit agreement of the still guilt-ridden West and, especially, the shekel-compromised United States, make its chances of success beyond challenging. Still, even though well over 200 of its employees have been killed in Gaza and despite Israel's campaign to undermine its importance – one that has been slavishly followed by many in the West – UNRWA keeps going. The need for its endurance has never been greater.

UNRWA is anathema to Israel precisely because it has, for decades, represented so well the interests of the Palestinian people. In most cases, refugee issues are resolved only by the political entities involved in the dispute that led to them having to leave. UNHCR includes Palestinians in its annual report on the State of the World's Refugees.

The rights of all Palestinians are, as they are for all the people of the world, in the 1948 Universal Declaration of Human Rights; but the accretion of more and more territory is critical to the Zionist ambition, which means denying the Palestinians any right to land because the annexation of their territory must be forever, something that any 'right to return' clearly undermines. For those who do leave, either allowed to do so or fleeing for their lives, there can be no going back as the purpose of Israel's remorseless annexation-creep would be worthless unless the settlement of the stolen land can be cemented forever.

This is why those driving the Zionist mission are so intent on destroying UNRWA. The esteemed Palestinian lawyer, Raja Shehadeh, says, 'among the issues unresolved after the Oslo Accords is the return of the refugees. Israel sees UNRWA as perpetuating the refugees' insistence on the right to return. It believes that if it succeeds in dissolving the organisation, the refugee problem will be forgotten. This is an illusion. There will be no lasting peace without resolving the refugee issue'.[146] Shehadeh is right that peace is impossible without resolving the refugee issue but were Israel to succeed in its determination to have UNRWA closed down, Palestine's cause would be massively damaged.

Jewish Israeli academic Ilan Pappé is no less sure of the intent of Israel to remove the Palestinians altogether. He uses the term 'settler colonialism'.[147] While there are different forms of colonialism, the specificity of the settler colonialist objective is the replacement of the majority population by the settlers, rather than its mere subjugation. When the land the colonists want isn't vacant, it needs to be emptied by whatever means necessary, and with it, if possible, all traces of the life that had existed before the colonisation.

UNRWA is a bulwark of the Palestinian defences against that Zionist mission. It is not a standard UN agency. In many respects, the organisation is Gaza. Its status there reflects the range and depth of its work. It builds schools, hospitals, community centres. Its own people create the social infrastructure, then those places are run by other UNRWA employees: teachers, healthcare professionals, social welfare officers, caterers, cleaning staff.

UNRWA is irreplaceable in the fabric of Gaza and this is why Israel is so intent on its destruction. It is why, in the summer of 2024, Israeli legislators voted overwhelmingly in the Knesset in favour of new legislation that would remove UN privileges from UNRWA staff and formally designate it a terrorist organisation; proof, if any were needed, that UNRWA threatens the Zionist project.

Seven

Israel's Wider Intent

The West Bank

After Israel's victory in the 1967 war, Moshe Dayan, who served as a government minister in three different Israeli governments between 1959 and 1979, declared, 'we are now an empire'.[148] In 1969, he gave an insight into Israel's approach to Palestine:

> In considerable areas of the country we bought lands from the Arabs. Jewish villages were built in the place of Arab villages. You do not even know the names of these Arab villages, and I do not blame you, because these geography books no longer exist; not only do the books not exist, the Arab villages are not there either. Nahalal arose in the place of Mahalul, Gevat – in the place of Jibta, Sarid – in the place of Haneifs and Kefar Yehoshua – in the place of Tell Shaman. There is no one place built in this country that did not have a former Arab population.[149]

These remarks – a warning of the inherent risk in trying to erase the past – were made two years after Israel annexed East Jerusalem, incorporating it into the West Bank, beginning a process of settlement that clouded any distinction between the lands it had occupied and its once sovereign self. Often this has involved the demolition of existing property, the killing of livestock and the destruction of orchards and olive groves before replanting something in order to claim rights over the stolen land. This part of Palestine now has 150 official settlements, with a further almost 200 that are not sanctioned (called outposts) by the Israeli government. The total number of 'settlers' who have stolen people's land with the direct support of the state of Israel is in excess of 700,000, almost three times the 250,000 settlers in the West Bank in 1993. In 2024, as its destruction of Gaza continued, Israel moved to strengthen the Zionist hold on the West Bank, with the objective of making the establishment of a Palestinian state more and more difficult. Since Israel's assault on Gaza following the Hamas attack, the rate and depth of state-sponsored land theft by Israelis in the West Bank have both increased exponentially.[150]

Yesh Din, a respected Israeli NGO, reported in early 2024 that there had been 225 incidents of Israeli violence in ninety-three Palestinian communities in the West Bank, including the shooting dead of nine Palestinians by settlers. In April 2024, *The Washington Post* reported from the West Bank on 'settlers' attacking anyone on the street. A 14-year-old shepherd boy had gone missing and was found murdered, which led to protests by the local people against the Israeli settlers. When townsmen were in the local mosque for prayers on the following Friday, hundreds of settlers arrived in the town, a young woman said it was as though they were coming from all sides. 'You see something running over the hills, something coming toward us.' At least 60 homes were attacked in the region and over 100 vehicles were set on fire, according to Yesh Din, which monitors settler violence. IDF soldiers arrived later but didn't stop the attack and Yesh Din reported that hundreds of the livestock of Palestinians were slaughtered during the attack.[151]

Social media lets us see much of this activity in real-time and brings home the levels of violence involved and how the actions are generally supported by the Israeli authorities on the ground. What it doesn't or cannot do is establish how coordinated this is, the extent to which these incidents are part of a state-sponsored programme of annexation-creep and how the system folds the abuse of Palestinians' rights, the theft of their land and destruction of their homes, into its bubble wrap of legal protection.

The West Bank has become almost unlivable for the indigenous people. The number of settlements, the separation wall across the occupied territories and the new road infrastructure that is only for the use of the settler community stretch the apartheid management of Israel into a land that is not theirs to govern. The Palestinians do not have freedom of movement even within their own land. There are an estimated 700 road obstacles, including 150 checkpoints, about half of which are manned by Israeli security companies: 'About 70,000 Palestinians with Israeli work permits cross these checkpoints in their daily commute.'[152]

This is where organisations like Yesh Din, B'Tselem and HaMoked are essential. Israel consistently refers to how, like other nations, it has independent bodies to examine allegations of abuse in all areas of public life. Specifically, the IDF references the FFA (General Staff Mechanism for Fact-Finding Assessments), which reports directly to the Military Advocate General. Yesh Din reviewed the FFA's work on 664 complaints submitted to it across three different military operations involving the IDF between 2014 and 2024. What it found was that 542 (81.6 per cent) of the complaints were closed without an investigation of any kind; 41 (6 per cent) led to investigations being opened, with one (0.17 per cent) indictment.[153]

Toward the end of summer 2024, without any prior warning, Israel undertook some military operations in the West Bank. The area was already dealing with extreme levels of 'settler' activity, which had markedly increased since 7 October, with groups of Jews, often backed by the IDF, taking the land of Palestinians. The thieves ('settlers') would burn dwellings and bring livestock, plant lemon trees or build shacks just so, by any means possible, they could lay claim to land in a manner that could then be defended by the authorities. The step change was when the IDF conducted military actions targeting areas in the northern part of the territory, claiming this was to break up Iranian-sponsored cells.

With this move, Iran and the spectre of Islamism were shoehorned into the global positioning of what Israel was doing and why. Netanyahu knew there was no surer way of cementing the support of his Western allies than suggesting that his government was protecting them from the particular evil that he wanted to suggest resides in Tehran. This idea was to underpin not just the aggression in the West Bank but, later, Israel's widening of its territorial ambition into Lebanon.

The military operations changed the dynamic in the West Bank. Israel's minister of foreign affairs, Israel Katz, said the operations were intended to 'thwart Islamic-Iranian terrorist infrastructures', claiming that Iran was 'working to establish an eastern terrorist front against Israel in the West Bank'.[154] The minister went further, suggesting that evacuation orders for civilians would be issued there, as had been done in order to empty districts before IDF operations in Gaza.

There had been another change, too, one that almost went unnoticed but was no less important. Over the decades since it commenced its forced 'settlement' of land in the West Bank, Israel has always denied that it was annexing the land. International law prohibits annexation but there's now a fine legal point that shields Israel – despite the thousands of hectares its people have stolen – from being held to account for the move of annexing territory that is not theirs.

Until the late summer of 2024, Zionists who had seized Palestinian land were under the supervision of the Israeli military but the government changed this administration to a civilian one by transferring much of the governance of the West Bank from the military commander to a new deputy head of the Civil Administration. This deputy is a purely political appointee, answering to the Settlement Administration led by Smotrich. This material change meant that the occupied land in the West Bank was no longer seen as being held for operational military reasons and therefore not subject to the laws regulating military occupation, formally denying Palestinians their rights in the process. In a joint petition on behalf of Yesh Din and the Association of Civil Rights in Israel, human rights lawyer Michael Sfard argued this constituted 'legal (de jure) annexation' and provided further evidence of Israel as an apartheid state.[155]

Israel has embraced apartheid. Inequality is constitutionally established so that there can be no alignment of the interests of Jewish citizens and those of other beliefs. This characteristic, openly worn in its statues and in the behaviour of its leadership, makes it more difficult to understand the unbroken support it receives from so much of the West but most particularly Germany, France, Britain, Canada and the United States.

When the state was founded, its declaration included the standard references to equality. But those commitments have gradually been withdrawn by the introduction of new legislation. That erasure started in the 1950s, but even with Israel continuing, however ludicrously, to claim to be among the West's modern democratic nations, the tightening of the apartheid noose continued. The Jewish Nation-State Law, passed in 2018, formalised statutory inequality among its civilians as only Jewish citizens were granted the right of self-determination. It also promoted Jewish settlement of land as a national value and downgraded the status of the Arabic language.

Under the Rome Statute of the ICC, apartheid is defined as 'inhumane acts … committed in the context of an institutionalized regime of systematic oppression and domination by one racial group over any other racial group or groups and committed with the intention of maintaining that regime'.[156] In a number of authoritative reports, including a 2017 report from the UN, it was established that by virtue of their self-identification, Israeli Jews constitute one racial group and the Palestinian people another, for the purpose of establishing apartheid.[157] Since 1948, Israel, through a series of discriminatory legislative measures, has engineered a regime of apartheid. It's not really a matter of debate: it is an apartheid state.

The founder of modern Zionism, Theodor Herzl, would have approved of the long-term, slow but relentless stealing of land in the West Bank; he would have liked how Israel went about colonising with such stealth. Herzl had no compunction in setting out on a course that would involve the Jewish people taking the entire land of Palestine for themselves. There was, he believed, no other course than to push the Palestinians out of the country in a 'process of expropriation' that needed to be enacted 'discreetly and circumspectly'.[158]

One hundred and thirty years on, that 'ideal' has found a new voice in the language of Benjamin Netanyahu, Bezalel Smotrich, Itamar Ben-Gvir and other members of Israel's coalition government assembled after the elections of November 2022. The important difference is that, in 2024, emboldened by the West's indifference to it being done slowly but assuredly, as war in Gaza raged, Israel set about taking more of the West Bank without feeling any need for the kind of 'discretion' or 'circumspection' that Herzl had counselled. The uber confidence with which many leaders of Israel today approach the business of cleansing Palestine of Palestinians is becoming more trenchant and considerably less cautious.

The horrific events of 7 October 2023 seemed to provide them with cause to ratchet up the tone of the hatred they have long espoused. Netanyahu himself vowed to turn Gaza 'into rubble'[159] and the number of political voices of support increased as the genocidal process gathered momentum, in a cabinet already known for remarks against Palestinians. Minister of Foreign Affairs Eli Cohen had said any Arabs in Israel or the West Bank who viewed themselves as Palestinian would receive every assistance from the government to move to Gaza 'on a one-way ticket'[160], while Minister Miri Regev, objecting to the US National Basketball Association referencing Palestine, said, 'Palestine is a country everyone knows doesn't exist.'[161]

The mission of this right-wing and ultra-Orthodox thirty-seventh government of Israel is to use any means possible to shift how the country is governed toward what is, at the most optimistic, a bastardised form of democracy. To give effect to their plans, they need to use the situation in Gaza as an opportunity to kill as many Palestinians as possible but also as a political shield as they increase the annexation-creep in the West Bank. Critically, designating Israel as a state 'at war' allows its government to do things it would find a great deal more difficult otherwise.

While social media plays a huge part in allowing the world to see, in real-time, excesses and injustices, there can be a tendency to focus on the distressing imagery of the shocking drama without enough attention being paid to the more systematic institutional means by which injustice is generally perpetrated and sustained. With Israel's campaign in Gaza, the daily images provided by those few journalists (over a hundred of whom have been killed) and the testimonies provided by brave civilians have both been essential to the mobilisation of public opinion in the West.

The West Bank is different; throughout most of 2024, even as Israel sponsored more aggressive and greater levels of 'settler' activity, the visual testimonials, no matter how moving, were neither as stark nor dramatic as what was being posted every hour of every day from Gaza. In terms of public attention and consciousness, there was very little that could stimulate the interest of the public. Yet, the number of incidents increased; the amount of land being stolen and the support of settler activity by Israeli security services were all at unprecedented levels. Events in the West Bank were considerably less dramatic or violent than the catastrophe unfolding in Gaza, but that made it no less important because to ignore it means allowing Israel free rein to facilitate land theft at unprecedented levels, which would represent a huge step toward the realisation of its Zionist ambition to take all of Palestine.

During a strange televised briefing to the nation in early September 2024, Benjamin Netanyahu displayed a large map of Gaza and Israel where there was, actually, no West Bank at all, the area appearing instead as Israeli territory. Apart from the usual places, the presentation received little or no critical attention in Israel, but those few elements in the international media that were not in thrall with Tel Aviv pounced on it as though it revealed something new about his country's intentions. It did not. As mentioned previously, just a year earlier, he had used a similar map of the Middle East without Palestine in a speech at the United Nations. It, too, had received little global attention.

The idea of Israel erasing Palestine is not new; how could it be when that has long been the real ambition of the Zionist cause? It may be that this resolve has been more transparent under the leadership of Netanyahu's Likud-led coalition than at other times, but it is known that at the time of the 1967 war, a Labor-led Israeli government had precisely the same intentions. The state of Israel is the means by which the objectives of modern Zionism – as set out by Theodor Herzl in 1896 – would be realised.

It may be that, if a solution is ever to be found to the conflict, neither the Palestinians nor the Israelis can expect to have all the land that they would want but, technically, only Israel could make that happen. Unfortunately, the evidence that Israel wants the complete opposite is everywhere. Those in power (the legislature as a whole, not just the government of Benjamin Netanyahu) want to control freedom of thought and, certainly, of expression. This starts with changing legislation and the aggressive policing and restriction of the press and all forums of public debate; beyond that, the long-term 'play' is to shape young minds, to corral their sense of self and that of their peers so that their mindset is exclusively Jewish-centric and Zionist-oriented.

The ambition is to promote Israel's supremacy and its dominance as a Jewish race. Israel wants the Jewish people to have an exclusive and unquestionable right to take over the entirety of Palestine and obtain territory over which – legally and morally – it has no rights at all. It is using the attack by Hamas as the basis on which it can pursue objectives that contravene international law and, if the ethnic cleansing were happening elsewhere, the West would be united in furious opposition to it. Instead, the West, or certainly its most influential and its most monied nations, are providing the aggressor, the terrorist, the thief, the cleanser, with the money and the armaments it needs in order to make considerable progress toward its genocidal end.

Gaza is only one part of the exercise and, just as 7 October provided Israel with some cover for what it set about doing, the scale of its military operation there distracted attention from its Zionist mission across the West Bank. There, since October 2023, the Israeli government has actively worked toward destabilising the situation in order to expedite plans to take complete control of the area, including East Jerusalem. The intent on the West Bank was lost on many because Gaza dominated the media's attention. Israel's wanton destruction of one part of Palestine allowed it to accelerate and deepen its longstanding policy of annexing land in another part of the territory it has illegally occupied for more than half a century. Israel's annexation-creep in the West Bank has been ongoing for decades at a consistent but not dramatic pace until, with its utterly disproportionate response to 7 October in Gaza, it could progress its broader ambitions almost sight unseen. With Gaza dominating attention both in Israel and across the world, the levels and aggressiveness of land theft increased markedly. The figures prove it.

At any other time, the killing of 650 civilians in the West Bank, at least 120 of them children, over the first eight months of 2024 would have generated significant global attention. Those figures represent a deadly campaign but, in 2024, it was largely ignored because, when compared to the demolition of Gaza and the killing of many tens of thousands of innocent civilians, including an estimated 18,000 children, the annexation-creep that had, since April, started to morph into a sprint seemed like a nothing. The intensity of the government-sponsored and supported theft of land became more and more aggressive over the course of 2024. Then, in August, the administration in Tel Aviv moved land forces into the West Bank and engaged in full-scale military activities under the noses of an international community led by a supine Washington.

B'Tselem, whose name refers to the universal and Jewish moral edict to respect and uphold the human rights of all people, monitors Israel's detention of Palestinians and its 'settlement' of the West Bank. Under the banner, 'Settler Violence = State Violence', it documents the forced expulsion of Palestinians from their land and the significant levels of state-sponsored violence. As far back as 2021, it was documenting the scale of land theft supported by the government of Israel.

> Since occupying the West Bank in 1967, Israel has misappropriated more than two million dunams of land (200,000 hectares) throughout the West Bank. Israel uses this land for its own purposes, including building new settlements, expanding the territory they control – including farmland and industrial zones – and paving roads that mainly serve the settler population ... Israel has taken over some of these areas using official means: issuing military orders, declaring the area 'state land', a 'firing zone' or a 'nature reserve', and expropriating land. Other areas have been effectively taken over by settlers through daily acts of violence, including attacks on Palestinians and their property. The two tracks appear unrelated ... in truth, there is only one track: Settler violence against Palestinians is part of the strategy employed by Israel's apartheid regime, which seeks to take over more and more West Bank land.[162]

The theft of such a huge amount of Palestinian territory represents the relentlessness with which the Zionist ambition is pursued. It's arguable too that, for all the work of agencies like B'Tselem and HaMoked in Israel, the accretion of land in the West Bank has largely occurred, as Theodor Herzl had counselled 125 years ago, 'discreetly'. The theft of land had started well before 1967.

In *Mapping My Return*, Abu Sitta recounts how he and his siblings lost the home that had been in his family for generations before they were forced to flee by Zionists, just as the state of Israel was formed. He was 10 years old when his home was destroyed and all their possessions burned. It was 15 May 1948, the exact date that Israel's first prime minister, David Ben-Gurion, formally declared the state of Israel. This is what happened to the land that belonged to the Sitta's family for generations before that fateful day:

> I have maps of how they divided the land, among them approximately 20,000 dunums (4,750 acres / 2,000 hectares) each, at the rate of 300 dunums (72 acres / 32 hectares) for each of the seventy families there. That means the density of the 'settlers' on my land is fifteen per square kilometre at most. Those of my family, the least privileged, who still live in a refugee camp in Gaza, live at a density of five thousand persons per square kilometre. Yet they live only a few kilometres from their home.[163]

This example of settler colonialism is not some unusual or rare feature of a period in history from many years ago. The annexation of land has continued ever since the boundaries were agreed in 1967, and the recent acceleration of land theft with its more aggressive character has the direct backing of the state.

In December 2023, a school built with EU funds and ten homes in the Bedouin village of Khirbet Zanuta were demolished by 'settlers'. This involved the use of a bulldozer to smash the front walls of the school and to completely destroy the fairly basic dwellings that were homes to families that had lived there for generations. The Star of David was painted in various places on what remained of the school. Khirbet Zanuta is a Palestinian village in the South Hebron Hills region of the West Bank, in Area C, where Israel has full security and civil control.

The villagers had abandoned their homes some months before the attack due to the persistent aggressive violence of the Israeli 'settlers'. When they went back to see about returning, they first realised that their village – home to 250 people – had been completely destroyed. The ruins were not all that met them there; they were intimidated by a group of settlers from an illegal settlement, the Meitarim Farm outpost, which human rights groups working with the local people profiled as a source of violence and harassment against Palestinians. The villagers' attorney wrote to the commander of the Hebron police district and the legal department of the IDF, demanding that they act to protect the property at Khirbet Zanuta and that they immediately investigate the threatening behaviour of the 'settlers'. To support the case, the attorney provided video evidence of the people involved, including the licence number of a vehicle used by the group directly responsible. The story of what happened with Khirbet Zanuta is illustrative of the Israeli state's intent in the West Bank.

A plaque on a wall of the destroyed school said it had been funded by the European Commission's Civil Protection and Humanitarian Aid department along with contributions from individual nations, including Belgium, Britain, France, Ireland, Luxembourg, Spain, and Sweden. This was the second occasion that a school in the area, funded by the EU, had been demolished. Before, in 2018, it involved those who were supposed to be governing the area, the Israeli-controlled Civil Administration, who justified the demolition by saying it had not granted permission for the school to be built. There was no consultation and no consideration of the community's needs; the occupying administration simply destroyed it without explanation.

In September 2024, as the local people made preliminary plans to return, they were warned against doing so by 'settlers' who said that if they chose to go back to Khirbet Zanuta, they would be met by a 'celebration'. These threats of hostility followed what was a very rare victory for the indigenous people in the High Court, which ordered the IDF and the police to enable their return. The law was followed in a fashion; the IDF met the Court's instruction to allow the villagers back, but then prohibited those forty who did from repairing the damage done to their homes by the 'settlers'. Then, the Civil Administration told the villagers that it was going to proceed with a demolition order that dated back to 2017 and relocate the residents.

It was very much a 'take it or leave it' offer as the agency told the lawyer acting for the villagers that, if they didn't agree, it would proceed with the demolition order within thirty days. The agency made no reference to the fact that where they were being moved to was subject to property claims by other West Bank residents. A small local Palestinian human rights organisation, Haqel, that co-produced a comprehensive report on Israel's occupation of Palestine in June 2024, said,

> There is no doubt that the timing of the state's proposal, precisely after the return of the villagers by order of the High Court to

> their village after the violent expulsion they underwent, is designed to formalize and complete the expulsion of Khirbet Zanuta's residents that was carried out by the settlers, and the ethnic cleansing that is being done in Area C.[164]

The Israeli NGO, B'Tselem, agreed, pointing out that generations of Khirbet Zanuta residents lived in natural caves in the area, as other people living in the area still do. Those families whose homes had been violated by 'settlers' lived in stone houses that relatives built in the 1980s when the caves began to collapse due to natural causes. They had built them without permits from Israeli authorities. When the High Court made its surprise intervention to support the villagers, the security services managed to fulfil the legal obligation by allowing them back to their homes but prevented them from carrying out the repairs essential to make them habitable. Then, they enacted an order from almost eight years previously and attempted, in trying to relocate the Palestinian residents to an area that was being claimed by others, to set Palestinians against each other.

The Civil Administration, which is meant to oversee equitably the governance of those parts of the West Bank where Israel has authority, instead works with the security services to support the actions of 'settlers'. Outside of Gaza, it is the 'settlers', whether they come from the United States, Europe or even from Israel itself, that are at the vanguard of the Zionist campaign, which requires the theft of all of the West Bank and East Jerusalem so that any idea of Palestinian nationhood being realised on the land that is, actually, Palestine, can be written-off forever.

In early 2024, Israel's approach to bringing settlers into the West Bank increased, as did its armed support of the 'settler' movement, so greater areas of land could be taken more speedily. The approach was different to the destruction of Gaza, but even still, the number of Palestinians killed increased markedly as the methods used to take their land became more aggressive. With each month that passed, there was more evidence of military involvement. In April 2024, fourteen Palestinians, including two children, were killed in a raid by the IDF on the refugee camp of Nur Shams.

The Nur Shams camp is an area of crude housing over 23 hectares that's home to around 6,000 Palestinians. The IDF had entered the area in 2023 but in what human rights groups described as an exercise in intimidation. This time, they came to kill and to destroy. Using ground forces, drones and bulldozers, they were met by militants determined to protect the indigenous population. UNRWA has run the camp, managing its two schools and its health centres since 1952 and, after the attack, the UN's Office for Human Rights said that it believed several Palestinians were unlawfully killed and that soldiers 'used unarmed Palestinians to shield their forces from attack and killed others in apparent extrajudicial executions'.[165]

Israel's defence was that some of those killed were armed militants. This narrative is largely accepted in the West without reference to the need for people to take up arms in order to stop the systematic theft of their land that has continued unchecked for decades. The other consideration for those brave enough to fight back – is the protection of the wider Palestinian population. Throughout 2024, Israel managed a coordinated campaign toward the realisation of its ambition, which means, as well as pursuing its interests in Gaza, it has supported over 1,000 settler attacks on Palestinians in the West Bank and arrested more than 10,000 Palestinian citizens. The attacks are generally reported, the arbitrary arrest of civilians less so, the sheer numbers making that impossible. B'Tselem and HaMoked say the IDF's policy of heavily restricting the Palestinians' freedom of movement means the numbers being held under administrative detention has increased significantly.

Seeking Refuge

I am the grandson of displaced people, of refugees. My grandfather, Joseph Connolly, travelled to Dublin at Easter time 1916, with every intention of fighting the British in the planned uprising. He had been a leading member of the Irish Volunteers in Belfast since 1914. When he arrived in Dublin, his superior officer ordered him to travel back in the direction from where he'd come to the town of Drogheda with countermanding orders, telling the volunteers there to stand down. Fate may have determined that he didn't fight in the Rising but he had trained to do so and had travelled with the clear intention of fighting. 'I'd heard Pearse [Pádraig Pearse, one of the leaders of the uprising] propounding clearly the need for blood sacrifice and, if the Rising was taking place, then there was only one thing to do and that was to join in with the others.'[166]

My grandfather was among those arrested by the British and imprisoned first in Dublin and then in Frongach. In the days before he travelled to Dublin for Easter 1916, the records show the great efforts he made to complete a will that included his brother

Alec, who flatly refused because he, too, was determined to take part in the Rising. My grandfather was a revolutionary, a 'freedom fighter', someone who opposed the later establishment of the Free State government but who circumstance determined would never fire that cliched shot in anger that he was trained and ready to fire. When he was released from prison, he returned to Belfast and his business, where he and my grandmother started their family. They were tense times, though and as his republican activities continued, their home became a 'safe house' for operatives of Sinn Féin and the Volunteers. Then, between June 1920 and June 1922, Belfast was ravaged by pogroms against Catholics.

It wasn't the first time he'd experienced such events. My grandfather was just 13 years old when the authorities allowed what were termed 'clearances' of about 700 Catholic workers from shipyards, linen mills and other Protestant-controlled businesses. He was 27 when, in 1912, about '2,400 catholics and 600 protestant trade unionists were, often violently, driven from their places of work.'[167] These experiences were nothing to what was experienced in Belfast between 1920–22. 'More than 500 people were killed in his native city, 500 were interned, 23,000 were made homeless and more than 50,000 fled.'[168] Most of the victims (73 per cent) were nationalist civilians.

Those figures were illustrative of a deeply fractured society, one which forced an estimated 50,000 nationalist or Catholic citizens to flee south. My grandfather was a high-profile member of the nationalist community who had stood unsuccessfully for Sinn Féin in Mid-Antrim in the 1918 Westminster (UK) election. With a young family, it became imperative to leave an increasingly dangerous West

Belfast. The life they wanted was threatened. They were educated, successful, with every reason to believe in what might lie ahead, but they were also nationalists who realised their young family was, to quote Warsan Shire, 'in the mouth of the shark'.[169]

Even though Dublin was only 170 kilometres south, it offered safety and prospects for their family, which Belfast could not. They were in fear. They fled. They were refugees in their own land or displaced people, as they would now be profiled. More than a decade later, Joseph Connolly served two terms as a minister in the government of the Irish Republic that made up most of the now partitioned island. Partition had become part of the political, business and social life of the island with an increasing drift toward acceptance of its permanency and away from any great interest in the welfare of those in the nationalist community who had, at the stroke of a pen, been cut adrift and remained under British rule in Northern Ireland.

With the passage of time, the government in Dublin paid less attention to the welfare of Irish people in the North and the British government did little to improve their welfare or to reverse the substantial levels of discrimination that pertained. The situation became more oppressive, and by the late 1950s, a sense of hopelessness had set in for many nationalists who, unlike their kin in the Republic, still lived under British control. It took another decade before the pressure that had been building spilled onto the streets. The civil rights movement was born but, when street protests were met by force, the seeds were sown for considerably more serious action. The IRA, which had been dormant for decades, was to reemerge as the Provisional IRA.

In Dublin, successive governments led by the former opposing factions in the Irish Civil War chose to distance themselves from the plight of northern Catholics. There was a difference in tone between the pro-Treaty Fine Gael, and those who had opposed it, Fianna Fáil, but neither party was prepared to go to the political gallows in the interests of those Irish people who had been caught by history's turn and remained living under British rule. That political distance reflected a growing disinterest in most areas of the country as, with the passage of time, the majority of the population became ever more focused on the future of the Republic. That part of the island that had gained independence started to evolve as a politically divided but largely coherent nation. Certainly, institutional Ireland moved beyond concern about those who, by dint of place of birth, were being governed by the same colonial power that their brothers and sisters elsewhere had successfully rejected.

It wasn't that the nation's recent history was ignored. In the homes and schools of the Republic, children were taught Ireland's modern history. The 1916 Rising was a hallowed moment marked by fiftieth-anniversary celebrations with specially commissioned books, commemorative medals and vinyl records, as well as a large military parade in central Dublin. Four years later, the country was to be convulsed by a scandal where it was alleged that a number of government ministers had been using funds raised through a public appeal to help arm the IRA in Belfast rather than for the intended purpose of helping poor nationalist families in the city. Ministers were forced to resign, some faced criminal charges, most of the media was scandalised and it became a hotly debated subject for a generation.

Strangely, given her own struggle, my grandmother was angry at that turn of political events. Only fifty years before, her husband, my grandfather, had precisely the same intent, yet she was appalled that those who hadn't escaped the 'mouth of the shark', who still lived under British rule, were, in the 1970s, as determined to do whatever it took to live free of the colonial power. My grandmother, whose husband had taken up arms and who'd served time in a British jail, was prepared to support poor nationalist people in the place of her birth but not to enable them to continue to fight for their equal right to the independence she and her family now enjoyed. So, over the decades between the War of Independence, the Civil War and the partition of Ireland, the critical importance of that most sacred of things to people the world over – land – was systematically diluted to the point where those who chose to fight for their rights were, by the 1980s and beyond, largely demonised by their own.

Twenty-five years after the Belfast Agreement, Ireland is awash with those who expound with authority about what happened over the course of the past fifty years or more and yet they may have never experienced discrimination. Much of what passed for commentary on political events in Northern Ireland over that time lacked understanding, never mind empathy, for the needs and rights of nationalist people in Northern Ireland, people who are stranded there by an act of political expediency. Empathy is often lacking, too, in the commentary on what is happening in the Middle East; my own family's experience in Ireland has helped to shape my perspective on the situation in Palestine.

◆◆◆

The process of stealing Palestinian land by forced eviction that is so in evidence today in the West Bank is long established. When the area was governed under the British Mandate (1920–48), Zionists were evicting Palestinians from their own land – land they would otherwise have worked and maintained for generations. At that time, with Britain's approval, Palestinians were reclassified as 'tenant farmers' rather than 'owners' and Zionists were allowed to purchase as much land as they could afford. Huge tracts of land were transferred illegally into Israeli hands and the West enabled the start of Israel's settler-colonialism. This is a particular type of colonising. In Ireland, our ancestors were colonised by a Britain that wanted to govern us and force us to live under its laws. However, the objective of settler-colonialism goes beyond this: it is the complete replacement of the indigenous population.

Over the decades, the conflict between Israel and Palestine has had different manifestations but what has remained constant is the desired removal of Palestinians by Israel. In his book, *A Very Short History of the Israel-Palestine Conflict*, Ilan Pappé writes of the methodology, in March 1948, of Israel's fourth plan – Plan Dalet (D) – for the colonisation of Palestine. This was the Nakba: 'each village and neighbourhood was to be surrounded from three sides, leaving the fourth side free for residents to leave as they were expelled or fled in terror. Then the village was to be reduced to rubble, and explosives planted in the rubble, so no one could return'. The plan was drawn up by the military but approved by the Zionist political leadership. Pappé says that in the orders sent to troops, it was clear that, underpinning the strategy, lay an intent to eradicate the Palestinians rather than colonise their land with respect to governance: 'Palestinian villages and neighbourhoods the Zionists coveted were doomed to be ethnically cleansed from the start.'[170]

The pogroms in the West Bank that were conducted by 'settlers' and Israeli security services in the summer of 2024 were reminiscent of those in Derry and Belfast that had ultimately forced my grandparents to flee to Dublin in the early twentieth century but, even as they were carried out in broad social media daylight, the international community was unfazed. Granted similar latitude to do as it wished as it had in Gaza, Israel set about dealing with Palestinians in the West Bank in exactly the same way. The sense was of further confrontation; Israeli ministers warned the Palestinian population of 2.5 million that its plans for the West Bank were the same as for the Gazan enclave; there would be no safe hiding place. This is consistent with the Zionist plan: to make all of Palestine a living hell, somewhere it would make sense to leave before you are killed or starved to death.

In July 2024, the ICJ declared Israel's occupation contrary to international law and called for it to evacuate all of its settlements and pay reparations to Palestinians for damages caused by the occupation. Since then, Israel's approach hardened significantly, increasing its direct involvement in the ongoing theft ('settlement') of Palestinian land through the engagement of its military, using helicopters, drones and ground forces.

The conflict in Gaza, more than any other, completely shattered any sense of a global order around land, security and the basis on which war can be conducted. It was as if the rest of the world was still in shock over the Hamas attack of 7 October 2023 and so traumatised that it had – even as autumn a year later approached –

abandoned any thought of keeping Israel's response proportionate. Israel has the fiddle; it knows how to play the right tune, and the West, in large measure, dances to it. This is not new. The Western world, for all its sense of self-importance as the arbiter of good over evil, has for a long time abandoned the Palestinians to their fate at the hands of Zionists.

On Gaza, it seemed the case for a measured response was lost from the very moment details of the Hamas attack became clear and, allowing for limited and softly whispered urgings not to stray beyond the rules of war, the US administration of Joe Biden gave Israel clearance to do whatever it wanted. The West Bank was, or should have been, different, but the stated intent of the Israeli government is to lay waste to it as it has done Gaza. It became increasingly clear that its military actions in the West Bank had the express intention of increasing the scale and pace of the land grab that had been underway for decades.

Strategically, this land theft in the West Bank is important for Israel because the establishment of a state of Palestine demands, at a minimum, the West Bank, Gaza and East Jerusalem – the 1967 borders. The day before the ICJ ruling, Israel's parliament, the Knesset, passed a resolution rejecting the idea of a Palestinian state. The Zionists do not just want their own nation. The Knesset vote reinforced Israel's determination to deny that the people of Palestine can have one. It meant Israel's legislature was doubling down on denying the right of those whose land they are stealing from ever having the right to self-determination.

The land in the occupied Palestine territory (the West Bank, East Jerusalem and Gaza) constitutes, under the Oslo Accords, 'a single territorial unit'.[171] Israel believes international law, the accepted codes of behaviour, apply to it only when convenient; its ambition hasn't changed since the Nakba. Taking the West Bank and forcing Palestinians to flee is part of the Zionist project; another critical factor is denying them any right to return. As with Gaza, it follows that removing the idea that they have a state to return to is critical to that outcome.

Israel's main backers, who for years had allowed its annexation-creep to continue unchecked, were unmoved when it took some of the tactics it had deployed throughout 2024 in the annihilation of Gaza and went after Palestinians in the West Bank. In September 2024, the UN reported that 136 Palestinians in the West Bank had been killed in Israeli airstrikes that year, which seems small until it's compared with the six who were killed between 2020 and 2023. The situation was to get progressively worse as the year went on.

But Israel's military campaigns, both in Gaza and the West Bank, have not only killed unprecedented numbers, they have also forced many Palestinians out of their homes. Since the start of Nakba II, almost the entire population of Gaza (close to 2 million people) has been internally displaced, often multiple times, with roughly 100,000 Gazans managing to escape out of the strip. Thousands more were made to flee in the West Bank: 'Nearly 6,200 Palestinians, including more than 2,700 children, were displaced from their homes in the West Bank since October 7, by Israeli military home-demolitions or attacks that destroyed homes, as well as by state-supported settler violence. The UN recorded more than 1,400 settler attacks as of October 2, 2024.'[172] These numbers are likely to keep rising, yet there is often no place left to flee, even in the West Bank; Israel has worked hard to make sure that those who have been displaced have nowhere to return to. This, again, goes to the heart of the Zionist project – one that the Israeli legislature seems more determined to achieve than ever.

Lebanon

Lebanon is a small country of 5.6 million people, where the GDP has fallen 40 per cent in five years, and the UN reports that 3:4 of the citizens live below the poverty line. The estimated population figure is hopelessly vague on demographics, which is unsurprising given that no census has been conducted since 1932. It is generally accepted that about 2 million of its citizens emigrated between 1975 and 2010. One of the main features of Lebanon today, beyond where it sits geographically, is that it is home to more than 1 million Syrian refugees and an estimated 400,000 Palestinians. Lebanon has a complicated relationship with Palestine.

The Paris Peace Conference, established after World War I, was arranged to set out the peace terms designed by the victorious allies for the defeated nations. It was attended by representatives of thirty-two nations and laid out various initiatives to prevent future conflict; it was, however, also intent on punishing the defeated. Some of the decisions led to decades of resentment, with some historians believing that the treatment of Germany helped fuel the nationalism that caused World War II. The nations that drove the agenda and the outcomes in Paris were Britain, France, Italy, the United States and Japan. The stated intention was to manage the process of penalty and reparation in a manner that would reduce the chances of further global conflicts.

The result of this is considered to be among 'the great watersheds of twentieth-century geopolitical history'.[173] It included five treaties that were finalised at various stages over the following three years, which, to varying degrees, altered the maps of Europe and parts of Asia, Africa and the Pacific Islands. Turkey – or rather the Ottoman Empire – was among the losing nations in World War I. Its future was considered within the wider Ottoman considerations but was not resolved until the Treaty of Lausanne in July 1923 after a previous attempt at an agreement in Sevres in August 1920 had failed.

At the original meeting in Paris, once the conference made the decision to separate the former Arab provinces from the Ottoman Empire and to apply the new mandate system to them, the World Zionist Organization submitted its draft resolutions for consideration. Its president, Chaim Weizmann, who would be the first president of Israel, and David Ben-Gurion, its first prime minister, presented a map of what they hoped would be the new Jewish state at the conference. Their formal pitch for territory, which they wanted the allies to sanction, was all of the land of Palestine, as well as parts of Syria, Jordan, Egypt, Saudi Arabia, and Lebanon. They asked that the conference formally recognise the right of the Jewish people to the land of Palestine as their 'National Home' and that it would recognise the borders outlined as they had done on the map.

Their map of desired land was revelatory of the Zionist ambition; it included Lebanon's Nahr el-Līṭānī – the Litani River. The Litani is central to why Israel wants to claim sovereignty over large tracts of southern Lebanon that it has occupied for generations. It is why the Israeli army is stationed along its northern border and why UNIFIL (United Nations Interim Force in Lebanon) has had to be stationed in a buffer zone to try to prevent Hezbollah incursions and ensure Israel's full withdrawal until the government of Lebanon can restore its effective authority in the area.[174] While some hardliners in Netanyahu's government have even made claims about Israel taking all of Lebanon, there is reason to believe that the administration's ambition stretches at least as far as the Litani.

The Zionists who presented the map of the home they wanted for the Jewish people included the territory just beyond the Litani, which runs for one hundred and 20 kilometres from the Bakaa valley, north of Beirut, down the centre of the country, before it turns east to west into the Mediterranean. Its pronounced bend toward the coast is across southern Lebanon, 25 kilometres from the border with today's Israel, and it has long been prized by Israel because it was and remains a major source of water supply and irrigation for Lebanon. The French were heavily vested in Lebanon; as with Syria, it was to fall under their mandate, so they torpedoed that part of the Zionist plan and the river remained within Lebanon's borders.

The Zionist ambition never went away, however. In 1978, then an independent nation for thirty years, Israel's first invasion of Lebanon was codenamed 'Operation Litani'. The IDF invaded south Lebanon, an estimated 1,500 Palestinians and Lebanese were killed and more than 200,000 were displaced within Lebanon. The week-long campaign resulted in the UN establishing the buffer zone and putting troops on the ground with a UNIFIL force of 10,000 that continues to patrol the area. In 1982, as Ronald Reagan's White House became increasingly concerned about Israel, *The Washington*

Post was given access to a CIA report that said, 'Hardliners in Israel have for years pointed out that Israel, by seizing territory up to the Litani River, would gain a more defensive border and a greater supply of water.'[175]

The Litani River is a critical part of UN Security Council Resolution 1701 of 2006, which called for a complete cessation of hostilities between Lebanon and Israel. It provided for a demilitarised zone – a buffer area – that ran from what it termed the Blue Line (the border between the two nations) and the river. The resolution allowed only UNIFIL and the Lebanese army to possess weapons and any kind of military equipment in the area. The width of the buffer zone, which runs along the 76-kilometre border from Shebaa Farms in the east to Ras Naqoura in the west, ranges from 6 to 28 kilometres. There are 30 kilometres of coastline south of the Litani.

The river irrigates about 60,000 hectares and supplies water to 280 towns and villages, home to just over 800,000, or 20 per cent of Lebanon's population, three-quarters of whom are Shia Muslim. When Israel launched its full military offensive on Lebanon in late September 2024, Prime Minister Benjamin Netanyahu gave his standard speech, where he claimed, erroneously, that Hezbollah had, without provocation, been attacking northern Israel and that it was essential that Israel protect its borders. It was true that Hezbollah had, in some form of solidarity with Hamas and the people of Gaza, significantly increased the level of missile activity but at nothing like the levels claimed by Israel and, also, with very limited success.

There was no cause within the activity of Hezbollah for Israel to attack southern Lebanon, even less for it to engage in its pager attacks across the country, which killed and maimed scores of civilians, and its bombing, however targeted, of suburban areas of Beirut. The reason why Israel chose to start a war with Lebanon as it continued its bombardment of Gaza and increased its aggression in the West Bank was that its leadership was committed to seizing as much of the territory as it could at the expense of the indigenous people. There is nothing new about Israel's beliefs or about its ambition to realise them.

With Gaza destroyed, it was inevitable that Israel would turn its attention to Lebanon. With the West standing by idly as the Gazan campaign continued with unprecedented levels of death and destruction, Netanyahu's government knew it could again make a play for as much of Lebanon as it wanted, knowing that ambition would not be challenged. The signals from Tel Aviv were not new as government ministers tripped over themselves to strike fear into the hearts of the Lebanese. Minister of Defence Yoav Gallant suggested that every Lebanese take an aerial photo of what Israel had done to Gaza and superimpose it on Beirut to see what awaited them. Minister of Education Yoav Kisch – the person responsible for the education of Israel's children – said there was no difference between Hezbollah and Lebanon and that the country would be annihilated: 'Lebanon, as we know it, will not exist.'[176]

These remarks mirrored those of Prime Minister Netanyahu, for whom the move on Lebanon also made personal political sense. As the destruction of Gaza headed toward its first anniversary, he was also edging closer and closer to a date when he would have to deal with his two remaining indictments of corruption. For him, the country being at war represented the strongest possible cause for staying the hand of justice, which, as the case against the prime minister is considered substantial, might be necessary for him to stay in office. To survive politically, what Netanyahu needed was time, and nothing was going to grant him that like an extensive conflict, which would advance Israel's expansionist plans but equally could, as the need arose, conveniently be presented as a defence against the great Islamic monster: Iran.

Iran has long been a bogeyman gift to modern Israeli leaders. It is rare that those forces that do threaten Israel – Hamas and Hezbollah – are ever referenced other than as sponsored by or as proxies of the regime in Tehran. Not only does this tactic offer cover with the Iranophobic Americans and British but it has served Israel's politicians well with their domestic audience too. No leader has been as adept at using Iran tactically to win support at home and internationally than Netanyahu. So, with most of Gaza reduced to rubble – just as he had promised – and more of the West Bank under Zionist control, Netanyahu took his chance. If there was going to be a moment in history to push for that part of Lebanon south of the Litani River, autumn 2024 was it.

Within a few days in the middle of September 2024, the modest trading of missiles that Hezbollah and Israel had been engaged in for years escalated to a declaration of war. There had been earlier signs that Israel wanted to pull Lebanon and Hezbollah into the conflict. On 27 July, twelve civilians, including children, were killed in an explosion in the Israeli-occupied Golan Heights. It came as tensions along the border had heightened – my own planned trip to the city of Tyre one day earlier had been cancelled based on security advice – but after the carnage in the predominantly Druze village of Majdal Shams, in the Israeli-occupied Golan Heights, Hezbollah and Israel accused each other of responsibility.

Interestingly, days later, when Netanyahu sought to exploit what had happened by going to the village to place a wreath, a crowd of Druze residents,

> dressed in black gathered outside the soccer field where 12 children were killed while Netanyahu toured with local leaders, and chanted in Hebrew for him to leave. A crowd of locals – about ten rows deep – pushed up against barriers as Netanyahu toured the area, some yelling at the premier, calling him a 'murderer' and demanding that he leave. Others held up signs calling Netanyahu a war criminal.[177]

Whatever the truth of that attack, the local communities knew that their safety was at great risk as the missile activity – a constant for years – increased, so did the precariousness of their position. The Lebanese government's priority was different; it wanted to ensure that Israel would not strike further south, most especially that there could be an agreement, however informal, that the capital, Beirut, would not be hit.

In Beirut, the official view was that Israel would be unlikely to escalate as to do so would risk 'the kind of response that Hamas could not deliver whereas Hezbollah could wreak real harm to parts of Israel, despite its dome system'.[178] The Lebanese government thought the Golan Heights attack was most likely the work of Hezbollah, caused by a failure with one of its rockets, but there was confidence that, unlike its response to the Hamas attack, Israel would not use the hit on the village of Majdal Shams as cause for a broad military response. It was Hezbollah's understanding too;

security sources working with it and with French and US diplomats were under the impression that Israel's military focus would only be on the border region.

Whatever the source or character of the attack on the Druze village, it was the first of its type along the border with Lebanon over the course of 2024. It allowed Benjamin Netanyahu to again position himself as the saviour of his people. Still in the United States, after his address to Congress and his meeting with Vice President Harris, his office announced that he would be returning ahead of schedule. The moment was seized to leverage its full potential with words that, as ever, offered nothing other than the threat of what was to come: 'Hezbollah will pay a heavy price, the kind it has thus far not paid.'[179]

Beirut airport, the morning I left for Jordan on 28 July 2024, was busier than normal and one traveller, a Lebanese now living in the UAE, told me that he had been home to visit his parents in Tyre and make plans to evacuate them if the situation became more volatile in the south. I texted a Dublin radio journalist from the airport before boarding my flight to Amman: 'Could do 5 mins on the mood here and how it's changed in 24 hours. It's not an alarm but there's a heightened sense of exposure.'[180] The diplomatic efforts to contain it to the border area were intense, but over that weekend, the assessment I'd received that Beirut was off-limits was confirmed across the Western media with experienced correspondents in situ.

Two days later, on 30 July, those expectations were shattered when an Israeli missile attack on Beirut's Dahiyeh suburb killed Hezbollah's top military commander, an Iranian military adviser and five civilians. Lebanese officials and Hezbollah questioned 'whether diplomatic assurances had been relayed to the group accurately'.[181] The government of Lebanon chose to emphasise the need for restraint and appealed for an immediate cessation of the hostilities. The US, in contrast, chose to commit itself fully to the bellicosity of Israel's prime minister: 'Our support for Israel's security is ironclad and unwavering against all Iran-backed threats, including Hezbollah.'[182]

So, again, the United States embraced Israel and told the world that, no matter what, they would be united; whatever it was that Israel, uniquely Israel, needed by way of support would be provided. The offer was not just 'iron-clad'; it was necessary because, for decades, the US narrative has been that any force opposed to Israel is backed by the Islamist bogeyman, principally the Republic of Iran.

It was to be another six weeks before the government in Tel Aviv turned its attention to Lebanon with real purpose. In early September, in a clever, sophisticated act of terror, using technology that it had used to corrupt pagers being used by Hezbollah members, hundreds of them exploded in Lebanon over a couple of days. Thousands were injured and a dozen were killed, two children and four healthcare workers among them. With only a limited and subdued international questioning of its direct engagement in a blatant act of terrorism, one that had placed the lives of the most innocent at risk, Israel chose to revert to its more familiar military approach.

A week later, it began a sustained and indiscriminate bombing campaign that killed hundreds of civilians and caused thousands of injuries. Prime Minister Netanyahu continued his tactic of exaggerating the threat posed by Hezbollah to Israel's sovereignty and both he and his minister of security, Ben-Gvir, started to raise the stakes by referencing the need for the IDF to prepare for a ground invasion of Lebanon.

The Israeli narrative of the threat posed by Hezbollah and how it alone represented the West's need to curb Iran's ambition for regional dominance, with the attendant 'curse' of Islamism, was as pure an act of fiction as anything it had said about Gaza. It was true that Hezbollah had fired missiles into Israeli territory on 7 October 2023, signalling its support for the actions of Hamas, but in the eleven-month period between then and Israel launching war on Beirut and southern Lebanon, 82 per cent of the missiles fired between the two countries had been fired by Israel.[183] Israel was as militarily threatened by Hezbollah as Netanyahu was by having to pay for his own dry cleaning.

Israel's actions in dealing with the security threat it claimed was posed by both Hamas and Hezbollah were similar; the conduct of each campaign showed a complete disregard for civilian lives. The abandonment with which it set about its campaign to wipe out the Palestinian people across the land it has illegally occupied for decades was matched by the potency of its purpose in the first weeks of its attack on Lebanon. In the deadliest strike of those first weeks, on 23 September, it killed hundreds of people, of which the Lebanese Health Ministry said, 'the vast majority, if not all of those killed in yesterday's attacks, were unarmed people in their homes'.[184]

In Lebanon, Hezbollah represented a threat to the ambition of Israel, which Netanyahu worked hard to camouflage. This Zionist objective meant that, just as Hamas had to be defeated if the Palestinians were, once and for all, to be run out of Palestine, Hezbollah was an obstacle to taking most of southern Lebanon. Just a couple of days before the 23 September attack and in the wake of Netanyahu's TV appeal to the Lebanese that Israel had no quarrel with them, only with Hezbollah, his minister of diaspora affairs, Amichai Chikli, posted on X (formerly Twitter), 'Lebanon, even though it has a flag and even though it has political institutions, does not meet the definition of a country.'[185] Interestingly, given Israel's history with its neighbour and its covetousness of the land south of the Litani River, the minister went on to reference the need for all Lebanese to be removed from southern Lebanon.

To coincide with the widening of Israel's aggression toward Lebanon, President Isaac Herzog, who had effectively snoozed through the firestorm that had engulfed his country over its conduct in Gaza, suddenly appeared on US TV networks being interviewed, or more correctly, being 'softballed' some questions about Lebanon. The man who, just eighteen months previously, had tried to use his position as president to mobilise some form of civilian opposition to his government's plans for judicial reform had, however belatedly, decided to jump aboard the 'Netanyahu express'.

Internationally, conflict with Lebanon may have needed the president's diplomatic imprimatur, which involved, to a large degree, him repeating the lie that Israel had no choice but to go to war with Hezbollah because 'Israel has been attacked from October 8th [2023] from Lebanon; endlessly'.[186] The Israeli narrative rarely changes; it is always the oppressed, always the threatened party, never the schoolyard bully. It is a storyline that found favour with the electorate. In the summer, as tensions were rising, a poll showed that 62 per cent of Jewish Israelis supported an attack on Hezbollah in Lebanon with 'full force', with 36 per cent of these respondents supporting an immediate attack and 26 per cent an attack only after the operation in Gaza.[187]

President Herzog, who had gone missing for much of 2024, knew that his chances of corralling Netanyahu as he had wished with his citizens' framework lay in the ruins of Gaza and the stolen homes, orchards and olive groves of the West Bank. Now Herzog decided that Lebanon was the cause with which he could publicly align himself with his autocratic prime minister. Where better to start than with the US networks, where tough questions are rare and much of the audience would appreciate his gratitude for the unstinting support of the United States?

President Herzog, mute on Gaza, had now found his voice, though it was only to be heard on Western media where he was sure he could pretty much say what he liked about Lebanon and Hezbollah. There was no surprise that he consistently played the oldest trope in the Western manual, saying how Israel regretted having to take the action it had, but Hezbollah 'are proxies of the Iranian empire of evil. And all of these proxies are trying to close in on Israel from all sides of our borders. That's the real situation. Now, Hezbollah's … a terrorist army, which basically hijacked a nation called Lebanon'.[188] It seemed he would adopt the media tactics of his prime minister and most of his cabinet in not letting the facts get in the way of Israel's narrative.

The facts – available to all the networks that interviewed him but never used – showed how easily he lied. ACLED's (Armed Conflict Location and Event Data) figures showed that, between 8 October 2023 and 6 September 2024, Israel had launched at least 7,845 attacks on Lebanon, killing at least 646 people, while Hezbollah and other armed groups were responsible for 1,768 attacks that killed 32 Israelis. The argument that Israel had to go to war with Hezbollah was nonsense, but the point of no return had been reached for Benjamin Netanyahu and it seemed President Herzog too. The other lie was that Hezbollah had 'hijacked' Lebanon. Hezbollah is more than just a guerrilla army; it is a political party as well; one of the two largest in Lebanon, it has 14 seats in the 128-seat parliament, has a place in government and is a political party recognised by a number of states and the European Union.

In 1982, Israel was also led by a hardline prime minister, Menachem Begin; his minister of defence, Ariel Sharon, was even tougher and militarily brilliant but also known to be ruthless in the pursuit of his plans. The PLO was fractured and much less active than it had been in the 1970s when it had carried out some audacious, if brutal, attacks. It was relatively quiet until an attempt was made on the life of Israel's ambassador to the UK, Shlomo Argov. Israeli intelligence told Sharon that the shooting had nothing to do with the PLO; it was in fact a renegade Arab group sponsored by Sadaam Hussein of Iraq. Sharon and Begin had plans, however, and given Israel's thirst for land, they capitalised on the event for their own ends; the truth could not be allowed to get in the way of an opportunity to invade neighbouring Lebanon.

Within a fortnight, the Israeli army had surrounded Lebanon, where Yasser Arafat, the father of the Palestinian movement and then head of the PLO, resided, along with his leadership cohort. The siege that followed lasted almost two months. While Ronald Reagan, two years into his first term as president, had given the invasion his blessing, he and his officials began to see and hear, even without the 24/7 exposure of today's social media, reports of thousands of Lebanese civilians perishing. The White House then leaned on Menachem Begin to bring hostilities to an end.

Arafat and all of his PLO leadership left Beirut for different locations across the region, allowing Israel to claim an important victory, which Ariel Sharon suggested represented a mortal blow to the cause of international terrorism. It was an idle boast, one that was shattered by the behaviour of the troops who, under his command as Israel's minister of defence, watched on as the Phalangists, a Lebanese Christian militia, massacred more than 2,000 Palestinian civilians in the refugee camps of Sabra and Shatila. The huge loss of life in such brutal circumstances, the slaughter of thousands of innocent people, done with the aid of flares used by the Israeli armed forces, had an added poignancy because the residents of the camps were among the 700,000 Palestinians expelled by Israel during the Nakba of 1948. They had fled Israel's genocide only to perish, decades later, at the hands of Christian militia whose night-time slaughter was carried out under floodlights provided by the IDF, who had sealed all exits to the camps and watched on, not unenthusiastically.

Many Lebanese do not trust the Palestinians. The history between them is fraught and connected to the Nakba of 1948. The influx of Palestinian refugees then and again in 1967 after the Six-Day War, with the annexation by Israel of what became termed 'the occupied territories', contributed to the growth of Lebanon's Muslim population. With almost 500,000 Palestinians living in Lebanon by the late 1960s, the country's Muslim minority grew, causing a consequent change in its demographic. The PLO was active in the camps where most of the Palestinian population lived and the Christian leadership of the country felt threatened.

In 1975, Lebanon fell into a civil war as fights broke out between Palestinian insurgents and Christian militias. Initially, the war was purely between domestic religious or ideological groups; subsequently, external parties, including Syria, Israel and Iran, became involved. The war lasted almost a decade and a half, with 150,000 deaths and more than 1 million Lebanese – mainly Christian – having to flee their homeland. Many went to France, were granted refugee status, and, having the right to return, did so in the years after the war ended.

Most refugees came back, and many now hold positions of influence in Lebanese society, business, academia, and public service. There are differences in their perspectives but there is a fundamental similarity: having been bruised by what war had done to them and their families, they all want peace. Christian Lebanese are more understanding of Israel's response to Hamas' 7 October attack; they were wary of Palestinians because they had fought them and considered them responsible for having to flee to France in the 1970s. There was no love of Israel, no sense that their cause was just, but there was, for many, a hangover from an experience that had been life-changing.

Lebanon's fragile economy supports more than 300,000 Palestinians, so any risk of the war in Gaza escalating had to be avoided, even if that meant keeping away from criticising Israel's actions in Gaza. The Lebanese were prepared to turn their gaze the other way. It was, they declared, a case of 'Lebanon First' – the country simply could not afford to go back to war. They had a clear appreciation of how Israel was abusing the Palestinians' rights but Lebanon's stability – its growth – had long been undermined by the Palestinian 'problem'.[189] They were horrified by what they'd seen of Israel's actions but not to the point where the future of their own land could be compromised.

In the months leading up to Israel's decision to widen its aggression and pursue land across its northern border into Lebanon, there was some concern that Israel might use Gaza as cover for taking land elsewhere, not just the West Bank but right along the Lebanese southern border and the Golan Heights. 'They will stop at nothing, even getting all the West Bank would not satisfy them. I'm not even a Palestinian but I know enough to see how they want to wipe out the whole Palestinian race.'[190]

The sympathy didn't translate into more than words, but it was an acknowledgement of the reality for the Palestinians. Even Lebanese who fought Palestinians in the war decades ago had a different view if it proved Israel's plans included taking any part of their homeland too. In that scenario, even Hezbollah critics would be turned into ardent supporters of the need to protect every metre of Lebanese soil.

The younger generations were more hardline; no political cause could justify genocide, as they believed Israel was conducting in Gaza. Their views on Israel and its war in the strip were well-informed, more in line with many younger people internationally, and allowed for no conditionality. The Hamas attack on 7 October was shocking but 'not unexpected given the brutality of Israel, its relentless annexation of land and the imprisonment of thousands of Palestinians without charge'.[191]

When it came to Lebanon, all agreed that none of its land could be lost to Israel and they would fight for it if that was required. There was unanimity across the generations that Israel had no right to be in Gaza but, selfishly, the fact that it seemed preoccupied with Hamas and the Palestinians made it less likely to engage with Hezbollah. The almost daily exchange of missiles in the south near the city of Tyre had been going on for so long that they were largely unaffected by it. Their sympathy for Palestine was about its loss of territory; it was the theft of land in Gaza and across the West Bank that they could relate to more than anything. It was this that united Lebanese of different ages and different faiths.

The demilitarisation of southern Lebanon and the return of that part of the country to its people was a *sine qua non* for all Lebanese; most would insist on each and every inch of it being restored to Lebanon. They wouldn't countenance Lebanon ceding fragments of its territory in the south in order to secure a lasting peace. Resolution 1701 must be implemented without alteration or any diminution of Lebanon's right to its land. It was or is an immutable position for the vast majority of Lebanese, including the millions scattered across the globe.

◆◆◆

The reality of Israel's approach to Lebanon and the Lebanese shows very little difference to its campaign in Palestine. Nor is it new. In 2006, it destroyed most of south Beirut, and in 2008, its military briefed Israeli media that the IDF had been given the go-ahead to use maximum force in its bombardment of towns and villages in southern Lebanon. Former IDF Chief of Staff Gadi Eisenkot made it clear: 'What happened in the Dahiya quarter of Beirut in 2006 will happen in every village from which Israel is fired on … We will apply disproportionate force and cause great damage and destruction there. From our standpoint, these are not civilian villages, they are military bases.'[192]

Whatever its ultimate course, the decision, in summer 2024, to extend its operations into Lebanon, at a time when its considerable resources were already stretched, represented a huge commitment for Israel. The decision to greatly increase its theatre of war had to have been strategic; it had to involve the prize of testing the Lebanese and the international community's resolve on southern Lebanon, maybe as far as the long-prized Litani. For Netanyahu, there was the additional benefit of putting the whole country on more of a war footing. Those political benefits were quickly apparent. In the last days of September 2024, for the first time since 7 October 2023, national opinion polls showed a sharp rise in support for Netanyahu and his Likud party after the attacks on Beirut and the assassination of Hezbollah leaders.

The continuing spectre of Israel's military campaign in Gaza and the West Bank as the giant folly of a rogue prime minister who desperately needed the conflict to stall his indictments was lessened by the escalation that a war with Hezbollah represented. It also allowed the pretence that the aggression was necessary to curb Hezbollah in moving to breach Israel's northern border and threaten its citizens in towns and villages in the area, which was hyped for months in advance in order to give the escalation greater credence operationally. It worked: the change for Netanyahu went beyond a strong, if relatively short-lived, uplift in public support. The escalating war with Hezbollah met with the approval of most of his most trenchant critics, both on the right and on the centre-left politically:

> opposition movements perceive the war in Lebanon as an offensive led by the military and the defense minister for 'objective' reasons … Unlike the differences of opinion (few, but they do exist) on how Israel is fighting in Gaza from a humanitarian perspective, there is no such dispute at all over the war against Hezbollah, which is perceived even by large parts of the Israeli left as just and necessary.[193]

The assassination of Hezbollah leader Hassan Nasrallah in Beirut at the end of September and a number of its other prominent figures seemed to invigorate the government, which, within days, had announced its intention to open up a ground war on its northern neighbour. Lebanon, Hezbollah certainly, and Israel had a long history. They had fought a war in 2006, only half a dozen years after Israel had ended its almost two decades-long occupation of southern Lebanon and there's long been a sense among many Israelis of 'unfinished business'.

Internationally, there was no outcry from the international community over the pager attacks on Beirut that so recklessly threatened civilian lives or over the aerial bombardment that followed over the ensuing days and took hundreds of them. With almost casual indifference to the way his words might fall across large parts of the globe, Joe Biden gave his public approval for the

Israeli airstrike that killed Nasrallah, saying that he was a 'terrorist' who was 'responsible for killing hundreds of Americans' and that, with his death, it was time for 'threats to Israel to be removed'.[194] Sentiments echoed in the remarks of his vice president and candidate for the November presidential election, Kamala Harris. The leaders of nations that took the opposite view, in statements offered with as much alacrity as the White House, accounted for almost half the world's population. Hezbollah is Iran's most prized regional ally, so there was no surprise when Ayatollah Ali Khamenei vowed that Nasrallah's death would not be in vain.

Nowhere in the West was there commentary on the irony of Israel's leaders congratulating themselves on the assassination of a political leader who had committed terrible crimes and had initiated campaigns that had led to the death of thousands of civilians. Nowhere were there words of caution about the number of civilian lives lost in Beirut over three nights of bombing when the strategic focus of the escalation was said to be southern Lebanon. Nowhere were the words of congratulations tempered with the attempts to 'stay' Israel's hand from continuing its aggression. There was no conditioning of the support for the assassination of Hezbollah leaders, no reference to Israel's murderous campaign against civilians in Palestine and how its actions in Lebanon had already taken the lives of approaching a thousand innocent Lebanese.

The general of the Iranian Revolutionary Guards was assassinated in the same attack, registering a shock to Iran's own capacity to defend itself against Israel and increasing, for a time, the risk of a much wider conflict. With Iran in the mix, Israel successfully reduced the potential for criticism by United States legislators to practically nothing and gave itself more space and scope to broaden its intent and to push for the Zionist dream of a state of Israel that extended across all of Palestine and to the north reaching into Lebanon as far as the Litani River.

With Lebanon as the new battleground and the genocidal campaign in Gaza continuing apace, the attitude of the Arab nations toward Israel hardened, including those like Qatar and Saudi Arabia that had been working toward positive diplomatic relationships. With continuing bloodshed in Lebanon and as the first anniversary of 7 October approached, Deputy Prime Minister of Jordan Ayman Safadi spoke on their behalf:

> We are members of the Muslim Arab Committee, mandated by 57 Arab and Muslim countries, and I can tell you unequivocally that all of us are willing, right now, to guarantee the security of Israel in the context of Israel ending the occupation and allowing for the emergence of a Palestinian state. Ask any Israeli official their plan for peace, you'll get nothing.[195]

EIGHT

The West's Asleep

See No Evil Hear No Evil

There was considerable diplomatic activity from 7 October 2023 right through 2024 but little of it focused on Israel's great lie: its false claim to rights over land it has occupied illegally since 1967. In the process, over just twelve months, Israel killed at least tens of thousands and perhaps even more than 100,000 civilians while it did everything possible to deny the rights of the Palestinian people to what was and is theirs.

It was alarming to watch the ease with which – in the face of overwhelming evidence that Israel was conducting a genocide – so much of the Western world contorted itself to appear 'concerned' for Palestinians without 'upsetting' Israel. The twelve months between 7 October 2023 and 2024 were like one long camera roll of distressing images and atrocities comprising the untold suffering of the children, women and men of Gaza, the increased level of land theft that communities in the West Bank experienced and, from late summer 2024, the death and destruction wrought by the IDF on southern Lebanon and its capital Beirut.

In the conclusion of his book, *The Hundred Years' War on Palestine*, Rashid Khalidi says,

> Settler-colonial confrontations with indigenous peoples have only ended in one of three ways: with the elimination or full subjugation of the native population, as in North America; with the defeat and expulsion of the coloniser, as in Algeria, which is extremely rare; or with the abandonment of colonial supremacy, in the context of compromise and reconciliation, as in South Africa, Zimbabwe, and Ireland.[196]

Ireland's history has been marked indelibly by the experience of being colonised by Britain, which is one reason the majority of Irish people have long supported the rights of the Palestinians. Over 2023–24, Ireland has, politically, stood firm with a small number of other Western nations in attempting to place Israel under some form of moral pressure. It is not just Ireland; there's a great deal about what people across the West have seen about Gaza that has stirred a deep sense of injustice and, for many, a sense of betrayal that the big powers in Europe, along with the US, have channelled massive resources to Israel to allow it continue its oppression of the Palestinian people. The protest marches, the social media posts, the various public displays of support for Palestine were as much about condemnation of the big Western powers for their enabling of Israel's colonial ambition as they were about drawing attention to Israel's genocide.

The scale of Israel's response to the Hamas attack of 7 October 2023 is unparallelled. What Hamas did was brutal and involved significant loss of life, including more than 800 civilians; it was an attack that will have scarred all those Israelis present and their families. But the military response and the number of civilian lives taken by Israel since, the destruction of places and of communities, all toward the obliteration of a whole people, has been completely disproportionate. It was impossible not to look on with a mixture of shame and helplessness at how the huge public response in support of Palestine across the West was neutered by the governments of the most powerful nations standing firmly behind the aggressor of fifty-seven years and counting.

That Israel used 7 October as the pretext for a long-planned demolition of Gaza and manoeuvred to widen the conflict as it did in autumn 2024 is not that surprising. Israeli society has never shifted far from the Zionist pulse. Its education system, its media and many parts of its public service have been influenced by right-wing Zionist idealism, which presumes Israel is entitled to do anything that is required in the establishment of its rights to the land of Palestine.

The institutional response in the West since 7 October 2023 was alarming from the outset. Israel launched attacks on Gaza within hours and, as its onslaught scaled up, it was met by only the meekest of global political mutterings. Its key allies supplied it with unlimited arms and cash as it continued the destruction of that part of the occupied territories with shocking numbers of civilian casualties right through 2024. As it did so, Israel dramatically increased its support of the long-established annexation of land in the West Bank by its citizens before, later, without anything approaching serious provocation, it chose to extend the conflict to its northern border with Lebanon up to that country's capital city, Beirut, by engaging with Hezbollah.

Throughout 2024, the onslaught on Gaza dominated the Western media. The number of fatalities being reported by the Hamas health authority was staggering, though later, the global medical journal, *The Lancet,* projected numbers that were multiples of those estimates. While Israel refused any access to international media, the testimonials that emerged on social media, the videos taken by local people, volunteer doctors, nurses and other aid workers served to make up for the absence of international news channels. In many respects, those largely civilian accounts seemed more real and more powerful than the Western networks' portrayal of events. The independence of many news outlets has been compromised by the power of pro-Israel voices.

Over 2024, the world of immediate, citizen-led, eyewitness reporting made it impossible to escape the reality of being observers of a genocide, of the latest attempt by the state of Israel to erase Palestine, its people and its history, with the active encouragement of some of the West's major powers. The added horror was that, unlike in the 1930s and 1940s when the Jewish people were themselves victims of a genocide, this time, there was no credible basis on which anyone in the West could claim not to have known what was afoot.

The Nazi echo chamber was a constant. World War II documentaries that feature footage of European cities like Warsaw, Rotterdam or Paris destroyed by the Luftwaffe seemed eerily similar to drone footage of vast swathes of Gaza devastated by the Israeli armed forces. That the descendants of the Jewish people who survived the

Holocaust and who, in an act of contrition by the Western powers for the failure to protect them, were assisted in the establishment of the state of Israel would engage in the oppression and destruction of another people, is hard to understand. To know, to observe, the extent to which they were being enabled in the pursuit of that project by most of the West's biggest political powers beggars belief. The truth is that much of the West is so absorbed by its sense of self, by its perceived status, that it cannot contemplate that its judgement of Israel could be so wrong. How is it even possible that the Middle Eastern nation that much of the West believes shares its values could be actively and deliberately conducting a genocide?

With the increased bombing of Gaza, more of its limited infrastructure was destroyed. While the number of civilians, the number of Gazan journalists, medics and NGO volunteers killed all increased markedly, the West's main powers watched on, unmoved. The media in the West remained generally uncritical. When Israeli airstrikes hit the schools run by UNRWA, even that brought no response other than the Israelis claiming that the buildings harboured Hamas militants.

In fact, illustrative of the environment in which Gaza has always existed and the certainty of future Israeli bombings, many UNRWA schools were built with bomb shelters so they could be used to protect the civilian population during the bombing campaigns that would inevitably occur. Most of the West's mainstream media made little or no attempt to understand the realities that dominated life in Gaza for decades, the war-like circumstances that had to be considered as infrastructure was built. Whenever a school was hit, generally with a large number of casualties, the Israeli military's claims that it had been hiding militants or that there was Hamas activity nearby would get considerable coverage, often at the expense of covering the civilian deaths.

Almost all of the time, across most outlets, the language used is that of the oppressor, Israel, so that, by rote, newsreaders and reporters describe Hamas fighters as 'terrorists' while, in the West Bank, groups of violent Jewish thugs that destroy people's homes as they drive them from their land are 'settlers'. So, when Hezbollah attacked an Israeli military base and killed four 19-year-old soldiers the same day as Israel bombed another school in Gaza and killed 23 civilians, including 5 children, the Sky News headline read, 'Israel names teenage soldiers killed in Hezbollah drone attack as 23 die in Gaza school strike'. This was by no means an isolated example; countless occasions of such biased reporting served to both undermine the moral credibility of the West and further Israel's view that it has a 'free pass' to conduct its business however it pleases.

Over the course of the first twelve months of Nakba II, this inherent pro-Israel bias was never more evident than when 7 October was presented as the cause of the conflict. Somehow, a credible narrative placed Israel as a modern, successful democratic state, going about the business of improving the lives of all its citizens when a group of terrorists crossed over its border and, without cause, killed around a thousand of its citizens, many of them young, and took 251 others hostage. Time and again, in political debate and media coverage in the West, this part of the narrative that exempted Israel from responsibility was embedded in the positioning of 7 October as the cause of the conflict and Israel's reaction as somehow understandable or reasonable.

The absence of historical context in most of the debate about the attack in the West points either to ignorance or deliberate misrepresentation. For most, it is the latter, necessary because only that line can feed the idea, so beloved of Benjamin Netanyahu's cabal, that Israel is the West's only defence against the menace that is Iran. The speed with which spokespeople for different Western leaders or indeed the leaders themselves will reference the 'Islamist threat' when Israel and Hamas or Hezbollah are on the agenda is remarkable. The wider cultural point, one that's dangerous, is a general portrayal of those from the Arab world as 'different', 'shady', 'untrustworthy' – all terms that are just a pause or clearing of the throat away from describing them as 'terrorists'.

With the West's influence on the wane simply by dint of its falling share of the global population – around 12 per cent – its institutions need to be more vigilant about how they manage relationships. Israel, at its most delusional, describes itself as a 'Western democracy', which might make it seem a natural partner; but the partnerships Western powers should be forging in the Middle East might be elsewhere. The West urgently needs to broaden its horizons and recognise its presumed morality is not particular to it and is as evident, if not more so, within different cultural environments.

Over the year of Israel's devastation of Gaza, killing a significant percentage of its population, the horror of citizen reporting on individual cases was often matched by the reports logged by Palestinians in the West Bank on the brutality with which the Israeli 'settlers' stole their land, abusing men, women and children in the process. In this part of occupied Palestine, the decades-long theft of land must be recorded as one of the most blatant acts of colonialism ever. The amount of land that Israel has annexed, despite its presence being in contravention of international law, makes the acceleration it initiated under cover of the Gaza onslaught all the more alarming. The Israeli NGO B'Tselem, which has been documenting the stealing of Palestinian land for decades, reported that the levels at which land was taken in 2024 were unprecedented. Later in the year, incidents where many groups of 'settlers' were aided in their endeavours by the IDF increased, and later still, the armed forces engaged directly in the violent removal of people from their farms and homes.

What emerged increasingly over the course of 2024 was an unsavoury similarity in the behaviour of Israel's protagonists in Gaza and the West Bank (whether that was soldiers or 'settlers') with the actions of many of those charged with policing peaceful pro-Palestine protests in cities and on university campuses across the West. In the midst of the thousands of images of destruction and criminal activity online, two short videos captured both the nature of the oppression Israel is purposefully deploying against the Palestinians and how most of the institutional West is doing what it can to suppress the efforts of those who want action taken to stop its excesses. Both involved young boys and were, sadly, representative of events.

In the first, security footage from a small shop in the West Bank shows a very young Palestinian boy approaching the counter to pay for a small bundle of goods he is carrying. IDF soldiers on foot patrol come to the entrance and look in. One of them, with his machine gun in one hand, motions to the boy to stop. The shopkeeper looks on as the soldier removes the kid's shirt, throws it on the ground and walks away, then turns to walk back, picks up some of what the boy is about to purchase and throws an item on the ground. In the second video, at a protest rally in Berlin, a 10-year-old carrying a Palestinian flag is chased by a handful of German police officers. Adults try to protect him, but after a short chase, the police bundle him into a police van and take him away.

In two places, thousands of miles apart, the experience of these two children shows the character of the Zionist mission. Its pursuit in the Middle East is very much intact, while in Europe, it has such strong support that even a 10-year-old is considered a threat by the German police. Israel's hold on the West is unnerving and unhealthy, perhaps particularly so for Israel and its people.

The public pronouncements of its political leadership, like, 'There are no Palestinians, because there isn't a Palestinian people … They [Arabs] invent a fictitious people and claim fictitious rights to the Land of Israel',[197] are consistent with the ambition of the founder of modern Zionism, Theodor Herzl, who wrote, over a century ago, 'Palestine is our ever-memorable historic home.'[198] The pursuit of this ambition has found new life over the course of 2024, not on account of the Hamas attack but because Israel was allowed to use that event as *casus belli* to engage in a murderous campaign of destruction by a largely supine Western political leadership.

Without the sponsorship of some and the 'blind eye' of most of the rest, Israel's utterly disproportionate response to the attack on its soil by Hamas on 7 October 2023 could never have happened. This Nakba, unlike the original, could not have unfolded without the active, direct support of the United States and other Western powers. The legal pursuit of Israel's leaders to face the rigours of international criminal prosecution for war crimes should be accompanied by one aimed at those who enabled them in their murderous intent. The Western world watched on as Israel conducted its campaign, and from spring 2024, it was clear to all nations what its intentions were and that it was destroying Gaza without the remotest interest in the protection of civilian life. No government, no political leader, could credibly claim that they did not know this was happening, and those – most especially the United States – that provided it with the bombs to carry out that devastation must be held equally accountable.

The US

The 51 Star-Spangled Banner

When the history of this period is written, it is the United States of America on whom, out of all of Israel's allies, the greatest burden of guilt will rest. Its political leadership has behaved as though it comprises fifty-one states, the fifty that are part of the Union and the state of Israel. Its flag, the Stars and Stripes, should really carry fifty-one stars, including the Star of David. The way in which Netanyahu ran rings around the Biden administration and won the support of Congress was as if what he proposed, the campaign of destruction he led against the people of Palestine, was as much in the interests of the United States as of Israel itself. Netanyahu correctly calculated that neither the incumbent administration nor the presumptive one of Donald Trump could, in an election year, behave in any other way than taking the position that Israel's interests and those of whoever wanted to govern the United States were, in fact, aligned.

The attack of 7 October 2023 had been coming. In fact, despite the great shock expressed by Israel, its government had been given prior warning by international allies of such an incursion. That was not, perhaps understandably, part of the initial assessment by Israel's main allies. The death toll was the highest in Israel's history in any attack on its territory and the number of hostages taken contributed greatly to the reaction of its friends in the West, most particularly the United States.

Despite its tawdry history of international relations always led by self-interest, the US continues to portray itself as a nation that, above all others, upholds democratic values. This is aided in no small measure by its mainstream media, whose lexicon is littered with pontifical terminology and rhetoric – especially the ubiquitous use of the term 'leader of the free world' to describe its president – that reinforces the nation's sense of itself as 'special'. In part, its ever-unwavering support of Israel has contributed to the country's very inflated view of its own standing.

In his book, *American Reckoning*, a historical act of soul-searching about the Vietnam War and the notion of American exceptionalism, the US academic and writer Christian G. Appy suggests that if the future of the United States was to be less involved militarily and its tendency toward regular international interventions was to be ended, a first step 'is to reject – fully and finally – the stubborn insistence that our nation has been a unique and unrivaled force for good in the world'.[199] The political scientist Samuel Huntington had written in 1996 that Americans needed to understand that it was both possible to reaffirm their Western identity yet not see it as having a universal appeal or relevance.

Nowhere in the world is the United States more politically compromised than in the Middle East, where its relationship with Israel makes it impossible for any US president, no matter their party, and the vast majority of those who serve in Congress, to act independently or to judge the actions of that state and those with whom it is in dispute with any semblance of impartiality. This is impossible because the strategic and economic interdependency has been institutionalised for generations. Impossible because the great majority of them have accepted financial support – in some cases large sums – from AIPAC and other pro-Israel lobby groups that have much of the United States legislature under their control.

In US politics, the pro-Israel lobby is the equivalent in international affairs of the gun lobby domestically. It is impervious to criticism and it seems that Israel can act with impunity, knowing that its excesses will receive support or, at worst, mild rebukes, generally tempered by a reaffirmation of the special relationship between the two nations. In the book *The Israel Lobby and US Foreign Policy*, the authors suggest that, leaving aside how US policy in the region has influenced events in the Middle East, many policies it has pursued on Israel's behalf jeopardise America's own national security. This has, they say, no equal in US history: 'no lobby has diverted that policy as far from what the American national interest would otherwise suggest … The Israel lobby has successfully convinced many Americans that American and Israeli interests are, essentially, identical.'[200]

In the US, research indicates that legislators categorised as supportive of Israel receive considerable financial backing from Israeli interest groups. Open Secrets, the US-based NGO that tracks funding of different pressure groups across a wide range of issues in US politics, highlights twenty different pro-Israel lobby groups that fund US legislators. The total over October 2023–24 was just over $50 million, with the largest single contributor being AIPAC, which contributed just over $19.5 million.[201] Overall, the financial contributions across the pro-Israel lobby are weighted about 60:40 toward the Democrats but, as evidenced even over the course of this most callous of military campaigns by any Israeli administration, all levels of government in the United States remained resolute in their support.

The journalist Robert Fisk, who reported on Palestine for decades, understood this dynamic intimately. In his last book, *Night of Power*, he wrote about how the US had sold itself:

> The craven genuflection of the American elite towards Israel is as shameful as it is unworthy of a great nation. Strength and cowardice do not have to walk hand in hand, but that is the nature of the American-Israeli relationship. US foreign policy in the Middle East belongs to Israel to such an extent that American policy is now Israeli policy. Trump's decision to recognise Jerusalem as the capital of Israel in 2018 was merely an enlarged mirror of all that had gone before.[202]

Over the course of the brutal destruction of Gaza and the continuing theft of Palestinian land in the West Bank, nothing could move either the White House or Capitol Hill to be anything other than completely supportive of Israel. The willingness of the ICC to pursue charges of genocide against members of Israel's government, including Prime Minister Netanyahu, brought a furious denunciation by President

Biden, once a fierce proponent of the cause of the oppressed. Ahead of the ICC issuing its arrest warrant, a group of US senators wrote to its chief prosecutor, warning, 'target Israel and we will target you'.[203] The use of such aggressive language was bad enough, but on 4 June 2024, the House of Representatives passed a bill to sanction the ICC officials.[204]

Six weeks later, when Israel's Prime Minister Benjamin Netanyahu addressed the Joint Houses at a special sitting on 25 July 2024, the death toll in Gaza was bordering 40,000 according to the Gazan Health Ministry or a projected c. 100,000 in figures published around the same time by the global medical journal, *The Lancet*. The death toll was largely of civilians. In allowing Netanyahu to address a joint meeting of Congress at a moment in history where his government was conducting a genocide, the United States legislature diminished its standing in the world more than it has ever done in modern history. It was, nonetheless, representative of how hopelessly compromised the United States had allowed itself to become; how, for all its apparent power, it was Israel's, certainly Netanyahu's, lapdog.

Two former US presidents had prophesied – in different ways and at different times – just such an outcome: that without firmness, Israel would stretch its entitlement. Jimmy Carter and Ronald Reagan, back-to-back Democratic and Republican presidents in the late 1970s through the early 1980s, had to deal with a very challenging geo-political Middle East situation. Relationships between Israel and Palestine were played out against the backdrop of the Lebanese War, which had led to 150,000 casualties and the exodus of about 1 million people from Lebanon.

Carter, who tried without success to change the narrative, was considered to have a better appreciation of the Palestinian cause than any other US president. Later in life, he was unafraid to commit his view to print: 'In the occupied territories, there's profoundly disturbing proof of apartheid in its worst form, and I would say it's much more damaging in some ways to the Palestinians under the subjection of a domination of Israel than what the black people suffered in South Africa.'[205] ANC leader Nelson Mandela agreed, more than once branding Israel as a terrorist state and asking how it was that the terrorist moniker was so often applied to the Palestinians while Israel had oppressed them for generations. It's a great deal easier to see clearly and to criticise when you are no longer in power, but in all that Jimmy Carter ever said, post his retirement, there was a sense of a man who had witnessed first-hand the Israeli government's trademark deceit and determination. Reagan, who succeeded him, addressed publicly and firmly his country's responsibility toward the Palestinians. In 1982 and just a year in office, Reagan said, 'I re-emphasize my call for early progress to solve the Palestinian issue and repeat the US proposals, which are now even more urgent … to bring a just and lasting resolution to the conflict between Israel and its Arab neighbors, one that satisfies the legitimate rights of the Palestinians, who are all too often its victims.'[206] Just as Carter did, Reagan failed in that endeavour despite his high profile and seemingly genuine efforts to change the paradigm. While, despite their understanding of the Palestinian cause, neither man moved the dial appreciably on Israel's hold on US foreign policy, it is remarkable that half a century and multiple US administrations after Carter and Reagan were on the political beat in Washington,

US institutional support for the Palestinians has diminished to a nothing. Israel has managed to cement its position as strategically critical to the interests of the United States, and of the West more generally, in the Middle East.

◆◆◆

Over the last decade and a half, Israel's position in the US strengthened even further. In February 2011, the administration of Barack Obama exercised its UN veto to prevent a Security Council Resolution condemning Israeli settlement expansion. It was an extraordinary decision; the resolution had, in fact, been carefully worded to accurately reflect the position of the Obama administration in order to secure its vote, so the decision to exercise its veto represented a complete *volte-face*.

It was so marked that, in calling the veto, as she had been instructed to do, Obama's representative at the UN, Susan Rice, even appeared uncomfortable at the sleight of hand involved. Rice said that, while the US would veto the resolution, that decision shouldn't be taken to mean that her country supported the settlement activity: 'On the contrary, we reject in the strongest terms the legitimacy of continued Israeli settlement activity.'[207] The reason she later gave for such an epic display of diplomatic manoeuvring was that, for the US, supporting the condemnation risked hardening the positions of both sides.

To veteran US foreign policy watchers, there was no great surprise that the US could be both strongly opposed to Israeli settlements in the West Bank and equally determined to veto their declaration as 'illegal'. Stewart Patrick of the Council on Foreign

Relations said, 'The US has a long history of trying to prevent the United Nations from becoming an instrument to coerce Israel.'[208] It was left to human rights organisations, including Human Rights Watch, to call it for the fudge that it was: 'President Obama wants to tell the Arab world in his speeches that he opposes settlements, but he won't let the Security Council tell Israel to stop them in a legally binding way.'[209]

While this UN vignette represented a very public display of how the US will always protect Israel, even when the administration is one that the Palestinians might reasonably have thought would offer them some respite, there were more concerning incidents during Obama's presidency. What was particularly shocking was how, so early in his first term, his team counselled Israel on mitigating the ramifications of a UN fact-finding mission on Gaza (the Goldstone report) and actively worked with Tel Aviv to prevent the international community from pursuing Israel over its military offensive (Operation Cast Lead) that had killed more than 1,400 Palestinians (and 13 Israelis) between 27 December 2008 and 19 January 2009.

When the Goldstone report – which claimed Israel had committed war crimes – was released in September 2009, Obama's administration went into overdrive to protect Israel. Clear instructions were given that the findings had to be questioned, the conclusions disputed, so that Israel would not be held to account internationally. Secretary of State Hillary Clinton sent an urgent memorandum to all US ambassadors so they could engage with their host nations to 'prevent efforts to refer the matter to the International Criminal Court.'[210]

Clinton's defence of this was that the Goldstone report (named after its author, a South African Jew) had denied Israel's right to self-defence when it, in fact, had explicitly referenced Israel's right to protect itself. Years later, in a letter to Israeli-American billionaire Haim Saban that was riddled with falsehoods, as she sought to secure the Democratic nomination for the 2017 presidential contest, Clinton proudly referenced her condemnation of the Goldstone report. The letter to Saban is a great example of how deeply compromised Democrats and Republicans are in their conduct on Israel. She excoriated BDS (Boycott, Divestment, Sanctions) activists opposed to Israel's occupation and was so eager to secure the Jewish vote that she decried the role of the UN in any attempt at a negotiated agreement, saying, instead, that the negotiations should be solely 'between the occupying power and those under occupation',[211] thus betraying a willingness to abandon a fundamental tenet of international law.

The Goldstone report may have been damaged by the subsequent conduct of some of its members, including its chair, but, in real-time, as its findings were released, the Obama administration used its considerable influence to enable Israel to elude accountability for the crimes it had committed, which the report had spelt out. The report was balanced; it had been unequivocal in its criticism of Hamas, but the problem was that it found Israel's conduct no more becoming. This presented the US with a diplomacy problem, so it worked with Israel to proactively undermine the report's value.

Barack Obama fell in line with institutional America in defending Israel at all costs, but he went even further; he undermined the PLO's campaign for Palestine to be recognised as a nation-state and to achieve full membership of the UN. In 2013, at the height of the Arab Spring, catching the coat-tails of what appeared to be happening, Obama had extolled the impulse for freedom and democracy underlying the protests that were sweeping the region: 'the current convulsions arising out of the Arab Spring remind us that a just and lasting peace cannot be measured only by agreements between nations. It must also be measured by our ability to resolve conflict and promote justice within nations.'[212]

This high-octane speechifying was in sharp contrast to the administration's campaign against the UN granting full membership to Palestine, led by Hillary Clinton. The Undersecretary for Political Affairs, Wendy Sherman, testified before Congress that 'there has been a very broad and very vigorous demarche,' against Palestinian membership in the UN, 'of virtually every capital in the world, that this is high on the agenda for every meeting the secretary [Clinton] has with every world leader'.[213]

By the start of his second term, Obama had dispensed with any pretence of even-handedness, naming Martin Indyk as his special envoy for Israeli-Palestinian negotiations. Indyk had been a researcher at AIPAC and co-founded its think tank, the Washington Institute for Near East Policy. Obama was proving himself every bit as partisan toward Israel as any US president, with echoes of what Gerald Ford had written to Yitzhak Rabin in 1975 to clarify that any proposals the US might bring forward would, 'make every effort to coordinate with Israel its proposals with a view to refraining from putting forth proposals that Israel would consider unsatisfactory'.[214]

As a gifted political orator, one of Barack Obama's skills has always been to present an informed, open and positive public image of Israel, regardless of the reality of their political management. By that standard measure, there was no inconsistency between many of his public utterances and what his team was doing to shore up the interests of the government of Israel. Neither was there a problem in appealing for an end to conflict and a just resolution, but it was clear where the administration saw the source of the problem.

> For decades, the conflict between Israelis and Arabs has cast a shadow over the region. For Israelis, it has meant living with the fear that their children could be blown up on a bus or by rockets fired at their homes, as well as the pain of knowing that other children in the region are taught to hate them. For Palestinians, it has meant suffering the humiliation of occupation, and never living in a nation of their own.[215]

It was a staggeringly one-sided perspective. What was even more revealing was how President Obama chose to address the AIPAC conference just a few days later: 'No vote at the United Nations will ever create an independent Palestinian state.'[216] In any examination of Israel's outsized global political strength and the USA's influence on this, it's instructive to look at how the Obama administration – one that might have been expected to try to break the mould – chose to do nothing. The president's speech to AIPAC, six months before the election seeking his second term, was explicit in the alignment of his administration with Israel. In his lengthy address, the Palestinians were pinpointed as the reason peace talks had not advanced, while Israeli reluctance was presented as reasonable as, he argued, no country should have to negotiate with terrorists. The approach he had taken to Goldstone was touted as evidence of the USA's preparedness to stand up for Israel's right to defend itself.

It is reasonable to dwell on Obama's eight years in the Oval Office; there was real hope among progressives in America and elsewhere that he could and would deliver change to US foreign policy, whatever domestic constraints he might face. He was a brilliant campaigner and often used social and global issues as a means of connecting with the electorate, but, in the end, as represented by his approach to the Middle East, he was, as one historian profiled him at the end of his presidency, 'a disappointingly conventional President'.[217] The young firebrand politician had, like most before and since, found that when he was in charge, when he was president of the US, there was little choice but to resolutely support the cause of Israel. It is exactly what he did over his two terms in the White House.

Whatever other advances the United States may have made in its eight years with Barack Obama in the White House, he did nothing for the cause of the Palestinians. Nothing. When he first evolved from his Chicago base into a national figure, attention was paid to how connected he was to the Arab American community and how those of the Jewish faith among his Illinois advisers were liberals, unattached to hardline Israeli Zionism. The Palestine-empathetic words and tone of the young Obama politician carried through to the early days of his presidency; five months in, he pledged to the president of the Palestinian Authority, Mahmoud Abbas, 'the establishment of a Palestinian state is a must for me personally'.[218]

It was as empty an assurance as any offered to Palestinian leaders by an American president. Under Obama, military aid to Israel increased. That was in part due to commitments made by the Bush administration but, so conscious had Obama become of the alignment of Israel's interests with his own and those of the

US establishment, that every opportunity was taken to brag of the special levels of support to Israel provided by his administration. Addressing the pro-Israel Saban Center for Middle East Peace at the Brookings Institution, one of his senior officials, Andrew Shapiro, said it was because of President Obama's enduring commitment to Israel's security that the bilateral relationship was 'broader, deeper and more intense than ever before'.[219]

◆◆◆

Each November for many years, the United Nations General Assembly has taken a vote on a resolution called 'The Peaceful Settlement of the Question of Palestine', which would involve Israel withdrawing from those territories it occupied in 1967. International law – what President Biden told Israel to respect when committing the 'unprecedented support'[220] of the US after the Hamas attack – prohibits nations from taking territory by war. This means, of course, that Israel has no legal right to the territories it stole in 1967: East Jerusalem, the West Bank and Gaza. Every year, when the UN puts this resolution to the members of its General Assembly, there are only two votes against the resolution: Israel and the United States of America.

Why should we expect that the US would hold Israel to account for its breaches of international law when its own legislature ignores laws it passed to protect against just the kind of situation that America has found itself in over the course of 2024? The Leahy Laws, or Leahy Amendments, are US Human Rights laws, named after their sponsor, Senator Patrick Leahy of Vermont, that prohibit the US Departments of State and Defense from providing (any) military assistance to foreign security forces when there's 'credible information that [they have] committed a gross violation of human rights'.[221]

The United States' sense of global importance is such that, since the Leahy Amendments were introduced in 1997, its foreign policy needs and ambitions have seen many occasions when their intent has been ignored. US military officials argue that it restricts their ability to train foreign forces but, over the last decade, much of the attention has been on loopholes within the law that have allowed different administrations to ignore its purpose. Many of these incidents have related to Israel and, in spring 2024, it was reported that Secretary of State Anthony Blinken had refused to use the powers under the Leahy Laws to sanction Israeli units that had participated in torture, rape and extrajudicial killings in the West Bank. The recommendation came from a special committee within Blinken's own department; importantly, the reported events predated the Hamas attack of 7 October.[222]

It is known that there have been occasions in the past where evidence of the complete abandonment of human rights has been difficult to establish, so despite the reservations of officials, Israel and other nations continued to receive US aid in contravention of the law. This case was different; it met the bar set by the secretary of state's own department to warrant sanction, but Blinken, with an approach he would repeat later, chose to ignore the findings and the recommendation. That this involved actions taken before Israel's onslaught on Gaza and that it had happened at least a year before Israel moved its attention back to the West Bank demonstrates its umbilical attachment to the United States.

In an essay written four decades before Israel's all-out attack on the Palestinians in Gaza, the Palestinian-American academic Edward Said addressed the destructive axis between Israel and the US, saying that while the legality and legitimacy of international law rests with Palestine, US policymakers had long failed to 'make connections, draw conclusions, state the simple facts.' The critical facts were rooted, he said, in a Palestinian truth, which 'stems directly from the story of their existence in and displacement from Palestine.'[223]

The US and Netanyahu

With the gathering storm around his indictments, the man leading the aggression against the Palestinians, Benjamin Netanyahu, may have been the person with the most to lose. No one in modern Israeli political history has had such a deep appreciation of how to tag along with the United States than he. Equally, he fully appreciated that no matter how many opportunities you get to achieve your ends in Israel, without the support of the United States, you are lost. In his previous term in charge, there was no great surprise that he could out-shallow the prince of shallowness, Donald Trump, to the point where, against all expectations, the US moved its embassy from Tel Aviv to Jerusalem.

Any hope that the legacy left by the Obama administration might be different with Joe Biden in the White House was to be short-lived. The 'real' in US realpolitik means always being deferential to the demands of Israel and so it was proved again. In his first detailed remarks after 7 October, President Biden, as the United States had done many times, proceeded to support Israel based on information sourced only from Israel. The nature of the attack was described in graphic, if incorrect, detail (babies being slaughtered; beheadings; rape; people burned alive) before building to the crescendo that, more than any other single assurance, allowed Israel to commit its genocidal campaign: 'I'm going to ask the United States Congress for an unprecedented support package for Israel's defense.'[224]

It was through that cast-iron commitment, that use of the word 'unprecedented', in the midst of hopelessly weak caveats about Palestinian rights and, effectively, the need for Israel to behave itself, that Netanyahu knew he'd received a *carte blanche* from the US to do whatever he wanted to do. That commitment and the utter failure of the United States administration, or any part of its legislature, to corral Israel when, over the months that followed, it became clear that its government was engaged in war crimes and in the annihilation of Palestinians, is what allowed Netanyahu and the Zionists in his cabal to do whatever they wished. The caveats were nothing more than weak defensive points to be used in the event Israel went rogue; Biden's commitment was a weak gesture and could be presented as more guarded than it actually was. It was, arguably, the most gutless political act of any US president in the history of the Middle East; certainly, it was the most costly in terms of the lives of innocent civilians.

There was, among the confetti of political balance, a commitment to humanitarian relief for Gaza and Biden's aides made sure that he reminded Israel of its status and the need for it to go about its business appropriately: 'when conflicts flare, you live by the law of war.'[225] It had all the value of a drunken father telling his teenage child not to party too much on their way out the front door; Biden's demands were, from the very outset, flagrantly ignored, with ample evidence that the US never seriously attempted to hold Israel to account. The Biden administration chose not to limit any element of Israel's aggression.

Just as with Obama's time as president, Biden was utterly beholden to Israel. The principled positions on human rights and apartheid in South Africa that had helped propel Joe Biden, then a young senator, to national attention had, when it came to Israel and the Palestinians, long gone through the AIPAC shredder. Even undoing the first Trump administration's decision to move the US embassy to Jerusalem – symbolically important – was beyond him, so any hope that his administration would take a stand on Gaza was, in fact, completely unrealistic.

International aid did not get through to the people of Gaza to prevent the humanitarian disaster that gradually unfolded. The US did not exert anything like sufficient pressure on Israel to protect civilian lives, to ensure hospitals were not targeted, or to act in a manner that prevented any risk of starvation. When, in late summer 2024, Israel set about widening the theatre of war by deploying large troop numbers on the Lebanese border and in the Golan Heights, the US muttered concerns about Iran but largely stayed quiet; so too as Israel set about enacting direct IDF interventions to support its 'settler' movement in the West Bank.

The United States' institutional arrogance and shallowness in managing foreign relations have rarely been more exposed than by its backing of Israel over the course of late 2023 and 2024. The US relationship with Israel is due to the currency of the Israeli shekel in US politics and the belief that only Israel can protect it from the threat posed by Iran. The consequences of the 'unprecedented' commitment made by the US in October 2023 meant that, by autumn 2024, with the death toll in Gaza hitting about 45,000, mostly civilians, Israel could announce that it had received its 500th aircraft carrying weapons and military supplies from the US since it commenced its operations in Gaza. There was no press announcement; none was needed. The equipment delivered – similar to the previous 499 aircraft drops and the 107 made by sea – included armoured vehicles, ammunition and personal protection gear, all of which were furthering the interests of a government led by a man who was facing indictment under international law for committing war crimes.

While the US did pause shipments for a short period, over the course of Israel's campaign, the US supplied it with 500-pound (225kg) and 2,000-pound (900kg) bombs, without which Israel could not have wiped out whole areas of Palestinian civilisation. As the evidence that it was conducting war crimes became undeniable, there was no change in the support of Israel by the United States and the Biden administration continued to fund and arm it as though the rules of engagement the president had referenced at the outset meant nothing. When it comes to Israel, they don't. Two sentences in Biden's first remarks on the day he bound his administration to support whatever course Israel took after the Hamas attack explain why: 'The State of Israel was born to be a safe place for the Jewish people of the world. That's why it was born. I have long said: If Israel didn't exist, we would have to invent it.'[226]

The fullness of that fraternal embrace would not have been lost on Benjamin Netanyahu, who, throughout his career, demonstrated a knack for how best to use the unwavering, uncritical commitment of the United States. Nor would he have missed how Joe Biden had too easily dismissed Hamas as not representing the interests of the Palestinian people when, in fact, it has been directly involved in the administration of Gaza since 2007, establishing political, legal and military institutions to meet the needs of its people. Hamas' approach may not appeal to the United States' view of how to govern but the evidence of Israel's conduct has also long since debunked the idea that it meets those standards. The idea that Israel could credibly cast aspersions on the morality of any other administration was totally absurd.

Netanyahu is a veteran at 'playing' the US in every scenario. He'd made over twenty visits to the White House over his five terms as prime minister since 2009, so he knew that the events of 7 October would allow him to ignore any requests for caution that Joe Biden might urge. There appeared to be increasing frustration in the White House at the lack of movement on a ceasefire, and the ICC prosecutor applied for arrest warrants against Netanyahu and two of his ministers.

This was the backdrop when Netanyahu was invited, for the fourth time in his career and at a moment when he stood indicted of war crimes by the ICC, to address a joint session of Congress on 25 July. While quite a sizable number of liberal Democrats didn't attend, Israel's prime minister seized the opportunity to show the world, but more importantly, his own citizens, that he was the person to lead Israel at this time. The great shame of what US legislators had enabled was that he was allowed to address his own people from the floor of what many of them, however naively, consider to be a temple of democracy.

At the time of the address, President Biden had received a letter from a group of American medical professionals who'd already documented for his administration just how out of control Israel was and just how robust the ICC's case was against Israel's leadership. In the letter, dated 25 July and also addressed to Vice President Harris and Joe Biden's wife, Jill, who is a professional educator, this group of forty-five doctors and nurses who all had volunteered in Gaza set out probative evidence that the human toll in Gaza was far higher than generally understood. They said the death toll was likely to be over 92,000 or, as they put it, 'an astonishing 4.2 per cent of Gaza's population.'[227]

They provided shocking first-hand evidence of emergency departments that were completely overwhelmed and said that they'd witnessed scenes of unbearable cruelty to women and children. Each of them testified that on at least a daily basis, they'd treated children who had been shot in the head. The medics' letter warned of what the administration of America's forty-sixth president was enabling. It said Israel had killed one out of every forty Gazan healthcare professionals, while those they hadn't killed were malnourished and both physically and mentally devastated. They said their Palestinian peers had all lost family members and their homes, which meant living with their surviving family in unimaginable conditions. They had not been paid since 7 October. The letter to the White House continued:

> Many of these colleagues of ours were taken by Israel during the attacks. They all told us a slightly different version of the same story: in captivity they were barely fed, continuously

> physically and psychologically abused, and finally dumped naked on the side of a road. Many told us they were subjected to mock executions and other forms of mistreatment and torture. Far too many of our healthcare colleagues told us they were simply waiting to die. We urge you to see that Israel has directly targeted and deliberately devastated Gaza's entire healthcare system … This makes a mockery of the protected status hospitals and healthcare providers are granted under the oldest and most widely accepted provisions of International Humanitarian Law.[228]

The depth of the testimony and the strength of the appeal may have been new but the basic message was not. Similar messages of deep concern about Israel's behaviour in Gaza had been brought to the White House by others over the preceding months. In April, InterAction, a group that represents NGOs in the US, wrote to Biden about the 'humanitarian catastrophe' in Gaza and, tellingly, called for a 'strict adherence to International Humanitarian Law, including demonstrable efforts to minimize civilian casualties'.[229]

That month, a group of seven former and serving US officials addressed similar concerns to the president, while in May, MSF (Doctors Without Borders), which had lost five staff members by then, had added its voice to the chorus of criticism:

> The Biden administration's analysis of Israel's war in Gaza has not proceeded as a good faith effort to uphold US law … As the leading provider of military and financial support to Israel,

> the US has an obligation to assess if the conduct of the war is consistent with international and US laws designed to protect civilians and to apply the appropriate legal procedures.[230]

The cumulative evidence provided to President Biden and his team for months was clear and unvarnished: Israel was conducting a genocide. Despite the clarity of the message of those presenting it, it went unheard, as did the direct appeal by the forty-five medical professionals to the White House who had offered the most damning testimony of all. The detail and tone of these different appeals to the president should have demanded that the United States pause and reflect on the commitments made. The administration was being given the clearest evidence possible from impeccable American sources that Israel had taken Joe Biden's commitment of 'unprecedented support' yet completely ignored his reminder, however whispered, that the backing would have to be used in a manner that stayed within the international rule of law.

The group of American medics, with first-hand testimony from their time volunteering in Gaza, chose the day when the genocide's architect-in-chief, Benjamin Netanyahu, was in Washington to make their public call for an immediate ceasefire and an international arms embargo on both Israel and all Palestinian armed groups. They put it up to Biden in blunt terms: 'Every day that we continue supplying weapons and munitions to Israel is another day that women are shredded by our bombs and children are murdered with our bullets.'[231] They told their president that the man who was the guest of the US political establishment that very day was leading a genocide. They were ignored.

The Address

The United States, arguably the most self-absorbed nation on earth, had beaten itself up about the attempted insurrection of 6 January 2021, led by Donald Trump and his cronies. It was nothing as to what it would witness on 25 July 2024. This time, there was only one criminal on the premises, but his hour-long speech, which wouldn't have been out of place at Nuremberg, was delivered in a place that many still consider a bulwark of democracy.

In Washington, on 25 July 2024, four minutes after the appointed time, House Speaker Mike Johnson introduced their 'honoured guest', the prime minister of Israel, Benjamin Netanyahu. There followed almost another four minutes of schoolyard whooping and hollering, interspersed with loud shouts of approval as the majority of America's elected elite welcomed Israel's prime minister. Netanyahu stumbled momentarily as he almost missed a step up to the podium from which he would address his largely adoring audience. That was as close as he came to failing to deliver what the supplicant legislators of the United States had come to witness.

Once he stood at the lectern, the ovation was recharged before, name-checking done and with no awareness of the heavy irony of how he opened his address, the 75 -year-old Israeli prime minister, facing serious criminal indictments at home as well as, internationally, the charge of being a war criminal, spoke to Congress and to the world. 'We meet today at a crossroads of history,' he intoned, with all the gravity he could muster. 'This is not a clash of civilizations. It's a clash between barbarism and civilization. It's a clash between those who glorify death and those who sanctify life.'[232]

When he continued, he introduced the standard fear factor without, at that point, naming Iran and insisted on how, for the forces of civilisation to survive, the US and Israel would have to 'stand together'. This brought the majority of the elected representatives and those in the public gallery to their feet in an act of rapturous genocidal-collegiality. At that moment, the institutional United States stood as one with one of the most immoral political leaders of modern history, someone who was so determined to avoid the consequences of the laws of his own land that he'd manoeuvred politically to change them and someone who chose to use the attack of a guerrilla army on his people as cause to unleash a wholly disproportionate military response, killing tens of thousands of innocent civilians in the process.

On that day, 25 July, the legislature of the United States, representing its more than 330 million citizens, took to its institutional bosom the words and the actions of a man who the ICJ and the UN – the world's leading adjudicators of law and order – had both, however powerless they may ultimately be, profiled as the leader of a nation embarked on a genocidal mission.

Around the world lie many sites of horrific and barbaric legacies. Visiting Belsen or Auschwitz, places where millions of Jewish people were exterminated by the brutal genocidal Nazi administration of Adolf Hitler, is harrowing. The killing fields in Cambodia, where you walk over the remains of the estimated 1.3 million people disposed of by the Pol Pot regime, are equally so. It's impossible to go to these sites of some of the foulest acts of barbarism in the history of mankind and not be moved. There are enough awful places around the world that were once awash with tears of the forsaken without our careless acquiescence to the begetting of yet more, but for all its assumed sophistication, mankind appears little better at preventing genocide than before. Those places are proof enough of the capacity of man to destroy the lives of others; we do not need any more.

Yet, in the moment of Prime Minister Netanyahu's address to Congress in July 2024, the institutional United States chose to walk over the remains of tens of thousands of dead Palestinians, the killing of whom it is enabling through the shipment of arms and its huge funding commitments. Worse, the majority of those elected to represent all Americans stood – metaphorically if not literally – as one, steadfastly committed to what Netanyahu and his glorified lynch mob want, which is the complete destruction of the Palestinian people and to erase their very existence from history. At that moment, if it had not already done so, the United States of America endorsed the Jewish Zionist mission.

Just a week before Netanyahu addressed Congress, the Knesset had passed a resolution overwhelmingly rejecting Palestinian statehood. This is critical to understanding Israel's ambition; Israel's identity depends on denying Palestinian identity. It is a *sine qua non.* It is how Israeli children are educated; that their existence isn't only dependent on their right to nationhood, to the territory that they consider theirs, but is predicated too on the denial of any similar right for the people of Palestine.

When it comes to Palestine and its right to exist, the problem isn't just about the complicity of many Western powers nor is it just about the genocidal ambitions of leaders like Netanyahu, Ben-Gvir or Smotrich. The problem is endemic to Israeli society. The largest party on the opposition benches, the National Unity Party, supported the motion, rejecting the very idea of Palestinian statehood. This is the strongest evidence possible that the settler colonial gene is embedded across Israel's political fabric, and it's how, as that fabric is stretched, any notion of balance and proportionality in how the state behaves is lost.

Israel has always deployed the defining features of settler colonialism to devastating effect, buoyed by its whiteness and its enduring need for recompense for what had been allowed to happen to the Jews in the 1930s. Regarding the former, Israel knows that the United States in particular suffers from a long-standing fundamental distrust of anyone in the region but the Israelis, based largely on institutional ignorance and political cowardice.

In his 25 July address, Netanyahu adopted the standard Israeli narrative of Iran as the Middle East bogeyman from which, without a powerful alliance with Israel, Americans could never be safe. In his opening, when he referenced a clash between those who 'glorify death and those who sanctify life',[233] Netanyahu was playing the Western and, particularly, American trope of the Arab or Muslim (interchangeable, it seems) as someone for whom death is preferred over life.

That done, his address was punctuated with fear-mongering, with Iran as the underlying threat and Israel as the partner that could protect the United States from doom. This was his message when he appealed for more military aid to be fast-tracked so Israel could 'dramatically expedite an end to the war in Gaza and help prevent a broader war in the Middle East'.[234] The sheer gall of this political leader, whose very actions were unquestionably most likely to prompt a wider conflict, the audacity of such a claim was undone only by how blindly this great deception was received. The United States Congress was as one with him, as unwavering as its president and with few exceptions, the American media was too.

Few political leaders in the West have warned against this simplistic narrative; few have chosen, in light of the frequent barbarism of Al Qaeda and the Islamic State, to remind their citizens that there is no basis in fact, no evidence from history, that makes Muslims or Arabs more prone to violence than others. In large measure, the political establishment in the West has fed the false narrative and has been doing so for generations. Demonising Arabs is and has long been part of the West's political narrative.

That anti-Arab narrative has allowed countless US presidents and British prime ministers (some of whom, long retired, shuffle around the world addressing conferences on conflict resolution when they should be part of a touring circus of political clowns) to defend reckless overseas interventions. Few have stepped away from this dangerous misrepresentation. One rare example is the former French prime minister, Dominique de Villepin, who, at the time of the Charlie Hebdo attack in 2015, warned of the risk that conflicts in the Middle East were simplified by 'seeing only the Islamist symptom.'[235] Over late summer/early autumn of 2024, de Villepin became an angry advocate for the West to end its support of Israel. 'France is fading away and it is France that is footing the bill. I cannot accept that … One must see that Israel is in the process of creating the conditions for a reoccupation of Gaza.'[236]

On 25 July 2024, in allowing its Congress to deify Benjamin Netanyahu, the United States chose to forget that when he'd last addressed them in 2015, he had bitterly opposed the nuclear deal with Iran that then-President Barack Obama was trying to secure. This same man, nearly a decade later, addressed them in worried tones about the necessity to speed up his ethnic cleansing of Palestine, urging belief in the falsehood that only the alliance with Israel could bring stability to the region. Most US legislators present applauded his call, knowing that the man making it was directly responsible for getting President Trump to withdraw the US from the nuclear agreement with Iran in 2018.

Wrong Side of History – Again

In 1967, that giant of human rights, Martin Luther King, gave a lengthy speech on the Vietnam War, one that drew sharp criticism because he referenced the United States government as 'the greatest purveyor of violence in the world today' and also said that, in respect of that war, the United States was on the wrong side of history.[237] Among those who condemned him for this assessment were many who were normally his supporters, but if the US was on the wrong side of history then, how does it stand almost six decades later as it performs political cartwheels to please Israel?

Neither President Joe Biden nor Vice President Kamala Harris can claim they did not know what Israel was doing. Their administration had arrogantly and recklessly dismissed the ICC's findings. It called the indictment of Benjamin Netanyahu 'outrageous' and said of the Court, 'We don't recognise their jurisdiction … the way it's been exercised, and it's that simple. We don't see an equivalence between what Israel did and what Hamas did.'[238]

President Biden would have been better advised to have only made the general point that the US did not recognise the jurisdiction of the ICC; it never has because doing so could be argued to be unconstitutional under US law, so that would have been a more credible argument. In saying there was no equivalence between the actions of Israel and Hamas, Joe Biden was saying that he had all the information required to make a decision, but that, based on its evaluation, the administration would continue to support Israel. That represents a political judgement that will forever haunt him and those around him who were party to it.

The 'support' of the United States, which represented well over 50,000 tons of military equipment over the first twelve months of Nakba II, was critical to Israel's pursuit of genocide; without it the Netanyahu government could not have realised the intention to reduce Gaza to rubble. It is utterly shocking that, as the overwhelming evidence of Israel's excesses grew, the Biden administration refused to act. There was precedent; he could have learned from Ronald Reagan's willingness to change course in 1982 when, after giving Israel the green light to invade Lebanon, he demanded that its prime minister, Menachem Begin, end its shelling of civilian areas when he realised Israel had greatly exceeded the actions that the US had sanctioned. Biden had all the evidence he needed to follow suit.

The refusal to countenance change appeared to deepen with the findings of international jurists but the source of information on Israel's conduct seemed irrelevant. It wasn't just the findings of the ICC that irked Biden and his people. So sure were they of the rightness of their unqualified support of Israel that they even ignored the independent and unequivocal testimony of the group of US medics who had volunteered in Gaza.

The US media showed no great interest in the president's indifference to what these US citizens had to say. Men and women who'd risked their lives in the service of others and who provided a first-hand account that completely supported the findings of the ICC were ignored. The United States may not like being addressed by international bodies whose remit it cannot control but, even when strong evidence of war crimes by a country it is arming to the hilt came from a cohort of its own medical professionals, its government refused to give it any credence. It was a missed opportunity for Biden's administration to stay Israel's hand. It wasn't the first.

The moment when the administration had really blown its chance to intervene and rein in Israel had come and gone two months earlier, when it was given the evidence and advice it needed to act by USAID and a number of its own civil servants, but chose, instead, to ignore them. In May, well before Netanyahu's address to the Joint Houses, USAID – an independent government aid agency – had reported to the State Department that Israel was preventing urgently needed aid from getting into Gaza and, as a result, was creating circumstances that could lead to a famine. It presented the case starkly and without equivocation. This information pointed to any decision to continue arming Israel as being in violation of US law.

Even allowing for the extraordinary level of arms shipments made to Israel and the unconstrained support of numerous funding rounds by Congress, it was in these events of spring 2024 relating to the emerging evidence of famine that the complete abandonment of the Palestinians by the United States was most manifest. On 1 April 2024, Jake Sullivan, President Biden's National Security Adviser, was meeting a delegation of Israeli officials at the White House. The Americans knew just how dependent Israel was on the continuation of the huge arms shipments that Congress was supporting. Biden's team, by then fully aware that Israel was scarcely allowing the bare minimum of food and other supplies into Gaza, knew that it was involved in a morally questionable approach that meant ignoring those concerns and continuing the arms shipments.

It had been decided, however, that Israel needed to be put on notice that its actions around aid were really straining the relationship, so Sullivan was primed to deliver a scathing assessment to the Israeli delegation and warn them of the possible consequences of not dramatically increasing the flow of aid to Gaza. There was a determination to reset the relationship on the issue of food – the US administration did not want to carry any responsibility for a famine. The message was to be clear and direct but it was never delivered. Just as Sullivan was preparing to tell the delegation that their country was 'about to be responsible for the third famine of the twenty first century',[239] the Israeli team started the meeting by telling him that Israel had bombed the Iranian consulate in Syria. With that stunning news, the priorities of the White House and its national security chief pivoted to damage limitation as it sought to distance itself from an attack on the consulate of another state, which, under international law, constituted Iranian soil. The incident gives an insight into the political *simpatico*, however fuelled by dollars, between the United States and Israel, but, as tellingly, it illuminates the paranoia within the United States over Iran and its near obsession with keeping Israel 'armed and loaded' as the protector-in-chief of its interests in the region.

Secretary of State Anthony Blinken was, at best, circumspect in how he managed information his department had that Israel's actions were posing a real threat of famine in Gaza. More likely, he was simply untruthful. Considerable evidence of famine conditions was in the public domain and a senior civil-military adviser in the State Department, Stacy Gilbert, who'd considered the USAID report and prepared a briefing for Blinken, resigned over the administration's failure to act. In doing so, Gilbert made no attempt to hide why she chose to leave public service. She spelt out that it was because Anthony Blinken – her boss – had chosen to present a dishonest report to Congress; in doing so, she prophesied that the 'flagrant untruths will haunt us'.[240] This was a rare insight into the extent to which US foreign policy is conducted and it came from a senior, reliable source, someone without an axe to grind. She was saying, and not without reason, that the US secretary of state had lied.

The problem with the USAID report and its accompanying letter was the implications for the administration's capacity to continue backing Israel. Gilbert knew that under US regulations, the USAID report and the State Department's conclusions would prohibit the continued provision of arms to Israel. It was a moment in time that report provided the government of the United States with the perfect opportunity to stop arming Israel. It was simply a matter of applying US Federal Regulations; she and other officials knew that, as did the secretary of state.

The report that Stacy Gilbert and others had considered was clear: Israel was knowingly allowing famine conditions to prevail in Gaza by restricting the provision of international humanitarian aid. Blinken had the report; he understood its import and he knew the consequences of failing to act. All he had to do was use its findings to squeeze Israel but, yet again, after Jake Sullivan's failure to address the issue in April, Blinken instead chose to mislead Congress by choosing not to share the USAID commentary. It was only months before a presidential election; the Jewish vote would be critical to the electoral prospects of his boss, and any weakening of his commitment to Israel's Gaza campaign would be seized upon by his opponent. Politics came before Palestinian lives, and in that moment, in choosing that course, the United States doubled down on its support of a genocidal Israel and abandoned Palestine to its fate.

In making the decision, the administration directly influenced the course of Israel's campaign. That decision, which constituted a breach of US Federal Regulations, enabled the Biden administration to continue providing Israel with arms and ammunition, without which it could not have continued to pursue its aggression in Gaza at the same levels. Nor could Israel have, months later, set out to broaden the conflict to Lebanon with a devastating impact on civilian life there.

Blinken's decision was an act of political complicity with a murderous regime but a regime that, with a presidential election ahead in the US, needed the continuing support of the Democratic party if the most powerful lobby in America was to be kept on side. In choosing as he did, Secretary of State Anthony Blinken took a direction that was not unrepresentative of much of US foreign policy for decades.

The consistency of this kind of political behaviour is remarkable; the United States has always protected Israel at all costs. The actions of Susan Rice at the UN on 'settlements' and Hillary Clinton's intervention on Goldstone were all in the catalogue of that unqualified support that Blinken could have consulted if he wanted to find precedent for choosing to misrepresent Israel's conduct in Gaza to Congress and to the world. Presidents Obama and Biden provided this support, along with the most high-profile secretary of state of modern times, Hillary Clinton – all icons of a Democratic party that claims to have a monopoly on being moral in its political decision-making.

Stacy Gilbert's resignation had been preceded by others who were concerned by the general lack of scrutiny the Biden presidency was giving to Israel's conduct. One of them, Josh Paul, a director at the State Department for over a decade, said, 'the U.S. has not provided protection [to Israel] – it has provided weapons; it has not eased suffering – it has enabled a famine; it has not resolved the plight of persecuted and forcibly displaced people in Palestine – it has provided the diplomatic cover for Israel to continue their persecution and to repeatedly forcibly displace them without accountability or justice.'[241]

Whether it's over the course of one particular campaign of violence toward the Palestinians or over the decades of oppression since 1967, there have been countless opportunities that the unrivalled influence of the US could have been harnessed to change the narrative around Israel and Palestine. Not one administration has come even close to doing so. In the twenty-first century, the United States has chosen, as it has always done, to support Israeli ambition no matter the consequences for the people of Palestine. What hope is there now if even the globally imagined beacon of change and freedom, Barack Obama, shied away from the challenge? The former president is widely regarded as a man of peace. The failure of his administration to even attempt to change the narrative stands as the strongest evidence of how beholden US politics is to the Israeli cause.

There's no disputing the strength of Israel's lobby. AIPAC et al. use their considerable resources to move the needle of political debate, to support those for whom Israel's interests are America's interests; but there's more to it than might appear on the surface. When, in the mid-nineteenth century, Britain's naval power allowed it to lay waste to and then claim much of Palestine, elements in the US wanted to assert its rights over those presumed by Britain. Approaching two hundred years later, whatever the US does in the Middle East is based first on its own interests. The Israel lobby matters in Washington's decision-making but not more than what serves the mercurial strategic foreign policy interests of America itself. This is lost in much of the analysis; it is this contemporary colonial-lite approach of the US that should drive a more aggressive approach by global institutions in their assessment of the Biden administration's support of Israel over the first twelve months of Nakba II.

Three months before 7 October 2023, Biden repeated the line that, if Israel didn't exist, the United States would have had to invent it. That position was consistent with his (and that of the general legislative view, both Democrat and Republican) throughout his time as a legislator. In 2007, he'd said, 'When I was a young senator,

I used to say, if I were a Jew I'd be a Zionist. I am a Zionist; you don't have to be a Jew to be a Zionist … Israel is the single greatest strength America has in the Middle East.'[242] Two decades earlier, addressing Congress in 1987 as a young senator, he said, 'There's no apology to be made [for supporting Israel]. None! It is the best 3-billion-dollar investment we make.'[243] So, while the Zionist lobby has a hugely significant direct influence on US policy toward Israel, wider economic and geopolitical factors are just as important in any analysis of the warped sense of justice that America applies to its assessment of Israel. Add to that how Israel's location is touted as a reason to offer some succour to a nation and its legislators who feel threatened by the Arab world and the predominance of Islam, which, like in much of the institutional West, is seen in the US as a threatening political movement, not a creed.

Since its foundation, Israel has been the most significant foreign political 'cause' of the United States and irrespective of whether the White House was dressed in its Democratic blue or Republican red, that support has never wavered. The levels of material and diplomatic support the US has provided to Israel dwarfs what it's offered to any other nation. 'That aid is largely unconditional: no matter what Israel does, the level of support remains for the most part unchanged.'[244]

The events of 2024 brought home, again, how essential it is for both parties to be steadfast in their support. Biden and his team should be in the dock for their actions but so too should Republican leaders like House Speaker Mike Johnson who, after he secured passage of the legislation that delivered $14 billion in military aid for Israel, received a substantial donation from AIPAC.[245]

Europe

The EU's response to Israel's genocidal campaign has been inept and immoral. The former is evident in the diplomatic mishandling of relationships, especially when its most senior official, Commission President Ursula von der Leyen, accompanied by Parliament President Roberta Metsola, rushed to visit Israel and backed its right to defend itself while adding, quite remarkably, 'Hamas is a threat not only to Israel, but also a threat to the Palestinian people.'[246] The presumptuousness and arrogance of a politician with no mandate to speak on behalf of the EU on international affairs making such a statement caused real alarm in Brussels.

The EU is a bloc of twenty-seven states, so it was never possible for it to present one single united position. While it has elements of federalism, the sovereignty of the individual member states takes precedence. What has evolved, however, is a splintered union of at least three groups ranging from those who have been steadfast in their support of Israel (Germany, Hungary, Austria and the Czech Republic) to those (Spain, Belgium and Ireland) who have condemned Hamas but have been consistently vocal in their criticism of Israel, charging it with breaking international law.

Most of the remainder are strongly supportive of Israel's right to defend itself but are also vocal in their demand that it commit to a ceasefire, and they regularly make noises about the need for it to temper its aggression. Apart from Germany, no member of these three groups has any direct impact on the narrative in the Middle East, adding to the sense that the union that was formed from the ashes of two world wars has become a purely economic body, one of the world's largest trading blocs, rather than a global political force. Again, there's a need for perspective on the West's somewhat exalted view of itself; population matters and, while it comprises 27 nations, the EU's 450 million inhabitants represent less than 6 per cent of the world's population.

There is a different kind of group among European nations. That group – like the United States – has the most direct impact on recent events in the Middle East. In fact, it's doing more than wielding influence; the group, which comprises Germany, Italy, the Netherlands and the still geographically European United Kingdom, all provided armaments and ammunition to Israel to enable its 2024 campaign. According to figures from the European External Action Service's COARM (Working Party on Conventional Arms Export) database, the EU is the second-largest arms supplier to Israel after the US. Its figures show that between 2018 and 2022, EU member states sold arms worth €1.76 billion ($1.9 bn) to Israel.[247]

The real problem with how the EU has conducted itself over the course of the Israeli campaign is about a great deal more than arms; the failure is, above all else, one of an almost complete absence of moral leadership. There should be a deep discomfort in Europe at the ease with which the EU has institutionally aligned itself with Israel, revealing that for all the efforts many member states have made to be inclusive multi-ethnic societies, the Union will back a state that has made a virtue of the complete opposite. Israel is the modern global exemplar of a state that aspires to a nationhood for one people, one set of beliefs, one ethnicity, and it is prepared to murder hundreds of thousands of Palestinians in the pursuit of that goal. The United States is not alone in its shameful support of that end; institutionally, the EU faces the same charge.

It is hard not to see a deeply embedded racism in the midst of this support of Israel's genocide. The rightful indignation and horror at the brutality of the Hamas attack were not and have since rarely been balanced by an acknowledgement of cause and effect within a historical context. Israel has been engaged in a brutal suppression of the Palestinian people and theft of their land for decades. Israelis are often seen as white, many are of European origin, their faith is culturally aligned to Christianity, or at least that is how it is perceived, and the suffering of the Jewish people in the 1930s and 1940s happened under the watch of many of those who choose to support it today. The Palestinians are none of those things; there's a resistance to cultural acceptance of the Arab world and the Muslim faith that allows Israel to drive a coach and four through the standard rules that should apply.

There's ignorance, too; some of it is genuine but it is also convenient as a means of shirking responsibility. Many European legislators want to imagine that 7 October was the start of something, oblivious to or disinterested in the decades of oppression and abuse that Israel has meted out to the Palestinians in direct breach of international law. It benefits that position not to know or not to acknowledge the back-story, the history that would render such a stance indefensible.

The German politician Ursula von der Leyen has personified this in her leadership of the EU Commission. In the days following the Hamas attack of 7 October, she immediately had the Israeli flag projected onto the exterior of the Commission's HQ in Brussels.

When she visited Tel Aviv just six days after the attack and spoke of Israel's 'right to defend itself', she went against what had been agreed by the member states by choosing not to balance her comments with any warnings about its response having to be proportionate. In saying, 'I know that how Israel responds will show that it is a democracy',[248] not only did she display a failure to understand Israel's decades-long oppression of Palestinians, but she also misrepresented the agreed EU position.

Its head of foreign policy, Josep Borrell, the president of the European Council, Charles Michel, and the chair of its security and defence committee, Nathalie Loiseau, were all quick to remind Israel of its obligations under international law. Questioning von der Leyen's motivation, Loiseau asked what she thought she was doing: 'I don't understand what the President of the European Commission has to do with the foreign policy of the EU, which she is not in charge of.'[249] The damage to the EU's standing was considerable. It may well be that von der Leyen has no direct role in its foreign policy but, with her global status and in choosing to position herself as speaking on its behalf, she has represented the EU poorly at a crucial time in world affairs. It may also be that her successful stand on Ukraine – the authority with which she was seen to have established the EU's support, even though it wasn't exactly her job – had led her to act so peremptorily on Israel.

Right after the attack of 7 October, one of Von der Leyen's commissioners, Olivér Várhelyi, who was responsible for relations with the EU's neighbours, unilaterally announced that the EU was suspending its aid to UNRWA, which, though quickly reversed, reflected a blinkered perspective on events. Later, he introduced the EU's first-ever aid package for Israel. However, conscious of the likely controversy that would ensue, the Commission chose not to announce it publicly. The drift toward supporting Israel and forgiving its failure to conduct war under the established international rules – or to come within even the broadest possible interpretation of acting morally – was institutional: both the EU and some of its sovereign states simply abandoned the Palestinians to their fate.

The last few decades, through the first and second Iraq wars, and the conflicts in Afghanistan and Libya, have shown that in such circumstances, most of Europe simply falls into line with the Americans and the UK. Over the course of 2023–24, as Israel has sought to destroy the Palestinian people, that is what has happened with the EU. It has chosen to slavishly follow the Biden administration line of full and resolute support of Israel. While the US is Israel's greatest ally, even when it comes to the supply of arms, Europe's hands are anything but clean. European countries not only exported weapons to Israel amid the growing international concerns that Israel was carrying out genocide in Gaza, but they also spent public money to support the arms manufacturers that produce them.

Warfare is not about armaments alone; increasingly, the sophistication of military and security information determines success or failure. There is no doubting the exceptional quality of Israel's tech industry but experts believe the development of its digital war capacity was perfected with the assistance of European research funding, with some debate in parliament as to whether some of these funds have, however indirectly, supported Israel's military. Since 7 October 2023, the EU has granted €126 million in funding to 130 research projects involving Israeli entities. While Europe is

Israel's second-largest source after the US, it is noteworthy that in Europe, it is Germany, one of the most powerful members of the European Union, that accounts for the vast bulk of the armaments Israel has purchased. Since 2019, German weapons and ammunition accounted for 30 per cent of Israel's import of arms and that trade 'increased tenfold' in 2023 'from €32.3 million [$35m] to €326.5 million [$354m] with the vast majority of new licences being granted in the period following 7 October'.[250]

By any measure, Germany's approach has been staggering; the position taken by its chancellor, Olaf Scholz, especially so. The Holocaust should increase Germany's awareness of the long-term consequences of what Israel is engaged in – it's inconceivable that German politicians cannot see this – yet it has continued in its support of the Netanyahu government. It is noteworthy, too, that while a number of European countries have followed the US lead on the aggressive policing of civilian protests against Israel, it is in Germany that this has been most visible and trenchant. The government has sanctioned its police to stamp out, often with excessive violence, the right of its citizens to protest. Chancellor Olaf Scholz's insistence that Israel has acted in accordance with international law while it was holding the entire Gaza population under siege and wiping out complete neighbourhoods with airstrikes was particularly damaging.

The anger in Europe and beyond over the active support of Israel by the United States is justified, but while some nations have attempted to distance themselves from the actions of the European Union, it's hard not to conclude that, just as with the US, at some point, the EU will stand accused of knowingly assisting Israel in committing genocide. It would be correct in such circumstances that some would be charged with sponsoring it but there's a risk that member states (even those like Spain, Belgium and Ireland that tried to hold Israel to some form of account) could be found to have been complicit. As an institution, the EU has failed a huge test of its capacity to provide moral leadership; more than anything, its approach to Gaza has exposed its incapacity to act as a coherent political bloc of global importance.

◆◆◆

The United Kingdom, too, no longer a member of the EU, but a king among colonists, could not find a voice based on reason and law even with the change of government from the Conservatives to the Labour Party in mid-2024. Its culpability goes well beyond its institutional silence; it is both a massive supplier of arms to Israel and it is an active participant in the war, flying almost 50 per cent of the reconnaissance missions over Gaza since Israel's campaign began.[251] The US-UK alliance on such matters remains intact – Israel only needed to undertake 20 per cent of the missions as the US took up whatever slack remained.

The commitment didn't change with the change of government in Britain. The new prime minister, Keir Starmer, and his foreign secretary, David Lammy, were no less lily-livered than their predecessors, Rishi Sunak and David Cameron, in 'worrying' over civilian deaths but – without a flicker of irony – continuing to support Israel in its 'fight against terrorism'.

Starmer's approach to Israel, both in opposition and since assuming power, has been as shallow as any politician in the West.

In November 2024, a year into Israel's annihilation of the Palestinian people, he told the House of Commons that he was 'well aware of the definition of genocide and that is why I've never described this as and referred to it as genocide'.[252] Either the British prime minister was being disingenuous or, despite his estimable standing as a lawyer, he erroneously believed the legal definition had changed. In 2014, at the ICJ, in a war crimes hearing into Serbia's three-month siege of the Croatian city of Vukovar in 1991, making the charge that Serbia had conducted a genocide, he said Serbian forces had carried out a 'sustained campaign of shelling, systematic expulsion, denial of food, water, electricity, sanitation and medical treatment'[253], which he said led to the death (c. 20,000) and displacement of the civilian population. This, Starmer argued, represented grounds for a ruling of genocide. Ten years ago, that met the threshold for Keir Starmer, but not now, not when he is prime minister.

What compromises political action, even political thought, in the UK – as elsewhere – is that it's a major supplier of arms to Israel. As long as they are driven by economic interests, neither Europe, the UK nor the US are likely to stem the course of Israel's genocidal mission as it continues to rage on, more than a year since 7 October 2023.

Nine

One Year On

A Rogue State

Even in the context of what followed and the brutal and disproportionate response of Israel, the violence of the Hamas attack on 7 October 2023 was shocking; the loss of life was very significant. The trauma of those taken captive – Israelis and others – and the impact on their families and friends has to have been immense. The great majority of those killed and injured were innocent civilians and the terror experienced by even those Israeli civilians who escaped completely unscathed is hard to imagine. The attack was perpetrated by motivated, highly trained and well-armed militants whose intention was to strike terror into the nation whose government had, for generations, colonised their land and terrorised their people. It worked.

There's no disputing the terror of that Saturday in Israeli towns and villages just over the border with Gaza or how the brutal outcome was just as intended by those responsible. Yet, in spite of what Israel and its most powerful allies have consistently suggested, the story did not begin on 7 October 2023. The narrative that brought Israel to that day was decades long and was of its own composition. The heartache for the thousands of families directly affected by the Hamas attack and the tremors felt more widely across Israeli society were caused by the suppression of the human rights of Palestinians, the illegal occupation of their land and the ongoing incarceration by the Israeli authorities of thousands of innocent civilians.

None of this was hidden. Israel's sense of entitlement was such that it felt no need to obscure its suppression, abuse and domination of the Palestinians, no requirement to camouflage the historical Zionist intent. It has been there for more than a century and has never gone away. In 1914, then-future Israeli Prime Minister Moshe Sharett said,

> We have forgotten that we have not come to an empty land to inherit it, but we have come to conquer a country from a people inhabiting it, that governs it by virtue of its language and savage culture ... If we cease to look upon our land, the Land of Israel, as ours alone and we allow a partner into our estate – all content and meaning will be lost to our enterprise.[254]

In 1947, Yosef Weitz, head of the Jewish Land Settlement Department, who was tasked with ethnically cleansing the indigenous Palestinians, wrote, 'The only solution is Palestine without Arabs. And there is no other way but to transfer all of them: not one village, not one tribe should be left.'[255]

The killing of innocent civilians by Hamas was an act of terror, a well-planned, brutal response to the multiple massacres of innocent Palestinians – in their hundreds and in their thousands – going back to 1948. Added to that was the arrest of hundreds of thousands of their people, the detention without cause of thousands of minors, the torture of tens of thousands and the decades-long occupation of their land in contravention of international law. To present Israel's campaign of 2023–24 as caused by the Hamas attack is facile and dangerous; it is to ignore the circle of life (or, more correctly, death) in Palestine over the decades of Israeli control. Ten years before it occurred, the eminent Israeli sociologist Lev Luis Grinberg wrote, 'Palestinian resistance is in a catch: when it uses violence it is oppressed, and when it uses diplomatic negotiations it is ignored.'[256]

Palestinians had been resisting for years but with little success; they engaged in civil disobedience, held protests and occasionally carried out acts of violence but they had no resources to fight militarily. Miko Peled, a former Israeli special forces soldier, son of a general who fought in the 1948 war and grandson of one of Israel's founders, Avraham Katsnelson, said non-violent protest didn't stop the Israelis from killing Palestinians or rounding them up, detaining and torturing them or arresting their children:

> when they tried unarmed resistance for years, they've been murdered and killed and their children have been arrested and tortured … and I was there from the very beginning [in the IDF] … Non-violent resistance against a violent oppressive regime does not work … So what would you do? They're getting killed either way. Palestinians are getting murdered whether they kill Israelis or whether they sleep in their beds.[257]

Peled's testimony, which echoed the 1967 prophesy of French President Charles de Gaulle, is not unique. Other former members of the IDF share his view and the work of human rights organisations – including Israeli NGOs – over decades supports his account. In the years leading up to the Hamas attack, the numbers being murdered, forcibly removed from their homes and the number of minors detained and tortured were all on the increase. Palestinians were no longer solely dependent on civil disobedience, or rocks and sticks, and Hamas was far from just a group of terrorist as Israel and its principal allies would suggest. The attack of 7 October 2023 was carried out by a well-organised, highly trained guerrilla army. The attack caused terror for those civilians who were enjoying a public holiday but also, doubtlessly, members of the Israeli security services who came to their aid.

For those unfortunate enough to be taken hostage, the terror for them and their families can hardly be imagined. The wider Israeli population will have been terrified too. To have been there on that day, at that moment, to have witnessed it or to be related to or friends with anyone caught up in it must have been absolutely horrifying, but that does not define it as an act of terror: it was an act of complete defiance, demonstrating that Hamas and Gaza's other combatant groups were prepared to take the fight to Israel, for reasons that were longstanding and, given the decades of oppression by colonialist Israel, justifiable.

The widely accepted narrative in the West needs to change. This must start with a refusal to accept Israel's sovereign gnashing of teeth as it promotes the idea that those from whom it has, for generations, sought to remove every shred of dignity, any sense of place, even the remotest fragment of worth, are, when they fight back, the terrorists. Slowly, far too slowly, parts of the world are starting to see this fable for what it is: an act of political fiction rarely matched on the contemporary world stage. Israel is not the victim; it is the aggressor: a criminal state that has done nothing other than threaten, invade, steal, humiliate and kill its neighbours. It has done this for generations. As Gabor Maté testifies, 'I used to be a Zionist … Zionism was very important to me as a salvation of the Jewish people until I understood that the state was founded, based on, the extirpation, the expulsion and multiple massacres of the local population.'[258]

Our understanding of Israel in the West is warped. It has been moulded by institutional hands that believe Israel represents a quasi-Western presence in a part of the world that we don't understand and have no wish to educate ourselves about. The West sees Israel as some form of Judeo-Christian defence against Islam; it is a state the West helped to create out of a need to salve its guilty conscience for a collective failure to prevent the Holocaust and the killing of six million Jews. One that conveniently morphed into a model that, surrounded by an Arab world that is largely alien to us, we somehow like to believe reflects our values. On so many levels, we are badly mistaken.

Israel is also incorrectly profiled as a democracy, which serves to enhance its value to Western eyes. Western media's representation of its needs and rights is not and never has been either informed or objectively presented. The West's political class that has influenced this twisted presentation of Israel in the West is dominated by those who represent nations with colonial histories, with, in some cases, a large measure of guilt over the plight of Jews in Europe in the 1930s and 1940s Europe. One part of the distortion rests on the conflation of Judaism with Israel, so that those who question the rights and the conduct of the state are often categorised as antisemitic. This lie is fundamental to the defence of Israel by its own political leaders and those in the West who are most committed to its cause. It is such a deviously manufactured lie that it is difficult to defeat but it is worth remembering that when Balfour made his infamous proposal to the British cabinet in 1917, the one minister who opposed it was the only Jewish member of that cabinet, Edwin Montagu. The reasons Montagu was opposed are informative:

> I assert that there is not a Jewish nation. The members of my family, for instance, who have been in this country for generations, have no sort or kind of community of view or of desire with any Jewish family in any other country beyond the fact that they profess to a greater or less [*sic*] degree the same religion … When the Jews are told that Palestine is their national home, every country will immediately desire to get rid of its Jewish citizens, and you will find a population in Palestine driving out its present inhabitants … I deny that Palestine is to-day associated with the Jews or properly to be regarded as a fit place for them to live in … It is quite true that Palestine plays a large part in Jewish history, but so it does in modern Mahommedan history, and, after the time of the Jews, surely it plays a larger part than any other country in Christian history.[259]

Over a century ago, this Jewish member of a British cabinet saw Zionism as a 'mischievous political creed', a phrase that veteran

Middle East correspondent Peter Oborne wrote, would today have 'had him thrown out of Keir Starmer's Labour Party and pilloried in the media'.[260] The one Jewish member of the British government, which had granted territory that was not theirs to the Jews, warned that what it did was actually antisemitic. Montagu believed that the establishment of the nation-state of Israel provided nations with Jewish citizens with reasons to promote the need for them to relocate to the new 'promised land', thus encouraging them to act in an antisemitic manner.

Nor, he argued, was the government meeting the needs of Jewish people but rather of Zionists. He asked, 'When the Jew has a national home, surely it follows that the impetus to deprive us of the rights of British citizenship must be enormously increased. Palestine will become the world's Ghetto. Why should the Russian give the Jew equal rights? His national home is Palestine.'[261] Most damningly, in light of events a century later, realising that he was a lone opposing voice and that the plan would proceed, Montagu asked the prime minister to do everything possible to secure, for those Jews who moved to Palestine, liberty of settlement on the basis of equality with the Palestinians. Montagu's concerns for the Palestinians were not of interest to the men who led the Zionist mission, nor were they generally reflected in the approach Britain has taken over the painful history of the region since. One of the House of Commons' most vocal critics in recent times was another Jew who had served in government.

Gerald Kaufman was a prominent Jewish British parliamentarian for fifty years. The son of Polish refugees, he served as a Labour MP for Manchester for almost half a century. He served as a junior minister for four years but was best known for his trenchant opposition to Israel and unwavering support of the Palestinian cause.

Speaking in the House of Commons in 2009, at the time of Israel's offensive that had taken 1,000 lives, he said his grandmother who'd been shot dead in her own bed by Nazi soldiers in World War II had not died to provide cover for Israeli soldiers murdering Palestinian grandmothers in Gaza. He accused Israel of cynically using the 'guilt of gentiles' over their slaughter of Jews in the Holocaust as justification for murdering Palestinians. Kaufman said that the implication in Israel's conduct and in its narrative was always that Jewish lives were precious and Palestinian lives were not. Then he warned that the Israeli government's refusal to deal with Hamas, which he described as 'deeply nasty', was a grave error because 'it was democratically elected, and it is the only game in town.'[262]

Kaufman deplored the British government's decision to boycott Hamas. With words that are chillingly prophetic, he said that no matter how many thousands of Palestinians Israel might murder in Gaza, they could not solve the problem by existential means. 'Whenever and however the fighting ends, there will still be 1.5 million Palestinians in Gaza and 2.5 million more on the west bank. They are treated like dirt by the Israelis, with hundreds of road blocks and with the ghastly denizens of the illegal Jewish settlements harassing them as well.'[263] Concluding, Gerald Kaufman said it was time for the British government to tell the government of Israel, which he accused of being war criminals, that its conduct and policies were totally unacceptable and that it should impose a total arms ban as well. It bears repeating; that speech was by a Jewish member of parliament and it was delivered fifteen years ago during an Israeli invasion of Gaza that took just over one thousand lives.

Over this latest horror, since October 2023, both Tory and Labour governments and most of their standard allies have, for more than a year, supported the intent of Israel to ethnically cleanse the very people Montagu had referenced forcefully throughout his memorandum as those whose land it was: the Palestinians. There has been no Tony Benn figure excoriating those in power for the racism at the heart of their decision-making as he did in 1998 on the imminent bombing of Iraq. Watched by a young Jeremy Corbyn seated two rows behind him, Benn warned those who supported the government that they would hold a responsibility for civilian lives lost: 'I was in London during the Blitz in 1940 … It was terrifying. Aren't Arabs terrified, aren't Iraqis terrified? Don't Arab women and Iraqi women weep when their children die?'[264]

◆◆◆

Since October 2023, the support of most of the West's heavyweights has allowed Israel to act across all of the different metrics of a campaign of ethnic cleansing and genocide without being held to account. This level of support without any assessment of the behaviour of Israel as the beneficiary is particular to Israel and has been a phenomenon ever since the state was founded in 1948. Arguably, it reached its nadir in 2024. The international community has continually failed the Palestinians with ever more dire consequences but never more so than over the last quarter of 2023 and throughout 2024.

Israel is a rogue state; even when there's overwhelming evidence that it is carrying out a genocide, the needs of those it wants to destroy – the people of Palestine – are secondary to the West's need to support Israel. The most powerful nations in the West, those that lay claim to being beacons of moral political leadership, have disgraced themselves in their active support of Israel since October 2023. The West's collective shame over the Holocaust, its institutional concern about being branded 'antisemitic' and its hidden but real fear of the presumed 'dark elements' within the Arab world that Israel continually stokes, means much of the West refuses to face up to the truth of what has happened and its culpability in the horror.

Many Western political leaders believe or want to believe that Israel offers a degree of protection from Islamist extremism, which, it seems, should grant it some form of immunity from standard rules of behaviour. It is a factor in trying to understand how, with the incontestable evidence of its genocidal campaign, there remains such reluctance to bring Benjamin Netanyahu and his closest allies to face the consequences of their actions at the ICC. Only a rogue state would so completely destroy the land of a neighbouring people, killing tens of thousands of civilians in the process, and impose such stringent controls around the delivery of humanitarian aid as to knowingly force those it hadn't killed to the brink of starvation. That is what Israel did between October 2023 and 2024; it is what it was allowed to do.

Decades of blockades had forced the population of Gaza to be ever more self-sufficient but, since the events of October 2023, Gazans faced starvation. With the unprecedented bombardment they suffered, the appalling programme of disabling their capacity to farm and feed themselves was overshadowed by the deliberate denial of essential resources like food and medical supplies, which have been allowed to enter Gaza only infrequently. The resulting famine conditions were a direct result of Israeli government policy, as had been the destruction of medical and educational infrastructure. They were supported by the US administration of Joe Biden, which chose to turn away from the overwhelming evidence presented to it of the prevailing famine conditions.

Israel is a nation so absorbed by its sense of entitlement, so certain of its destiny, that it has no real sense of being part of a wider community of nations. Its relationship with others is exclusively about what it can get. It is utterly selfish, abusive even. For decades, it has 'played' the international community, most especially the United States, Britain and the EU, without whose money and arms it could not have engaged in its determined colonialism. It has shown such disrespect for international institutions, most particularly the United Nations, that, were it another place and another people, it would have been treated differently. Were it not seen by much of the West as a nation that serves the interests of Jews who suffered such unbelievable barbarism in Europe eighty years ago, its behaviour would long ago have been challenged. It has engaged in war, the theft of land, apartheid and the massacre of civilians, all of which have been documented, while it tells itself, and those whose support it has purchased, that it is the only defence the world has against Islamists and the often wildly exaggerated threat of Iran.

But the facts paint a different picture. Never has the poisonous bile of a rogue state been as clearly manifest as with the behaviour of Israel over the course of 2023 and 2024. Never in modern history has a nation killed so many people, bulldozed and stolen their land with such active support from countries like the US, Britain, France, Germany, Italy and Canada, and still laid claim to being among the most democratic in the world.

One year on from the Hamas attack, the Civil Defense Directorate in the Gaza Strip released the following unverified and possibly unverifiable statistics. In the twelve months between 7 October 2023 and 6 October 2024, there had been 3,654 violent incidents attributed to the IDF or other Israeli actors, with 51,870 people either dead or 'missing'. Strikingly, 902 families had been wiped out, resulting in their removal from civil registries. Among the dead, 986 were medical personnel, 750 teachers, 175 journalists, 130 academics and scientists and 85 officers in the Civil Defense. Almost 70 per cent of those missing or dead were women and children.

The damage to infrastructure was also listed: 462 schools and universities were destroyed; 34 hospitals, 80 health centres and 131 ambulances were rendered inoperable; 815 mosques, 3 Christian churches and 200,000 housing units were destroyed. Roads, electricity and water supplies have all been targeted to maximise the impact on people's daily lives. Estimates of the overall devastation range from 70 to 89 per cent of Gaza being destroyed by more than 85,0000 tonnes of explosives.

If the attack of 7 October is profiled as an act of terrorism rather than guerrilla war, then the response of the state of Israel since has, too, been one of terrorism, not war. This goes to the heart of the issue; what has threatened world peace is not Hamas or Hezbollah, which Israel and its Western allies are quick to profile as terrorist groups, but the terrorist state of Israel. With the continued acquiescence of the West's most powerful nations, it has set off in pursuit of its Zionist ambition. This ambition cannot be achieved without inflicting unimaginable levels of terror on the people of Palestine and, if taking southern Lebanon to the Litani River is to be part of the grand design, on the Lebanese too.

The decades-long accommodation of Israel by the West is the problem. It is not credible that, one year into Nakba II, the United States, Britain, et al., are unaware of the scale of Israel's abandonment of any moral integrity, never mind international law. The word rogue state has long been used in international commentary to describe despotic or malevolent nations. But, since the term was coined by experts to describe those that are considered a threat to world peace, Israel qualifies. There are those who argue that it is not the state but its prime minister and his closest allies that have 'gone rogue' but 'Being a rogue Prime Minister has one inevitable consequence: turning Israel into a rogue state.'[265] The main evidence to support the charge is the tens of thousands of civilian deaths resulting from its wildly disproportionate response to the Hamas attack on its soil and the disingenuity with which it entered into the protracted peace process.

Israel never wanted peace. Even a ceasefire that could have involved a hostage deal was not of interest to Netanyahu and his inner circle. The decision to assassinate the Hamas leader Ismail Haniyeh in Tehran in late July, at a time when he was involved in peace talks, represented the strongest evidence that it did not want peace. The idea that it was Hamas that was stalling any hopes of a negotiated truce was another lie emanating from Tel Aviv, one that the United States helped to amplify. Endless White House briefings by its different spokespersons told frustrated media that Hamas was the stumbling block to a deal. 'Hamas will not come to the table' became the weekly, if not daily, mantra of President Biden's hopeless and hapless spokespeople.

The independent nations involved in the process and some in the Israeli media, especially *Haaretz*, were quick to discount this falsehood: it was Israel that did not want peace; it was Netanyahu and his key ministers who continually shut down any consideration of a hostage deal that would be part of a ceasefire agreement. The independent evidence of that is overwhelming, but most commentary in the West, led by the White House, presented the failure to move toward a ceasefire as the fault of Hamas.

Israel's conduct over the course of 2024 and the unquestioning support of the government of the United States and some of the larger countries in Europe reinforced the value it realised from its heavy investment in the direct purchase of political influence. This was augmented by the penetration of important elements of Western media by strong Israeli interests, which have, for years, fomented a fear of Islam as the sole perpetrator of terrorism. As a result, many of those with influence on decision-making immediately promoted Israel's right to act as it so chose post 7 October 2023. There was little or no context, barely any serious attempt to offer a historical perspective on the shocking events of that day. Israel was allowed to respond to the Hamas attack so disproportionately it beggared belief and, sadly, the acquiescence of most in the West and the sponsorship of a substantial minority emboldened it to accelerate its programme of land annexation in the West Bank and, in late summer, to conjure a dispute with Hezbollah that seemed to justify expanding its aggression to Lebanon.

Playing the Iran Card

The events of summer 2024 presented Israel with a singular opportunity to reignite its full Zionist ambition. It was not going to be wasted. The widening of the war to include Lebanon was managed with some political and military ingenuity. The initial forays took out a few Hezbollah targets in Beirut, then the IDF concentrated on southern Lebanon for a period, then shifted focus back to Beirut, before launching its real intent with the use of technology to turn pagers into explosives, causing not just death and injuries but generating great panic across Lebanon. Then, with only the tamest of warnings by the US and with wider political support at home (even the opposition parties supported going to war with Lebanon), Netanyahu ordered a wider wave of bombings and missile attacks on Beirut. In doing so, he brought the war to Iran's door without, it seemed, a thought for the wider consequences, including for those that, however foolishly, had chosen to back Israel to the hilt.

Knowing the West's fear of the Islamist bogeyman, Israel had already used its standard playbook to defend its military actions in the West Bank, citing the involvement of Iranian-backed militia in the area. It was nothing new. Electioneering in March 2015, Benjamin Netanyahu told Israeli news site NRG, 'Anyone who is going to establish a Palestinian state, anyone who is going to evacuate territories today, is simply giving a base for attacks to radical Islam against Israel. This is the true reality that was created here in the last few years.'[266] This kind of fable has always served the interests of the Zionists, so, at the most sensitive tipping point for generations, when Israel most needed to play the Iranian card to dull any hint of criticism, it found that it worked again and again.

The critical factor in moving to engage Hezbollah and launch a series of lethal attacks on Lebanon was Netanyahu's personal political imperative. Just as with Gaza, it wasn't only his political career he was trying to extend; as we've seen, he needed to ensure that he stayed a free man for as long as possible. But the ultimate prize would be for his government to convince all Israelis that an Iranian wolf was dressed up in Hezbollah's clothing; opening up that flank would likely prove more appealing to his people and certainly to his Western allies than continuing to annihilate Gaza, which represented no threat at all to the West – Hamas has never brought its fight beyond Israel's borders, and has made it clear it doesn't intend to.

Whatever the truth behind the July attack on the playing fields in the Golan Heights that had killed twelve youngsters in the Druze village of Majdal Shams, it gave Israel the opportunity to test what it had long planned, a widening of the battleground to Lebanon. The killing of a dozen youngsters on the border might seem nothing compared to the platform the Hamas attack had provided Israel. However, managed carefully, the calamity in Majdal Shams could give it grounds to move against Hezbollah and flex its military muscle in Lebanon.

With the passage of time, as the nature and scale of Israel's intent became ever more evident, there continued to be factors that facilitated its warmongering. Among those was the creeping palsy of Joe Biden's last months in office as US president, with a Democratic party that was both AIPAC-contaminated and scared to death that any move to criticise, never mind sanction, Israel could advantage

Kamala Harris' opponent in the November election, Donald Trump. The West issued its usual mild pleas for diplomacy, but without even the hollow warnings Biden had offered when he approved Israel's offensive in Gaza in October 2023. The new president of Iran, Masoud Pezeshkian, just elected on a moderate stance, had been sworn in and, allowing for power ultimately resting with the ayatollah, had made encouraging noises about Iran's relationship with the West – a shocking prospect for a state of Israel that depends on being able to play the card of Tehran as the home of a terror industry focused on the annihilation of the non-Islamic world.

In Israel itself, some of the politics had changed. President Isaac Herzog, who was largely absent as his political foe Netanyahu had used the military campaign in Gaza to divert attention from his efforts to curtail the government's moves against the judiciary, changed his tune by issuing a public and wholehearted support of the idea of going to war with Lebanon. Over a few days in late September, on Sky TV and a number of US networks, he echoed the government's lies about Hezbollah's aggression of the previous twelve months, warning grimly of the threat Iran posed to the West and Israel's determination to defend itself against all-comers.

In the Knesset, too, there was strong support; elements of the opposition were more enthusiastic about war with Hezbollah than the pursuit of Hamas, and in the earliest weeks of the Lebanon campaign, Netanyahu let it be known he was considering replacing his minister of defence, Yoav Gallant, with the leader of the main opposition party, United Right, Gideon Sa'ar. In the end, he kept Gallant but added Sa'ar as a minister without portfolio and a member of the cabinet security committee. Sa'ar had, for months, been vocal on the merits of war with Lebanon. The attendant risks were that Hezbollah had the capacity to fight back in a way that would have been beyond Hamas or that Iran would step in. To someone as desperate to hold on to power as Netanyahu, even if Israel started a war as a result of attacking Lebanon, it was a risk worth taking. There was also the opportunity to bring the hardline Zionists in the Knesset with him, with the prospect of reversing the country's withdrawal from Lebanon in 2000, advancing into Lebanese territory and re-imagining the prospect of a state of Israel that ran north of where the Litani River sweeps across Lebanon to the Mediterranean.

Iran did respond, quickly and efficiently, hitting Israeli military bases in Tel Aviv, though most of its hypersonic ballistic missiles were shot down by US naval vessels and Israeli ground defence systems. The strike represented a sign of just how close Israel was shifting the dynamic to a regional war, with the United States again quick to assert its iron-clad support for the aggressor: Israel. The White House adviser, Jake Sullivan, who only months before had been shocked by Israel's attack on the Iranian consulate in Damascus, Syria, an attack Iran had not responded to, gave oxygen to Joe Biden's mumbled affirmation that he continued to support Netanyahu. With classic White House verbal dexterity, Biden's people called for everyone to remain calm to avoid the threat of a wider conflict. While stressing the need for calm, Sullivan was bullish about how the administration viewed the Iranian actions: 'We have made clear that there will be consequences – severe consequences – for this attack, and we will work with Israel to make that the case.'[267]

◆◆◆

The events of 2024 in the Middle East have also exposed the shrinking importance of the West, where many of the colonisers of the past continually fail to allow international law and human rights to override all other foreign policy considerations. The position of the United States is particularly marked. Israel was constructed on the ruins of another civilisation without so much as a thought, gifted it by one of the great colonisers, Britain, as though, to paraphrase former US President John F. Kennedy in a letter to his father, it was theirs to give in the first place.[268] Israel was given a place to pitch the Zionist tent in part as recompense for Europe's wider failings, but the land it was given wasn't in the West, and this 'gifting' was done without the merest consideration of the impact on the population whose land it was. This was considered acceptable because the indigenous people were Arabs, desert people, whose rights could be made secondary, at best, to those of white Europeans who needed somewhere to go. The first episode of ethnic cleansing, the Nakba of 1948, left the Palestinians adrift, scattered across the Arab world and further afield, with communities that had lived for centuries on the land of Palestine completely destroyed, obliterated.

The Israeli hold on Western political thinking is alarming. Even the Oslo Accords, which had seemed to offer some small hope, said Israel bore 'no responsibility for the costs of the occupation'.[269] This wording is extraordinary; so eager was the West not to offend Israel that in the settlement it proposed, it was to have no liability for the occupation of land it had no rights to but that it had controlled for a quarter of a century. Israel had destroyed the Palestinian economy and a whole way of life, forced people to live in abject poverty, forced them into camps, but the much-vaunted Oslo deal meant Israel bore no responsibility for any of this, so there was no requirement for compensation.

It was worse. The accords were illusory, a trick of the light to benefit Israel, to allow it to continue as before, with the only differences being a demilitarisation and the recognition of the Palestinian Authority. Oslo was 'a project to reorganize Israeli authority, through the establishment of the PA [Palestinian Authority] as an institution of indirect rule to which Israel outsourced its responsibilities for the occupied population.'[270] In 2012, a former adviser to Ariel Sharon, Dov Weisglass, wrote, 'Israel has the authority of the sovereign in the territories – without the obligations. This situation is a direct result of the Oslo Accords.'[271] Others put it more prosaically, that the effect was to establish the only prison in the world where those incarcerated had to provide for themselves.

The West has never learned that whatever Israel is offered, it will take what it considers its entitlement and then more. It is a state with no concern for fairness or a balance of interests; the evidence is that it has little interest in peace. Post the catastrophe, the Six-Day War had presented an opportunity to reset Israel's territorial ambitions but without success. Approaching six decades later, the best that the West can do is to invoke more UN resolutions in the certain knowledge they will be blocked by Israel's most powerful allies. Even were they not, Israel will ignore them and carry on its annexation of land, its detention of Palestinians and its administration of fear, knowing that, as long as it can invoke the threat of Islamists and of Iran as a notional nuclear threat, the United States and its allies will continue to look the other way.

Whatever resistance to Zionist ambition has emerged – and much of its source is among Jews across the globe – it has not been able to shift those in control of the state or to dampen the drive to spread the territory of the state of Israel as far west and north as possible. Any and all opposition to that ambition is countered with questionable biblical references and the horror of the Holocaust without recognising that, if the Bible is a reliable source, then Christians have a stronger case for much of modern-day Israel, and that, for the Arabs of Palestine, their Holocaust was the Nakba of 1948.

While it loves to tout Iran as a threat to the whole region, it is Israel who, time and time again, behaves as the aggressor. There is no limit to its ambition, no end to its needs. With Israel, there can be no satisfactory outcome that would allow a state of Palestine anywhere within sight, and with Israel, peace is not possible – not even desirable – if it means compromising on the Zionist mission. The borders set after the Six-Day War, ones that granted Israel territory on which to build a prosperous and peaceful state at some cost to the indigenous Palestinian population, were never accepted by Israel. It has occupied much of the land it has long coveted and has refused to leave, awaiting its moment to again expand west to Jordan and north into Lebanon, or move further into the Syrian Golan Heights. In the more than five decades since, apart from occasional bouts of diplomatic diarrhoea, the West did nothing to ensure the implementation of international law that affirmed 'the right of the Palestinian people to self-determination and to independence'.[272] This is at the root of Nakba II; the decades of neglect of the West allowed Israel to ride roughshod over international law, assert its dominance over Palestinians and, whenever it encountered a violent reaction, to call 'foul' – to wield the terrorist threat and to remind Western allies of its claim to be the one democracy in the region that could protect them from the 'threat of Iran'. Powerful elements in Israel watched and waited for the chance to give effect to the Zionist ambition.

The circumstances that brought about the latest opportunity may have been personal to the needs of Israel's prime minister, coinciding with the ambitions of those more hawkish politicians around him, but the Zionists have thirsted for this moment since their ambition has been allowed to fester since 1967. Without the West collectively turning on the Zionist state, and its biggest supporters placing it on notice that it will receive no further backing, Israel will go to war again and again and again. That is its history; it is its way. Through all the unfolding conflict, the Zionist intent is being slowly realised.

◆◆◆

When the United States and Britain launched the invasion of Iraq in 2002, one of those who pushed them to do so was Benjamin Netanyahu, who had long been obsessed with the threat posed by Iraq and Iran. Among the intelligence sources drawn on by the Bush and Blair administrations in their disastrous decision to invade was Israel's view that Iraq had developed a nuclear capability that threatened the West. In 2003, Shlomo Brom, formerly a senior intelligence officer and later a senior research associate at Tel Aviv University, wrote a deeply critical assessment of how Israel had got it so wrong; among his conclusions was that 'Israeli intelligence tends to adopt the worst-case scenario'.[273] Brom argued that this was not new, that right back to the Yom Kippur War in 1973, Israel's intelligence services had failed and that its overly simple tendency to assume the worst would mean more failures in the future.

What Netanyahu has done since October 2023, right through 2024, is straight out of that playbook. With his trademark deviousness, he has brought the US with him, knowing that, for all its frustration with Israel's neediness, there is no administration that cannot be bounced into acquiescence by even the most oblique reference to Iran or by teasing the Islamist word. The result is that while it's always been the case that the relationship between the US and Israel has been tight, Netanyahu has managed it to the point where they are 'as one'. The US has long bought the lie (not just Netanyahu's) that Israel is its most critical ally against the consistently overhyped threat posed by Iran. In October 2024, Netanyahu brought back that policy of deploying the Iranian threat to obtain unprecedented (the word Biden used when first addressing the response to 7 October 2023) and, arguably, unconditional levels of support.

Netanyahu used Biden's weakness and the perilous nature of Vice President Kamala Harris' campaign to defeat Donald Trump in the 2024 election as a means of enticing the US into a potential quagmire in the Middle East. When he extended the 'battlefield' to southern Lebanon, when he tried to order UNIFIL troops to leave their posts in the buffer zone and when he bombed Beirut, the risk to the West increased exponentially that, by pushing further into Lebanon, toward Tyre and Sidon, he could provoke Iran.

There was a method to this. First, it was Gaza, then an extension into the West Bank before, in July initially, gently poking Hezbollah and Lebanon, eliciting a response that allowed Israel to cry foul over Iran's backing of Hezbollah before increasing the intensity of its attacks on Beirut and southern Lebanon and drawing Iran into the conflict at a level that would allow it claim the need to strike Iran back. So, it turned out that, on 7 October 2024, on the anniversary of the Hamas attack and just a month short of the US presidential election, Netanyahu told Biden he needed to strike Iran in a manner that showed not just that he meant business but that so too did Israel's guardian angel, the United States of America.

The US was deep into its election cycle. The Democrats were increasingly confident that Vice President Harris would win, so disturbing the massively influential Israel lobby by any dilution in support of Israel's 'right to defend itself' was not going to happen. The Republican candidate Donald Trump was no less attentive to its importance but his credentials were such that his team could point to his dislike of war and to the fact that – at a time when his core voters were struggling to make ends meet – the Biden administration was found by the War Project at Brown University in Providence, to have had spent a record $17.9 billion on military aid to Israel between 7 October 2023 and 7 October 2024, a record for any one year. One of the report's other findings was that the US-backed Israeli military operations since 7 October 2023 would lead to far higher indirect than direct death rates.[274]

What makes the approach of the United States and the EU throughout this period most alarming is that they've enabled, and in the case of the US, Britain, Germany and maybe some others, sponsored the genocide of the Palestinian people by a political leader whose single greatest motivation is to avoid the prospect of going to jail for corruption. It is hard to think of a case in modern history where a country has taken such aggressive and sustained military action, killing tens of thousands of civilians on such grossly immoral grounds. Yet Netanyahu's thirst for war seemed unquenched as he edged his allies closer to a widening of the conflict in the autumn of 2024.

Nakba II

For the people of Palestine, the events since 7 October 2023 have been another Nakba, a complete catastrophe; for the beleaguered people of Gaza, the West Bank and East Jerusalem, it is hardship upon hardship upon hardship; for the six million diaspora of Palestinians around the world, it has been a heartbreak, one that, given their history, is hard to see ending in the near-term. The heartbreak is all the greater because nations like the United States and others that claim to hold some particular position of moral democratic leadership have funded and supported Israel in its genocidal campaign over the twelve months from 7 October 2023 to 7 October 2024. Some senior political voices in these places questioned the proportionality of Israel's response to the Hamas attack but very few have used the only word that can accurately profile what Israel has done: genocide. Fewer still have drawn attention to the depravity of the Netanyahu government's pursuit of a genocide against the Palestinians.

To those who object to this description, to those for whom Israel remains some unique nation with a set of rights that are so special that they believe it was entitled to react to the attack it suffered on its soil on that October Saturday in 2023, the following may be worth consideration:

- When 70 per cent of the population killed in a conflict are women and children, it's hard to conclude that the intent of those responsible is not genocidal.
- When the population is being deprived of essentials for even the most basic form of life, it's hard to conclude that the intent of those responsible is not genocidal.
- When the delivery of emergency food and medical aid is consistently and deliberately stalled, it's hard to conclude that the intent of those responsible is not genocidal.
- When hospitals and health centres, schools and humanitarian NGOs are repeatedly attacked, it's hard to conclude that the intent of those responsible is not genocidal.
- When over 900 families have had to be removed from the civil registry, it's hard to conclude that the intent of those responsible is not genocidal.
- When over 15,000 children are reported to have lost one or both parents, it's hard to conclude that the intent of those responsible is not genocidal.
- When rehabilitation hospitals and orphanages are targeted, it's hard to conclude that the intent of those responsible is not genocidal.
- When 85,000 tonnes of explosives are dropped on one of the most densely populated areas on earth, it's hard to conclude that the intent of those responsible is not genocidal.

The experts do not all agree with the campaign in Gaza being profiled as a genocide, but none who are reputable dispute that Israel has conducted war crimes that are as morally reprehensible as they are contrary to international law.

The esteemed Israeli-American historian Raz Segal, who is an Associate Professor of Genocide Studies at Stockton University, New Jersey, decided only a week after the Hamas attack that Israel's response was 'genocidal'. At a time when the loss of civilian life was 1,800 and only 400,000 Palestinians had been displaced, he described in detail why, even then, Israel's campaign amounted to 'a textbook case of genocide'.[275] One part of his case was the clear intent of those leading Israel, something that later received attention from the ICJ in clearly establishing the 'intent' of those responsible.

The ICJ and independent human rights legal experts are generally more cautious than historians about formulating a charge of genocide on the basis of 'intent' as, from a legal perspective, it is more difficult to establish. The 1948 Nakba came about because of the shared political ambition of the Jewish population. It was clear that in order for the Jewish state to be established as intended, the millions of Arabs who lived there would have to be removed. There was never any evidence found then of an actual plan drafted by Jewish leaders to destroy the non-Jewish people. So, from a legal perspective, what happened failed the 'intent' test, which is why the Nakba is generally documented as a campaign of ethnic cleansing, not genocide. The same legal argument is made by those who argue, including many who believe Netanyahu et al. should face trial as war criminals, that without proof of an actual military or political plan to wipe out the whole Palestinian people, the charge of genocide cannot be made.

A year after the Hamas attack of 7 October, the Israeli academic Amos Goldberg, Professor of Jewish History at the Hebrew University of Jerusalem, took a different view, arguing that it was a clear case of genocide:

> the level and pace of indiscriminate killing, destruction, mass expulsion, displacement, deliberate famine, executions, the wiping out of universities, cultural and religious institutions, the crushing of elites (including the killing of journalists), and the sweeping dehumanization of the Palestinians create an overall picture of genocide, of the intentional and conscious shattering of Palestinian existence in Gaza. Palestinian Gaza, as a geographical, political, cultural, and human entity no longer exists. Genocide is the deliberate destruction of a collective or part of it, not of all of its individual members – and that is what is happening in Gaza today … The result is undoubtedly genocidal.[276]

Silence is Acquiescence

I am a 66-year-old European. I am also Irish but the European piece represents a great deal when your parents were born just after the catastrophe of the Great War and lived through the even greater one of World War II, which killed 73 million people, almost 50 million of whom were civilians. The European Union emerged as a force to, above all else, provide a means by which humanity, in the West at least, would ensure that no such horror could again occur. The Schuman Declaration of 1950 said the construct of such a supranational foundation would make war 'not merely unthinkable, but materially impossible'.[277] While the declaration was focused on Europe's old warring factions, it went much further in its original ambition, one it said would be offered to the world as a whole, 'without distinction or exception, with the aim of contributing to raising living standards and to promoting peaceful achievements'.[278]

Today, in 2024, twenty-seven European nations believe in most of those basic principles – however different the emphases – but there's overwhelming evidence of a failure to act in anything approaching the coherent fashion that the EU's architects would have expected in response to Israel's genocidal campaign in Palestine.

Whatever about the people of Europe, institutionally, the European Union and most of its member states have done nothing approaching enough about Israel's genocide as it was carried out in full public view by a state that's allowed to continue to trade, to have its diplomatic representatives in situ across Europe's capital cities, to be fully involved in most sporting activities at both national and club level and to participate in global music and arts festivals.

The fact that Nazi Germany targeted the Jewish people, killing six million, in the single largest genocide in history, has always tempered Europe's capacity to address Israel's long-established abuse of its legal entitlements and its decades-long oppression of the Palestinians. What is different about the events of 2023–24 is the extent to which – in full knowledge of the scale of Israel's destruction of Palestine and the wholescale killing of its people – many of Europe's largest nations have provided it with armaments to enable its repugnant campaign.

There are various degrees of culpability involved, starting with the sponsors of the genocide, but even nations like Ireland, which has been at the forefront of condemnation in Europe, have not done enough in response to this horror; it has not banned all trade, has not policed US military use of Shannon, its airport on the west coast, nor did it expel Israel's ambassador. I am a citizen of Ireland, a citizen of Europe; I have marched and argued Palestine's case when I could but I have done nothing close to enough to qualify as being 'outraged'. In spite of my long interest in the situation, in spite of informing myself well before 7 October 2023, I had no answer to the most relevant question posed by UNRWA officials, residents of the West Bank and even Israelis who have chosen to leave, so horrified are they by what they have witnessed: where, oh where, is the outrage?

It seems that the complicated politics of the Middle East have been with us forever. In part, many of us, despairing of really understanding it, choose its apparent complexity as a reason to either accept the mainstream presentation of events or just decide not to 'engage'. I count myself among that group even though, as a journalist in the 1980s, I read all I could about it. I met and interviewed Robert Fisk many times, one of the most knowledgeable commentators on the subject. I believed way back then that Israel was prepared to trade its status as a state born out of the ashes of a genocide to dominate the territory it had been gifted, irrespective of the consequences for those others whose land it was.

Over the decades since, I watched with bemusement the attempts by different US administrations to work toward the achievement of lasting peace, all of which were effectively, hopelessly compromised by the stranglehold of the Israel lobby on American politics. I had first witnessed this covering the US presidential election of 1984. Reagan won a second term in a landslide but his targeting of the Jewish vote four years earlier, in 1980, was crucial to his success against incumbent president Jimmy Carter, who was seen as having leanings toward the Palestinians.

The Camp David Accords garnered considerable media attention across the West but my own interest only spiked again with the Oslo Accords of 1993 when Israel and the PLO included provisions for Israel to withdraw its troops from parts of Gaza and the West Bank. There was hope, but it was a mirage, a diplomatic sleight of hand that allowed Israel to continue with its colonialist behaviour. Globally, the accords were presented as considerably more profound than they were in reality and while Israel's parliament, the Knesset, narrowly voted in favour of the agreement and, the following year, the signatories received the Nobel Peace Prize, cause for real optimism among those who really understood their limitations was limited. Nearly all of the commitments of importance were heavily caveated, and most independent commentators stated that there remained little or no trust between the two sides.

Lord Mayor of Jerusalem Ehud Olmert, later prime minister of Israel and by no means the most right-wing Israeli political figure of the past half century, opposed the agreements and called for Jerusalem to expand further into the West Bank. Most Palestinian groups – including Hamas – opposed the accords too, arguing that Israel would use them as an opportunity to expand its settlement programme. Most interestingly, almost a decade later, in 2001, Benjamin Netanyahu was recorded as saying that he'd been asked before the election if he would honour the agreements. Here was his response: 'I said I would, but … I'm going to interpret the accords in such a way that would allow me to put an end to this galloping forward to the '67 borders.'[279]

Even a cursory review of Israel's conduct over its history is enough to raise serious questions about its claim to be a democracy. It is too engrossed by its origins, by the awfulness of the tragedy that was allowed to befall Europe's Jews in the 1930s and 1940s and too sure of its entitlement to land that, by its twisted perspective, was promised to the Jews alone, for it to be capable of behaving democratically. Even within its own sovereign borders of the twenty-first century, there's overwhelming evidence that some of its laws and their application are so discriminatory as to represent an apartheid form of government. Israel's failure, for decades, to recognise scores of UN resolutions places it outside the global structure that – however flawed – attempts to bring some order across all but a handful of the nations on earth.

Still, for all Israel's decades-long display of contempt for the international community, despite its belief that the history of the Jewish people – both in the biblical sense and in their experience of the horror of Nazism – gave them an entitlement to behave in a manner that could never be fundamentally questioned, never mind challenged, the West took little or no notice. The people who were suffering at the hands of this despotism were not of our place and we knew little enough about them. The situation was complex. Those people – the Palestinians – were themselves divided, and like the homeless on our streets, they had no real identity, certainly not one that Westerners could relate to.

Israel, on the other hand, was like an extension of our world – we knew its cities, its football clubs and its politicians; it even competed in Eurovision – in short, it was a place, a state, a nation, whereas the Palestinians were homeless, rudderless, without status and that was just the way it was. We were Israel-washed, and, to an extent, it wasn't Israel's fault.

There was more to this quasi-identification with Israel, of course; there was and is our deep-seated white, Judeo-Christian cultural bias that makes many of us outwardly racist or, perhaps, closet believers that our whole world is threatened by Muslim extremists. This prejudice, which can translate into an unease with Arabs, is rarely vocalised but it is an unpalatable truth of why so much of the West remains slow to outlaw Israel. As Arabs, the Palestinians are predominantly Muslim, and the West has come to see terrorism or serious 'trouble' of any scale as having its origins in Islam. There are so many different groups involved on the Palestinian side – the PLO, Fatah, Hamas – that it feels impossible to follow who represents the people. Some of these groups have carried out acts of terror so they are conflated with Islamists who have perpetrated attacks in the West, while we have long been fed a belief that the state of Israel conducts its affairs politically as a reputable democratic state.

These many confused and confusing images or emotions are what have long dominated how most in the West think about the issue of Palestine and Israel – if we think about it at all. Our perspective is informed by what we've absorbed through our own experience and whatever historical perspective we've received, all of which is augmented by a mainstream media whose ownership lies mainly in the hands of those who support Israel. In the West, we cannot escape the clutches of its exceptionally well-managed narrative that positions it as a victim whose very survival as a state is threatened by the existence of Palestine and those in the region – especially Iran – that might choose to protect it.

Much of the West's most established and best-followed traditional media chose a pro-Israel stance over the course of its onslaught on the Palestinians. Overall, the reporting line was that Israel was simply defending itself, protecting its sovereign borders from attack by Islamist terrorists represented either by Hamas or Hezbollah. The storyline has, generally, suggested that its military action in

Gaza, its occupation of land in the West Bank and later, in 2024, its moves into southern Lebanon were all part of a need to protect its citizens from harm.

It was and is a lie, one that most mainstream media in the West understand but few are prepared to call out. Most acquiesce or stay silent when it is offered as a justification for the continuing destruction of land that is not Israel's to take and the annihilation of a people who are its rightful owners.

◆◆◆

In 1948, the Swedish diplomat Folke Bernadotte, who had saved more than 30,000 prisoners of war from Nazi concentration camps, most of whom were Jews, was mandated to try and bring the dispute between the Jewish and Palestinian people to an end. The fledgling United Nations thought Bernadotte was the best person to work towards securing a peaceful settlement between the parties. When he travelled to Palestine, Bernadotte toured the country to see what had occurred and was struck by the destruction of the indigenous people's towns and villages. Later, he met representatives of the local population when he visited refugee camps in Palestine and Jordan.

The scale of the crisis was said to have shocked him. The lack of food and medicines, allied to the destruction of people's homes, led him to advise that the Palestinians must be allowed back to their homes or what was left of them. He reported to the UN that 'It would be an offence against the principles of elemental justice if these innocent victims of the conflict were denied the right to return to their homes while Jewish immigrants flow into Palestine, and, indeed, at least offer the threat of permanent replacement of the Arab refugees who have been rooted in the land for centuries.'[280]

The first proposal Bernadotte suggested was for fixed boundaries through some form of agreed negotiation and economic union between the two states and the return of Palestinian refugees. The proposal – an early iteration of the 'two-state' solution – failed. Bernadotte spoke with reporters, acknowledging the failure of his proposal but saying that he remained confident that a resolution could be found. The following day, 14 September 1948, the motorcade he was travelling in was ambushed in Jerusalem and he was assassinated. The paramilitary Zionist group Lehi, better known as the Stern Gang, carried out the assassination. It was to be the group's last action; most of its members had, months earlier, been inducted into the newly formed IDF.

Almost exactly seventy-two years later, on the anniversary of the Hamas attack, another death somehow symbolised the futility of asking Israel to see the error of its ways, the hopelessness of expecting it to do anything other than steal, kill, maim and terrorise in the pursuit of its ambition. Omar Khalil Al-Balawi was a young school teacher in Northern Gaza who continued to teach right through the destruction that raged all around him, believing it was essential to educate children as the Israeli onslaught continued. Three other members of his family had already been killed when, on 7 October 2024, an Israeli drone hit the family home. Omar was killed. Colleagues described him as resolute in his determination not to let the children of Gaza down or allow Israel progress its ambition to colonise his homeland.

With a striking similarity to how Folke Bernadotte had unknowingly written his last words in his report to the UN the day before his execution in September 1948, Omar Khalil Al-Balawi wrote a testimonial of sorts the day before he was killed. In 1948, Bernadotte's words were available only to those in the UN who read his last dispatch; but, just hours before his death, Omar posted what he'd written on his Facebook page. It seems appropriate that, with a genocide that the world could follow live, the final commentary of a young Gazan schoolteacher was instantly available to the whole world:

> The war has decimated livelihoods in Gaza where most people rely on daily wages to survive. In the northern regions, nearly every home has been partially or completely destroyed, or burned. Electricity has been cut off since the onset of the war and internet access is almost completely severed, with some relying on eSIM technology to maintain contact with family and friends. The education system has been devastated, with schools, learning centres and kindergartens reduced to ruins and the loss of countless teachers and students. Moreover the closure of all crossings into Gaza has trapped the population, preventing any escape to safety. We are confined to an area where death looms from all sides. After a year of this ongoing crisis, we ask: Who is listening to our plight? Who cares enough to intervene? Who will stop this war and prevent further loss of life? Who will hold Israel accountable for these actions? Who will ensure our survival in the midst of this catastrophe? Despite everything, we remain resolute. As the indigenous people of this land, we will stay. This is our home – Palestine.
>
> WE WILL NOT LEAVE!

Endnotes

1 Khalidi, R., *The Hundred Years' War on Palestine* (London: Profile Books, 2020).

2 Ibid.

3 Pappé, I., *A Very Short History of the Israel–Palestine Conflict* (London: Oneworld Publications, 2024).

4 President Charles de Gaulle's press conference on the state of Israel (ORTF, 27 November 1967).

5 Elbagir, N. and others, 'Qatar Sent Millions to Hamas – with Israel's Backing' (CNN, 12 December 2023).

6 'EU's Borrell Says Israel Financed Creation of Gaza Rulers Hamas' (Reuters, 19 January 2024).

7 See Elbagir, 'Qatar Sent Millions'.

8 Personal interview (UNRWA HQ, Amman, July 2024).

9 Personal interview (Amman New Camp, July 2024).

10 'Amman New Camp, Jordan: Camp Profile' (UNRWA, April 2023).

11 Personal interview (Ramallah, August 2024).

12 Ibid.

13 Personal interview (Paris, September 2024).

14 Ibid.

15 Personal interview (Beirut, July 2024).

16 Maltz, J., 'Will Israel Become a Theocracy?', *Haaretz* (3 November 2022).

17 'Israel's Security Must Not Fall Victim to Politics', *The Jerusalem Post* (31 March 2023).

18 'President Herzog Speech Before Presenting the People's Directive for Changes in the Justice System' (Gov.il, 15 March 2023).

19 'Letter to President of the State of Israel, Mr. Itzhak Herzog' (Commanders for Israel's Security, 17 February 2023).

20 'Tens of Thousands Rally Against Judicial Overhaul', *The Times of Israel* (11 February 2023).

21 'Israel is Hurtling Toward Dictatorship', *Haaretz* (17 March 2023).

22 See 'Herzog Speech'.

23 Ibid.

24 '"Unacceptable, Insulting": Coalition Dismiss Herzog's Judicial Reform Framework', *The Times of Israel* (15 March 2023).

25 Chappell, B. and D. Estrin, 'Here's Why Netanyahu's Court Overhaul, Now on Hold, Brought Israel to Brink' (NPR, 27 March 2023).

26 See 'Herzog Speech'.

27 'Warning of Civil War, Herzog Unveils Framework for Judicial Reform', *The Times of Israel* (15 March 2023).

28 Ibid.

29 Keller-Lynn, C., 'Gantz's National Unity Accepts Herzog Framework', *The Times of Israel* (15 March 2023).

30 Shamir, J., 'Judicial Coup and Occupation "Directly Linked"', *Haaretz* (7 August 2023).

31 Ibid.

32 'Israeli Supreme Court Decision Prompts Polarized Response in a Nation at War', *The New York Times* (1 January 2024).

33 'Zionist Union Quotes Netanyahu in Massive Billboard Urging Him to Quit', *The Times of Israel* (15 February 2018).

34 'Corruption Charges Suggested for Netanyahu', *The New York Times* (13 February 2018).

35 Wootliff, R., 'State Prosecutor Hands Indictment Recommendations against PM to Attorney General', *The Times of Israel* (19 December 2018).

36 Hudson, J., 'Israel's Netanyahu Brings His Dirty Laundry to Washington. Literally', *The Washington Post* (23 September 2020).

37 Colonel Richard Kemp's remarks on UN Gaza protests inquiry (UN Watch Conference, 18 March 2019).

38 'Egypt Warned Israel Days Before Hamas Struck' (BBC Online, 12 October 2023).

39 Hanauer, L. and M. P. Connell, *Political Priorities, Poor Intelligence Tradecraft, and the Suppression of Dissenting Views: Why Israel Failed to Warn of Hamas's October 7 Attack* (Institute for Defence Analyses, September 2024).

40 Kubovich, Y., 'The Women Soldiers Who Warned of a Pending Hamas Attack', *Haaretz* (20 November 2023).

41 Dover, R., 'Why Israel's Intelligence Chiefs Failed to Listen to Warnings' (University of Hull, 8 December 2023).

42 'IDF Intel Warns Netanyahu of Israel's "Historic Weakness" Seen by Iran and Hezbollah', *Haaretz* (28 July 2023).

43 See Hanauer and Connell, *Political Priorities*.

44 See BBC, 'Egypt Warned Israel'.

45 *World Report 2023: Israel and Palestine, Events of 2022* (Human Rights Watch, 20 April 2023).

46 *Report on UNCTAD's assistance to the Palestinian people* (UNCTAD – United Nations Conference on Trade and Development, 11 September 2023).

47 Data on Casualties in the Occupied Palestinian Territories (OCHA – United Nations Office for the Coordination of Humanitarian Affairs, 1 January 2023 to 7 October 2023).

48 'Data sheet: Law enforcement against Israeli soldiers suspected of harming Palestinians and their property – Summary of figures for 2017–2021' (Yesh Din, 21 December 2022).

49 'Data Sheet, December 2023: Law Enforcement on Israeli Civilians in the West Bank (Settler violence) 2005–2023' (Yesh Din, 21 January 2024).

50 King Abdullah II of Jordan address at the UN General Assembly, 78th session (19 September 2023).

51 Dr Majed Al Ansari, M., Post on X (Twitter) (24 January 2024).

52 Kearns, E. M., A. E. Betus, and A. F. Lemieux, 'Why Do Some Terrorist Attacks Receive More Media Attention Than Others?' *Justice Quarterly*, 36, 6 (2019).

53 'The Peace Index' (Conflict Resolution and Mediation, University of Tel Aviv, November 2023).

54 Hermann, T. and O. Anabi, 'Even on the Right, Israelis Want Elections Immediately After the War' (The Israel Democracy Institute, 19 December 2023).

55 '72% of Israelis Say Aid Deliveries to Gaza Must Be Stopped, Survey Finds', *The Middle East Monitor* (31 January 2024).

56 Silver, L. and M. Smerkovich, 'Israeli Views of Israel-Hamas War' (Pew Research Center, 30 May 2024).

57 Yashiv, E., 'Autocrats of a Feather', *Haaretz* (28 August 2024).

58 'The Declaration of the Establishment of the State of Israel' (Gov.il, 14 May 1948).

59 Herzl, T., *The Diaries of Theodor Herzl*, Trans. M. Lowenthal (New York: Grosset and Dunlap, 1962).

60 Shehadeh, R., *What Does Israel Fear from Palestine?* (London: Profile Books, 2024).

61 Lubell, M. and N. Al-Mughrabi, 'Israel Rescues Four Hostages in Gaza Raid' (Reuters, 8 June 2024).

62 'Broadcaster Bias Is Failing to Hold Israel to Account', *The Independent* (1 November 2024).

63 Mishal, S. and A. Sela, *The Palestinian Hamas* (New York: Columbia University Press, 2000).

64 Wintour, P., 'Hamas Presents New Charter Accepting a Palestine Based on 1967 Borders', *The Guardian* (1 May 2017).

65 'The Right of the Jewish People to the Land of Israel' (Likud Party: Original Party Platform, 1977).

66 'Public Opinion Poll No (93)' (PCPSR, 17 September 2024).

67 Jenkins, J. P., 'Terrorism' (Britannica.com).

68 Fisk, R., *Night of Power* (London: 4th Estate, 2024).

69 Ibid.

70 Prime Minister Benjamin Netanyahu address at the UN General Debate, 78th session (22 September 2023).

71 Ibid.

72 Ibid.

73 'Netanyahu Vows to Turn Gaza "Into Rubble"', *The Middle East Monitor* (8 October 2023).

74 Segal, R., 'Israel Must Stop Weaponising the Holocaust', *The Guardian* (24 October 2023).

75 Minister of Settlements and National Missions Orit Strook speech in the Knesset (19 February 2024).

76 'Smotrich: It May Be "Justified" to Starve 2 million Gazans', *The Times of Israel* (5 August 2024).

77 *Welcome to Hell: The Israeli Prison System as a Network of Torture Camps* (B'Tselem, 1 August 2024).

78 '"Security" Inmates Held In Prisons Inside Israel' (HaMoked, July 2024).

79 '880 Palestinian Children Detained by Israel this Year, *The Middle East Monitor* (20 November 2023).

80 'Palestinian Children Abused in Israeli Detention' (Al Jazeera, 10 July 2023).

81 See B'Tselem, *Welcome to Hell.*

82 Personal interview (HaMoked senior legal advocate, August 2024).

83 Ibid.

84 *Bitter Legacy: State Impunity in the Northern Ireland Conflict* (Committee on the Administration of Justice, Pat Finucane Centre and Norwegian Centre for Human Rights, April 2024).

85 Ibid.

86 Ibid.

87 Albanese, F., *Report of the Special Rapporteur on the Situation of Human Rights in the Palestinian Territories Occupied since 1967*, (OHCHR – Office of the High Commisionner for Human Rights, 10 July 2023).

88 'Israel's Unlawful Carceral Practices in the Occupied Palestinian Territory Are Tantamount to International Crimes' (OHCHR, 10 July 2023).

89 See B'Tselem, *Welcome to Hell.*

90 'In response to HaMoked Habeus Corpus Petition' (HaMoked, 5 May 2024).

91 See HaMoked interview.

92 See B'Tselem, *Welcome to Hell.*

93 'Close the Sde Teman Detention Center' (The Association for Civil Rights in Israel, 17 September 2024).

94 See HaMoked interview.

95 Fassin, D., *Moral Abdication: How the World Failed to Stop the Destruction of Gaza*, Trans. G. Elliott (London: Verso Books, 2024).

96 See HaMoked interview.

97 'Scabies Spreading Among Prisoners; Visits Cancelled: Prisoners' Organizations' (WAFA, 3 September 2024).

98 Ibid.

99 See B'Tselem, *Welcome to Hell.*

[100] *'No Traces of Life': Israel's Ecocide In Gaza 2023–2024* (Forensic Architecture, 29 March 2024).

[101] Ibid.

[102] *A Spatial Analysis of the Israeli Military's Conduct in Gaza since October 2023* (Forensic Architecture, 15 October 2024).

[103] Ibid.

[104] *Famine Review Committee: Gaza Strip*, (IPC – Integrated Food Security Phase Classification, 18 March 2024).

[105] Ministry of Defense Coordination of Government Activities in the Territories, *Food Consumption in the Gaza Strip: Red Lines*, Trans. Gisha NGO (Originally published 1 January 2008, translation by Gisha published 17 October 2012).

[106] Prime Minister Benjamin Netanyahu address at the UN General Debate, 79th session (27 September 2024).

[107] Murphy, B., 'Israel Deliberately Blocked Humanitarian Aid to Gaza', *ProPublica* (24 September 2024).

[108] President of the European Commission Ursula von der Leyen special message for the 75th Anniversary of the foundation of Israel, Post on X (Twitter) (26 April 2023).

[109] Kamala Harris address at the AIPAC Policy Conference in Washington DC (28 March 2017).

[110] Gjevori, E., 'Gaza's Cultural and Religious Heritage Lies in Ruins After a Year of Attacks by Israel', *Middle East Eye* (11 October 2024).

[111] 'Israel Destroys Second Largest Historical Mosque in Gaza', *The Middle East Monitor* (4 July 2024).

[112] Al-Houdalieh, S., 'The International Order Is Failing to Protect Palestinian Cultural Heritage', *SAPIENS* (6 June 2024).

[113] *Policy on Cultural Heritage* (Office of the Prosecutor of the ICC, June 2021).

[114] Recommendation Concerning the Preservation of Cultural Property Endangered by Public or Private Works (General Conference of UNESCO, 15th session, 19 November 1968).

[115] Universal Declaration of Human Rights, Article 22 (UN General Assembly Resolution 217 A(III), 10 December 1948).

[116] *Cultural Apartheid: Israel's Erasure of Palestinian Heritage in Gaza* (Al-Haq, January 2022).

[117] Ibid.

[118] Shehadeh, R. and P. Johnson, *Forgotten* (London: Profile Books, 2025).

[119] Shwed, U. and others, 'Integration of Arab Israelis and Jews in Schools in Israel' (Taub Center for Social Policy Studies in Israel, October 2014).

[120] Feniger, Y., Y. Shavit and S. Caller, 'Schooling and Equity in Israel' in G. W. Noblit, *Oxford Research Encyclopedia of Education* (Oxford: Oxford University Press, 2021).

[121] Feniger, Y., Y. Shavit and S. Caller, 'The Israeli Education System', in G. Ben-Porat and others (ed.), *Routledge Handbook on Contemporary Israel* (London: Routledge, 2022).

[122] 'Nation-State Law to Be Included in Israeli High School Curriculum', *The Times of Israel* (16 August 2019).

[123] Masarwa, L., 'Reading, Writing and Racism: "Nation-State" Law Now Official Israeli Curriculum', *Middle East Eye* (4 September 2019).

[124] 'Basic-Law: Jerusalem the Capital of Israel', Trans. S. Hattis Rolef (Originally adopted in Knesset session 5740, 30 July 1980, translation published 1 May 2022).

[125] Personal interview (Paris, August 2024).

[126] Ibid.

[127] Ibid.

[128] Sokol, S., 'Knesset Passes Law Allowing Government to Fire Teachers It Asserts Identify with Terror', *The Times of Israel* (5 November 2024).

[129] Shire, W., 'Conversations about Home (At the Deportation Centre)', in *Teaching My Mother How To Give Birth* (London: Flipped Eye Publishing, 2011).

[130] Personal interview (London, August 2024).

[131] Graham-Harrison, E., and M. Cohen, 'Draft Israeli Law to Limit Academic Speech Labelled "McCarthyite"', *The Guardian* (21 July 2024).

[132] Rich, D., *Everyday Hate* (Hull: Biteback Publishing, 2024).

[133] 'Jerusalem Declaration on Antisemitism' (Jerusalemdeclaration.org, 2020).

[134] Appy, C. G., 'UMass Arrests: What Would Daniel Ellsberg Do?', *Common Dreams* (20 May 2024).

[135] Saifi, Z., 'Jordan King Warns of "Red Lines" in Jerusalem as Netanyahu Returns to Office', (CNN, 28 December 2022).

[136] King Abdullah II of Jordan address at the UN General Assembly, 79th session (24 September 2024).

[137] Abu Sitta, S., *Mapping My Return: A Palestinian Memoir* (Cairo: American University in Cairo Press, 2017).

[138] See Shehadeh, *Fear*.

[139] Moshe Dayan address to Technion University students (19 March 1969).

[140] Herzl, T., *The Jewish State*, Trans. S. D'Avigdor (Originally published as *Der Judenstaat*, 1896, translation published 1946).

[141] Ibid.

[142] See Abu Sitta, *Mapping*.

[143] Ibid.

[144] Lindsay, J., *Evaluating UNRWA After the Colonna Report* (Washington Institute, June 2024).

[145] Lindsay, J., *Fixing UNRWA: Repairing the UN's Troubled System of Aid to Palestinian Refugees* (Washington Institute, January 2009).

[146] See Shehadeh, *Fear*.

[147] See Pappé, *History*.

[148] Shehadeh, R., 'When Will This Horror End? When Israel Realises That the Cost of Destroying Us Is Too High', *The Guardian* (5 October 2024).

[149] See Moshe Dayan address.

[150] 'The Government Declares 12,000 Dunams in the Jordan Valley as State Lands' (Peace Now, 3 July 2024).

[151] Loveluck, L. and S. Taha, 'Homes Burned, Animals Killed, Palestinians Describe Settler Rampage', *The Washington Post* (16 April 2024).

[152] Haddad, M. and A. Chughtai, 'Israel-Palestine conflict: A brief history in maps and charts' (Al Jazeera, 27 November 2023).

[153] 'The General Staff White Washing Mechanism: The Israeli Law Enforcement System and Breaches of International Law and War Crimes in Gaza' (Yesh Din, 9 July 2024).

[154] Borger, J. and S. Taha, 'Israeli Forces Kill At Least 10 Palestinians in West Bank Raids and Strikes', *The Guardian* (28 August 2024).

[155] Sfard, M., 'Demand for Immediate Repeal of the *Order Regarding the Establishment of a Civil Administration*', Letter to the minister of defence, the commander of the IDF forces in the West Bank and the head of the Civil Administration (8 July 2024).

[156] Rome Statute of the International Criminal Court, Article 7(2)(h) (ICC, 17 July 1998).

[157] 'Israeli Practices towards the Palestinian People and the Question of Apartheid' (ESCWA – United Nations Economic and Social Commission for West Asia, 2017).

[158] See Herzl, *Diaries*.

[159] See '"Into Rubble"'.

[160] '"Business as Usual" with Current Israeli Government Not an Option, Says CJPME', *The Hill Times* (5 April 2023).

[161] 'Israel Pushes NBA to Delete "Occupied Palestine" from Website', *The Middle East Monitor* (30 December 2017).

[162] 'Settler Violence = State Violence' (B'Tselem, 25 November 2021).

[163] See Abu Sitta, *Mapping*.

[164] 'Israel Warns Palestinian Village Will Be Demolished if Residents Refuse to Relocate', *The Times of Israel* (9 September 2024).

[165] 'Mass Graves in Gaza Show Victims' Hands Were Tied, Says UN Rights Office' (UN News, 23 April 2024).

[166] Gaughan, A., *Memoirs of Senator Joseph Connolly* (Dublin: Irish Academic Press, 1996).

[167] McCluskey, F., *Tyrone: The Irish Revolution, 1912–23*, (Dublin: Four Courts Press, 2014)

[168] See Gaughan, *Memoirs*.

[169] See Warsan, 'Home'.

[170] See Pappé, *History*.

[171] Israeli-Palestinian Interim Agreement on the West Bank and the Gaza Strip (a.k.a. 'Oslo II') (28 September 1995).

[172] *World Report 2025: Israel and Palestine, Events of 2024* (Human Rights Watch, 16 January 2025).

[173] Showalter, D. E. and J. G. Royde-Smith, 'World War I' (Britannica.com).

[174] UN Security Council Resolutions 425 and 426 (19 March 1978).

[175] Anderson, J., 'South Lebanon Annexation by Israel Feared', *The Washington Post* (27 September 1982).

[176] Minister Yoav Kisch TV interview (Channel 14 News, 4 July 2024).

[177] Berman, L., 'Netanyahu Met by Angry Crowd on Visit to Site of Deadly Attack', *The Times of Israel* (29 July 2024).

[178] Private briefing of Lebanese government officials (Beirut, 26 July 2024).

[179] 'At Least 12 Killed in Rocket Attack in Israeli-Occupied Golan Heights' (Al Jazeera, 27 July 2024).

[180] WhatsApp message to RTÉ (28 July 2024).

[181] Gebeily, M., A. Timour and L. Bassam, 'Israeli Attack on Beirut Shatters Diplomatic Understandings' (Reuters, 1 August 2024).

[182] National Security Council Spokesperson Adrienne Watson statement on rocket attack on Majdal Shams (White House Briefing Room, 28 July 2024).

[183] Hussein, M., 'Mapping 11 Months of Israel–Lebanon Cross-Border Attacks' (Al Jazeera, 11 September 2024).

[184] 'Lebanon Says 558 Killed as Israel Bombs Hezbollah' (CBS News, 24 September 2024).

[185] Israeli Diaspora Minister Amichal Chikli, Post on X (Twitter) (21 September 2024).

[186] 'Interview with Israeli President Isaac Herzog', *Capital Connection* (CNBC, 24 September 2024).

[187] *Israeli Society Index* (Jewish People Policy Institute, 16 June 2024).

[188] See *Capital Connection*.

[189] Lebanese Focus Group 1 (Beirut, July 2024).

[190] Ibid.

[191] Lebanese Focus Group 2 (Beirut, July 2024).

[192] Katz, Y. and A. Ahronheim, 'Outgoing IDF Chief of Staff Gadi Eisenkot – A Look Back', *The Jerusalem Post* (11 January 2019).

[193] Landau, N., 'Israel's Opposition Doesn't Trust Netanyahu on Gaza. Why Are They Backing Him on Striking Lebanon?', *Haaretz* (23 September 2024).

[194] President Joe Biden statement on the death of Hassan Nasrallah (White House Briefing Room, 28 September 2024).

[195] Foreign Minister Ayman Safadi statement on behalf of Arab Islamic Ministerial Committee, Post on X (Twitter) (28 September 2024).

[196] See Khalidi, *Hundred Years' War*.

[197] 'Arab States Condemn Israeli Minister's "No Palestinians" Remark' (Al Jazeera, 21 March 2023).

[198] See Herzl, *Diaries*.

[199] Appy, C. G., *American Reckoning: The Vietnam War and our National Identity* (New York: Penguin, 2016).

200 Mearsheimer, J. J. and S. M. Walt, *The Israel Lobby and US Foreign Policy* (London: Penguin, 2008).

201 Pro-Israel Summary 2023–24 (Open Secrets, October 2024).

202 See Fisk, *Night*.

203 Majid, J., 'Republican Senators Warn ICC Prosecutor: "Target Israel, and We Will Target You"', *The Times of Israel* (6 May 2024).

204 Foran, C. and H. Talbot, 'House Passes International Criminal Court Sanctions Bill After Prosecutor Seeks Netanyahu Warrant' (CNN, 4 June 2024).

205 'Jimmy Carter Interview', *Charlie Rose* (PBS, 30 November 2006).

206 'Transcript of President Reagan's Speech on Sending Marines into Lebanon', *The New York Times* (21 September 1982).

207 'United States Vetoes Security Council Resolution on Israeli Settlements' (UN News, 18 February 2011).

208 Knickerbocker, B., 'If Obama Opposes Israeli Settlement Activity, Why Did US Veto UN Vote?' *The Christian Science Monitor* (18 February 2011).

209 'Israel: US Veto on Settlements Undermines International Law' (Human Rights Watch, 18 February 2011).

210 'Action Request: Constructive Outcome from the Goldstone Report' (Secretary of State, 23 September 2009).

211 Zunes, S., 'Answering Obama's UN Address' (Foreign Policy in Focus, 10 September 2011).

212 President Barack Obama address to UN General Assembly, 68th session (24 September 2013).

213 Rogin, J., 'Wendy Sherman Promises U.S. Veto of Palestinian Statehood at U.N.', *Foreign Policy* (7 September 2011).

214 Letter from President Ford to Israeli Prime Minister Rabin (National Archives: Records of Henry Kissinger, 1975).

215 'Obama's Mideast Speech', *The New York Times* (19 May 2011).

216 President Barack Obama remarks at the AIPAC Policy Conference (22 May 2011).

217 Wise, D. W., 'Obama's Legacy Is as a Disappointingly Conventional President' (London School of Economy Blog, 30 April 2019).

218 Ruebner, J., 'Obama's Legacy on Israel/Palestine', *Journal of Palestine Studies*, 46, 2016).

[219] Assistant Secretary of Political-Military Affairs Andrew Shapiro remarks at the Brookings Saban Center for Middle East Policy (16 July 2010).

[220] President Joe Biden remarks on the 7 October attack (White House Briefing Room, 18 October 2024).

[221] Leahy Laws, 22 US Code 2378d: Limitations on Assistance to Security Forces (Amendments to the Foreign Assistance Act of 1961).

[222] 'Blinken Sitting on Staff Recommendations to Sanction Israeli Military Units Linked to Killings or Rapes', *ProPublica* (17 April 2024).

[223] Said, E., 'Permission to Narrate', *Journal of Palestine Studies*, 13, 3 (1984).

[224] See Joe Biden remarks on the 7 October attack.

[225] Ibid.

[226] Ibid.

[227] 'American Physicians' and Nurses' Observations From the Gaza Strip Since October 7, 2023', Letter to President Joe Biden, Vice President Kamala Harris, and Dr Jill Biden (25 July 2024).

[228] Ibid.

[229] 'InterAction Member CEOs Send Public Letter to Address Crisis in Gaza' (Norwegian Refugee Council, 29 April 2024).

[230] 'Doctors Without Borders responds to Biden report on Israel's war in Gaza' (MSF USA, 11 May 2024).

[231] See 'American Physicians'.

[232] Prime Minister Benjamin Netanyahu address to the Joint Houses of Congress (25 July 2024).

[233] Ibid.

[234] Ibid.

[235] Hearst, D., 'History Did Not Start in Paris on Sunday', *Middle East Eye* (13 February 2015).

[236] Dominique de Villepin interview, *Le 7/10* (France Inter, 12 September 2024).

[237] Martin Luther King address at Riverside Church, Manhattan (4 April 1967).

[238] '"We Don't Recognize Their Jurisdiction", Biden Says of International Criminal Court', *NewsHour* (PBS, 23 May 2024).

[239] Foer, F., 'The War That Would Not End', *The Atlantic* (5 September 2024).

[240] See Murphy, 'Israel Blocked Aid'.

[241] Paul, J., 'A Further Resignation', Post on LinkedIn (28 May 2024).

[242] 'You Don't Have To Be Jewish To Be A Zionist' (Israel National News – Arutz Sheva, 26 August 2008).

[243] Senator Joe Biden speech at US Senate session (5 June 1986).

[244] See Mearsheimer and Walt, *Lobby*.

[245] Caruso, C., 'After House Speaker Mike Johnson Pushed Through Israel Aid Package, AIPAC Cash Came Flowing In', *The Intercept* (20 January 2024).

[246] Apelblat, M., 'Ursula von der Leyen Responds to Protest Letter by EU Staff on Israel–Gaza War', *The Brussels Times* (24 October 2023).

[247] Akkerman, M. and N. Ní Bhriain, *Partners in Crime: EU Complicity in Israel's Genocide in Gaza* (Transnational Institute, June 2024).

[248] See Apelblat, 'Ursula von der Leyen'.

[249] Wax, E. and J. Barigazzi, 'Von der Leyen Accused of "Unacceptable Bias" Toward Israel', *Politico* (14 October 2023).

[250] See Akkerman and Ní Bhriain, *Partners*.

[251] 'How US and UK Military Airlifts Have Supported Israel's War on Gaza' (Al Jazeera, 24 October 2024).

[252] Prime Minister Kier Starmer remarks during Prime Minister's Questions in the House of Commons (13 November 2024).

[253] Asem, S., 'Kier Starmer Has Previously Argued Serbia Waged Genocide against Croatia', *Middle East Eye* (18 November 2024).

[254] Morris, B., *Righteous Victims: A History Of The Zionist-Arab Conflict, 1881–1999* (New York: Albert A. Knopf, 1999).

[255] 'Situation in the OPT – SecCo Debate – Verbatim record' (UN, 14 May 1976).

[256] Grinberg, L. L., '"Resistance, Politics and Violence": The Catch of the Palestinian Struggle, *Current Sociology*, 61, 2 (2013).

[257] '#80: Miko Peled: HEATED DEBATE on Israel-Palestine', *For the Sake of Argument* (16 October 2024).

[258] 'Gabor Maté Debates Israel and Palestine', *Piers Morgan Uncensored* (TalkTV, 28 November 2023).

[259] Montagu, E., 'The Anti-Semitism Of The Present Government' (23 August 1917).

[260] Oborne, P., 'Why Ilan Pappe's New Book on the Israel Lobby is a Must-Read', *Middle East Eye* (24 June 2024).

[261] See Montagu, 'Anti-Semitism'.

[262] Sir Gerald Kaufman, MP address to the House of Commons (15 January 2009).

[263] Ibid.

[264] Tony Benn, MP address to the House of Commons (17 February 1998).

[265] Pinkas, A., 'A Rogue Prime Minister is Turning Israel into a Rogue State', *Haaretz* (30 Aug 2024).

[266] McLaughlin, E., 'Israel's PM Netanyahu: No Palestinian State on My Watch' (CNN, 16 March 2015).

[267] National Security Adviser Jake Sullivan remarks on Iranian attack on Israel (White House Briefing Room, 1 October 2024).

[268] Letter from John F. Kennedy to his father following his trip to Palestine (JFK Library, 1939).

[269] Said, E., 'The Myth of "The Clash Of Civilizations"' (Media Education Foundation 1998).

[270] Arafeh, N., 'The Illusion of Oslo', *Diwan* (Carnegie Middle East Center, 13 September 2023).

[271] Weisglass, D., 'Oslo Deal Was Good for the Jews' (YNetnews.com, 21 August 2012).

[272] Status of Palestine in the United Nations (UN General Assembly Resolution 67/19, 29 November 2012).

[273] Brom, S., *Israel's Intelligence Failure & The Iraq War* (Carnegie Endowment for International Peace, 11 December 2003).

[274] Stamatopoulou-Robbins, S., *The Human Toll: Indirect Deaths from War in Gaza and the West Bank, October 7, 2023 Forward* (Costs of War Project, Brown University, 7 October 2024).

[275] Segal, R., 'A Textbook Case of Genocide', *Jewish Currents* (13 October 2023).

[276] Goldberg, A., 'The Problematic Return of Intent', *Journal of Genocide Research* (2024).

[277] Schuman Declaration (9 May 1950).

[278] Ibid.

[279] Kessler, G., 'Netanyahu: America Is a Thing You Can Move Very Easily', *The Washington Post* (16 July 2010).

[280] Letter accompanying the first progress report of the UN Mediator on Palestine, Folke Bernadotte (16 September 1948).

Bibliography

Books/Journal Articles

Abu Sitta, S., *Mapping My Return: A Palestinian Memoir* (Cairo: American University in Cairo Press, 2017).

Appy, C. G., *American Reckoning: The Vietnam War and our National Identity* (New York: Penguin, 2016).

Fassin, D., *Moral Abdication: How the World Failed to Stop the Destruction of Gaza,* Trans. G. Elliott (London: Verso Books, 2024).

Feniger, Y., Y. Shavit and S. Caller, 'The Israeli Education System', in G. Ben-Porat and others (ed.), *Routledge Handbook on Contemporary Israel* (London: Routledge, 2022).

Fisk, R., *Night of Power* (London: 4th Estate, 2024).

Gaughan, A., *Memoirs of Senator Joseph Connolly* (Dublin: Irish Academic Press, 1996).

Goldberg, A., 'The Problematic Return of Intent', *Journal of Genocide Research* (2024).

Grinberg, L. L., '"Resistance, Politics and Violence": The Catch of the Palestinian Struggle, Current *Sociology*, 61, 2 (2013).

Herzl, T., *The Diaries of Theodor Herzl*, Trans. M. Lowenthal (New York: Grosset and Dunlap, 1962).

Herzl, T., *The Jewish State*, Trans. S. D'Avigdor (Originally published as Der Judenstaat, 1896, translation published 1946).

Kearns, E. M., A. E. Betus, and A. F. Lemieux, 'Why Do Some Terrorist Attacks Receive More Media Attention Than Others?' *Justice Quarterly*, 36, 6 (2019).

Khalidi, R., *The Hundred Years' War on Palestine* (London: Profile Books, 2020).

McCluskey, F., *Tyrone: The Irish Revolution*, 1912–23, (Dublin: Four Courts Press, 2014)

Mearsheimer, J. J. and S. M. Walt, *The Israel Lobby and US Foreign Policy* (London: Penguin, 2008).

Mishal, S. and A. Sela, *The Palestinian Hamas* (New York: Columbia University Press, 2000).

Morris, B., *Righteous Victims: A History Of The Zionist-Arab Conflict, 1881–1999* (New York: Albert A. Knopf, 1999).

Pappé, I., *A Very Short History of the Israel–Palestine Conflict* (London: Oneworld Publications, 2024).

Rich, D., *Everyday Hate* (Hull: Biteback Publishing, 2024).

Ruebner, J., 'Obama's Legacy on Israel/Palestine', *Journal of Palestine Studies*, 46, 2016).

Said, E., 'Permission to Narrate', *Journal of Palestine Studies*, 13, 3 (1984).

Shehadeh, R. and P. Johnson, *Forgotten* (London: Profile Books, 2025).

Shehadeh, R., *What Does Israel Fear from Palestine?* (London: Profile Books, 2024).

Shire, W., 'Conversations about Home (At the Deportation Centre)', in *Teaching My Mother How To Give Birth* (London: Flipped Eye Publishing, 2011).

Newspaper Articles/ News Websites/Online Sources

Al-Houdalieh, S., 'The International Order Is Failing to Protect Palestinian Cultural Heritage', *SAPIENS* (6 June 2024).

Anderson, J., 'South Lebanon Annexation by Israel Feared', *The Washington Post* (27 September 1982).

Apelblat, M., 'Ursula von der Leyen Responds to Protest Letter by EU Staff on Israel–Gaza War', *The Brussels Times* (24 October 2023).

Appy, C. G., 'UMass Arrests: What Would Daniel Ellsberg Do?', *Common Dreams* (20 May 2024).

'Arab States Condemn Israeli Minister's "No Palestinians" Remark' (*Al Jazeera*, 21 March 2023).

Arafeh, N., 'The Illusion of Oslo', Diwan (*Carnegie Middle East Center*, 13 September 2023).

Asem, S., 'Kier Starmer Has Previously Argued Serbia Waged Genocide against Croatia', *Middle East Eye* (18 November 2024).

'At Least 12 Killed in Rocket Attack in Israeli-Occupied Golan Heights' (*Al Jazeera*, 27 July 2024).

Berman, L., 'Netanyahu Met by Angry Crowd on Visit to Site of Deadly Attack', *The Times of Israel* (29 July 2024).

'Blinken Sitting on Staff Recommendations to Sanction Israeli Military Units Linked to Killings or Rapes', *ProPublica* (17 April 2024).

'Broadcaster Bias Is Failing to Hold Israel to Account', *The Independent* (1 November 2024).

Borger, J. and S. Taha, 'Israeli Forces Kill At Least 10 Palestinians in West Bank Raids and Strikes', *The Guardian* (28 August 2024).

Brom, S., Israel's Intelligence Failure & The Iraq War (*Carnegie Endowment for International Peace*, 11 December 2003).

'"Business as Usual" with Current Israeli Government Not an Option, Says CJPME', *The Hill Times* (5 April 2023).

Caruso, C., 'After House Speaker Mike Johnson Pushed Through Israel Aid Package, AIPAC Cash Came Flowing In', *The Intercept* (20 January 2024).

Chappell, B. and D. Estrin, 'Here's Why Netanyahu's Court Overhaul, Now on Hold, Brought Israel to Brink' (*NPR*, 27 March 2023).

'Corruption Charges Suggested for Netanyahu', *The New York Times* (13 February 2018).

'Cultural Apartheid: Israel's Erasure of Palestinian Heritage in Gaza' (*Al-Haq*, January 2022).

Dover, R., 'Why Israel's Intelligence Chiefs Failed to Listen to Warnings' (*University of Hull*, 8 December 2023).

Elbagir, N. and others,'Qatar Sent Millions to Hamas – with Israel's Backing' (*CNN*, 12 December 2023).

'EU's Borrell Says Israel Financed Creation of Gaza Rulers Hamas' (*Reuters*, 19 January 2024).

'Egypt Warned Israel Days Before Hamas Struck' (*BBC Online*, 12 October 2023).

Foer, F., 'The War That Would Not End', *The Atlantic* (5 September 2024).

Foran, C. and H. Talbot, 'House Passes International Criminal Court Sanctions Bill After Prosecutor Seeks Netanyahu Warrant' (*CNN*, 4 June 2024).

Gebeily, M., A. Timour and L. Bassam, 'Israeli Attack on Beirut Shatters Diplomatic Understandings' (*Reuters*, 1 August 2024).

Gjevori, E., 'Gaza's Cultural and Religious Heritage Lies in Ruins After a Year of Attacks by Israel', *Middle East Eye* (11 October 2024).

Graham-Harrison, E., and M. Cohen, 'Draft Israeli Law to Limit Academic Speech Labelled "McCarthyite"', *The Guardian* (21 July 2024).

Haddad, M. and A. Chughtai, 'Israel-Palestine conflict: A brief history in maps and charts' (*Al Jazeera*, 27 November 2023).

Hanauer, L. and M. P. Connell, Political Priorities, Poor Intelligence Tradecraft, and the Suppression of Dissenting Views: Why Israel Failed to Warn of Hamas's October 7 Attack (*Institute for Defence Analyses*, September 2024).

Hearst, D., 'History Did Not Start in Paris on Sunday', *Middle East Eye* (13 February 2015).

'How US and UK Military Airlifts Have Supported Israel's War on Gaza' (*Al Jazeera*, 24 October 2024).

Hudson, J., 'Israel's Netanyahu Brings His Dirty Laundry to Washington. Literally', *The Washington Post* (23 September 2020).

Hussein, M., 'Mapping 11 Months of Israel–Lebanon Cross-Border Attacks' (*Al Jazeera*, 11 September 2024).

'IDF Intel Warns Netanyahu of Israel's "Historic Weakness" Seen by Iran and Hezbollah', *Haaretz* (28 July 2023).

'Interview with Israeli President Isaac Herzog', Capital Connection (*CNBC*, 24 September 2024).

'Israel Destroys Second Largest Historical Mosque in Gaza', *The Middle East Monitor* (4 July 2024).

'Israel is Hurtling Toward Dictatorship', *Haaretz* (17 March 2023).

'Israel Pushes NBA to Delete "Occupied Palestine" from Website', *The Middle East Monitor* (30 December 2017).

'Israel Warns Palestinian Village Will Be Demolished if Residents Refuse to Relocate', *The Times of Israel* (9 September 2024).

'Israel's Security Must Not Fall Victim to Politics', *The Jerusalem Post* (31 March 2023).

'Israeli Supreme Court Decision Prompts Polarized Response in a Nation at War', *The New York Times* (1 January 2024).

Katz, Y. and A. Ahronheim, 'Outgoing IDF Chief of Staff Gadi Eisenkot – A Look Back', *The Jerusalem Post* (11 January 2019).

Keller-Lynn, C., 'Gantz's National Unity Accepts Herzog Framework', *The Times of Israel* (15 March 2023).

Kessler, G., 'Netanyahu: America Is a Thing You Can Move Very Easily', *The Washington Post* (16 July 2010).

Knickerbocker, B., 'If Obama Opposes Israeli Settlement Activity, Why Did US Veto UN Vote?' *The Christian Science Monitor* (18 February 2011).

Kubovich, Y., 'The Women Soldiers Who Warned of a Pending Hamas Attack', *Haaretz* (20 November 2023).

Landau, N., 'Israel's Opposition Doesn't Trust Netanyahu on Gaza. Why Are They Backing Him on Striking Lebanon?', *Haaretz* (23 September 2024).

'Lebanon Says 558 Killed as Israel Bombs Hezbollah' (*CBS News*, 24 September 2024).

'Letter to President of the State of Israel, Mr. Itzhak Herzog' (Commanders for Israel's Security, 17 February 2023).

Loveluck, L. and S. Taha, 'Homes Burned, Animals Killed, Palestinians Describe Settler Rampage', *The Washington Post* (16 April 2024).

Lubell, M. and N. Al-Mughrabi, 'Israel Rescues Four Hostages in Gaza Raid' (*Reuters*, 8 June 2024).

Majid, J., 'Republican Senators Warn ICC Prosecutor: "Target Israel, and We Will Target You"', *The Times of Israel* (6 May 2024).

Maltz, J., 'Will Israel Become a Theocracy?', *Haaretz* (3 November 2022).

Masarwa, L., 'Reading, Writing and Racism: "Nation-State" Law Now Official Israeli Curriculum', *Middle East Eye* (4 September 2019).

'Mass Graves in Gaza Show Victims' Hands Were Tied, Says UN Rights Office' (*UN News*, 23 April 2024).

McLaughlin, E., 'Israel's PM Netanyahu: No Palestinian State on My Watch' (*CNN*, 16 March 2015).

Montagu, E., 'The Anti-Semitism Of The Present Government' (*Wikimedia Commons*, 23 August 1917).

Murphy, B., 'Israel Deliberately Blocked Humanitarian Aid to Gaza', *ProPublica* (24 September 2024).

'Nation-State Law to Be Included in Israeli High School Curriculum', *The Times of Israel* (16 August 2019).

'Netanyahu Vows to Turn Gaza "Into Rubble"', *The Middle East Monitor* (8 October 2023).

'Obama's Mideast Speech', *The New York Times* (19 May 2011).

Oborne, P., 'Why Ilan Pappe's New Book on the Israel Lobby is a Must-Read', *Middle East Eye* (24 June 2024).

'Palestinian Children Abused in Israeli Detention' (*Al Jazeera*, 10 July 2023).

Pinkas, A., 'A Rogue Prime Minister is Turning Israel into a Rogue State', *Haaretz* (30 Aug 2024).

'President Herzog Speech Before Presenting the People's Directive for Changes in the Justice System' (*Gov.il*, 15 March 2023).

Rogin, J., 'Wendy Sherman Promises U.S. Veto of Palestinian Statehood at U.N.', *Foreign Policy* (7 September 2011).

Said, E., 'The Myth of "The Clash Of Civilizations"' (Media Education Foundation 1998).

Saifi, Z., 'Jordan King Warns of "Red Lines" in Jerusalem as Netanyahu Returns to Office', (*CNN*, 28 December 2022).

'Scabies Spreading Among Prisoners; Visits Cancelled: Prisoners' Organizations' (WAFA, 3 September 2024).

Segal, R., 'A Textbook Case of Genocide', *Jewish Currents* (13 October 2023).

Segal, R., 'Israel Must Stop Weaponising the Holocaust', *The Guardian* (24 October 2023).

'Settler Violence = State Violence' (*B'Tselem*, 25 November 2021).

Shamir, J., 'Judicial Coup and Occupation "Directly Linked"', *Haaretz* (7 August 2023).

Shehadeh, R., 'When Will This Horror End? When Israel Realises That the Cost of Destroying Us Is Too High', *The Guardian* (5 October 2024).

'Smotrich: It May Be "Justified" to Starve 2 million Gazans', *The Times of Israel* (5 August 2024).

Sokol, S., 'Knesset Passes Law Allowing Government to Fire Teachers It Asserts Identify with Terror', *The Times of Israel* (5 November 2024).

'Tens of Thousands Rally Against Judicial Overhaul', *The Times of Israel* (11 February 2023).

'The Government Declares 12,000 Dunams in the Jordan Valley as State Lands' (*Peace Now*, 3 July 2024).

'Transcript of President Reagan's Speech on Sending Marines into Lebanon', *The New York Times* (21 September 1982).

'"Unacceptable, Insulting": Coalition Dismiss Herzog's Judicial Reform Framework', *The Times of Israel* (15 March 2023).

'United States Vetoes Security Council Resolution on Israeli Settlements' (*UN News*, 18 February 2011).

Wax, E. and J. Barigazzi, 'Von der Leyen Accused of "Unacceptable Bias" Toward Israel', *Politico* (14 October 2023).

'"We Don't Recognize Their Jurisdiction", Biden Says of International Criminal Court', NewsHour (*PBS*, 23 May 2024).

Weisglass, D., 'Oslo Deal Was Good for the Jews' (*YNetnews.com*, 21 August 2012).

Wintour, P., 'Hamas Presents New Charter Accepting a Palestine Based on 1967 Borders', *The Guardian* (1 May 2017).

'Warning of Civil War, Herzog Unveils Framework for Judicial Reform', *The Times of Israel* (15 March 2023).

Wise, D. W., 'Obama's Legacy Is as a Disappointingly Conventional President' (London School of Economy Blog, 30 April 2019).

Wootliff, R., 'State Prosecutor Hands Indictment Recommendations against PM to Attorney General', *The Times of Israel* (19 December 2018).

Yashiv, E., 'Autocrats of a Feather', *Haaretz* (28 August 2024).

'You Don't Have To Be Jewish To Be A Zionist' (Israel National News – Arutz Sheva, 26 August 2008).

'Zionist Union Quotes Netanyahu in Massive Billboard Urging Him to Quit', *The Times of Israel* (15 February 2018).

Zunes, S., 'Answering Obama's UN Address' (Foreign Policy in Focus, 10 September 2011).

'72% of Israelis Say Aid Deliveries to Gaza Must Be Stopped, Survey Finds', *The Middle East Monitor* (31 January 2024).

'880 Palestinian Children Detained by Israel this Year, *The Middle East Monitor* (20 November 2023).

Official Reports and Legal Texts

Akkerman, M. and N. Ní Bhriain, *Partners in Crime: EU Complicity in Israel's Genocide in Gaza* (Transnational Institute, June 2024).

Albanese, F., *Report of the Special Rapporteur on the Situation of Human Rights in the Palestinian Territories Occupied since 1967*, (OHCHR – Office of the High Commisionner for Human Rights, 10 July 2023).

'American Physicians' and Nurses' Observations From the Gaza Strip Since October 7, 2023', Letter to President Joe Biden, Vice President Kamala Harris, and Dr Jill Biden (25 July 2024).

'Basic-Law: Jerusalem the Capital of Israel', Trans. S. Hattis Rolef (Originally adopted in Knesset session 5740, 30 July 1980, translation published 1 May 2022).

Bitter Legacy: State Impunity in the Northern Ireland Conflict (Committee on the Administration of Justice, Pat Finucane Centre and Norwegian Centre for Human Rights, April 2024).

Data on Casualties in the Occupied Palestinian Territories (OCHA – United Nations Office for the Coordination of Humanitarian Affairs, 1 January 2023 to 7 October 2023).

'Data Sheet, December 2023: Law Enforcement on Israeli Civilians in the West Bank (Settler violence) 2005–2023' (Yesh Din, 21 January 2024).

'Data sheet: Law enforcement against Israeli soldiers suspected of harming Palestinians and their property – Summary of figures for 2017–2021' (Yesh Din, 21 December 2022).

'Doctors Without Borders responds to Biden report on Israel's war in Gaza' (MSF USA, 11 May 2024).

'Close the Sde Teman Detention Center' (The Association for Civil Rights in Israel, 17 September 2024).

Famine Review Committee: Gaza Strip, (IPC – Integrated Food Security Phase Classification, 18 March 2024).

Hermann, T. and O. Anabi, 'Even on the Right, Israelis Want Elections Immediately After the War' (The Israel Democracy Institute, 19 December 2023).

'In response to HaMoked Habeus Corpus Petition' (HaMoked, 5 May 2024).

'InterAction Member CEOs Send Public Letter to Address Crisis in Gaza' (Norwegian Refugee Council, 29 April 2024).

'Israel: US Veto on Settlements Undermines International Law' (Human Rights Watch, 18 February 2011).

'Israel's Unlawful Carceral Practices in the Occupied Palestinian Territory Are Tantamount to International Crimes' (OHCHR, 10 July 2023).

'Israeli Practices towards the Palestinian People and the Question of Apartheid' (ESCWA – United Nations Economic and Social Commission for West Asia, 2017).

Israeli Society Index (Jewish People Policy Institute, 16 June 2024).

Leahy Laws, 22 US Code 2378d: Limitations on Assistance to Security Forces (Amendments to the Foreign Assistance Act of 1961).

Lindsay, J., *Evaluating UNRWA After the Colonna Report* (Washington Institute, June 2024).

Lindsay, J., *Fixing UNRWA: Repairing the UN's Troubled System of Aid to Palestinian Refugees* (Washington Institute, January 2009).

Ministry of Defense Coordination of Government Activities in the Territories, *Food Consumption in the Gaza Strip: Red Lines, Trans. Gisha NGO* (Originally published 1 January 2008, translation by Gisha published 17 October 2012).

'No Traces of Life': Israel's Ecocide In Gaza 2023–2024 (Forensic Architecture, 29 March 2024).

Policy on Cultural Heritage (Office of the Prosecutor of the ICC, June 2021).

'Public Opinion Poll No (93)' (PCPSR, 17 September 2024).

Report on UNCTAD's assistance to the Palestinian people (UNCTAD – United Nations Conference on Trade and Development, 11 September 2023).

Rome Statute of the International Criminal Court, Article 7(2)(h) (ICC, 17 July 1998).

'"Security" Inmates Held In Prisons Inside Israel' (HaMoked, July 2024).

Shwed, U. and others, 'Integration of Arab Israelis and Jews in Schools in Israel' (Taub Center for Social Policy Studies in Israel, October 2014).

Silver, L. and M. Smerkovich, 'Israeli Views of Israel-Hamas War' (Pew Research Center, 30 May 2024).

'Situation in the OPT – SecCo Debate – Verbatim record' (UN, 14 May 1976).

A Spatial Analysis of the Israeli Military's Conduct in Gaza since October 2023 (Forensic Architecture, 15 October 2024).

Stamatopoulou-Robbins, S., *The Human Toll: Indirect Deaths from War in Gaza and the West Bank*, October 7, 2023 Forward (Costs of War Project, Brown University, 7 October 2024).

Status of Palestine in the United Nations (UN General Assembly Resolution 67/19, 29 November 2012).

'The Declaration of the Establishment of the State of Israel' (Gov.il, 14 May 1948).

'The General Staff White Washing Mechanism: The Israeli Law Enforcement System and Breaches of International Law and War Crimes in Gaza' (Yesh Din, 9 July 2024).

'The Peace Index' (Conflict Resolution and Mediation, University of Tel Aviv, November 2023).

'The Right of the Jewish People to the Land of Israel' (Likud Party: Original Party Platform, 1977).

UN Security Council Resolutions 425 and 426 (19 March 1978).

Universal Declaration of Human Rights, Article 22 (UN General Assembly Resolution 217 A(III), 10 December 1948).

Welcome to Hell: The Israeli Prison System as a Network of Torture Camps (B'Tselem, 1 August 2024).

World Report 2023: Israel and Palestine, Events of 2022 (Human Rights Watch, 20 April 2023).

World Report 2025: Israel and Palestine, Events of 2024 (Human Rights Watch, 16 January 2025).

Acknowledgements

Where to start? My little grandchildren, Bahia and Ruan: their largely safe, secure world was motivation enough to explore how any state could kill innocent children. The Irish Palestine Solidarity Movement which, for decades, has kept Ireland Palestine-focused. The remarkable courage of some NGOs, especially those in Israel. With little recognition in the West, organisations like B'Tselem, HaMoked, Al Haq, YeshDin, the Association for Civil Rights in Israel, swim furiously against the state-controlled current that aims to wash away any and all dissent. Their work has never been as necessary or as dangerous as now.

The courage of Palestine's official media. Along with Gaza's civilian-media, these journalists risked their lives to bring the horror of Nakba II to the world in realtime. The bravery and objectivity of Israel's *Haaretz* daily newspaper must also be acknowledged.

Thanks to Palestine's Ambassador to Ireland, Jilan Wahba Abdalmajid; you are a wonderful representative of your nation. Ireland's Department of Foreign Affairs, in particular its team in Jordan led by Ambassador Marianne Bolger. Thanks to UNIFIL and one officer in particular whose advice was particularly helpful.

In Lebanon, all those who provided me with critical insights on events, its complex relationship with Palestine and its people, and special thanks to Dave Mulville, once of that place. In Jordan, thank you Juliette Tuoumo and Laurane March, and in the West Bank, to Tanya Habjouqa, Faris and Munif Treish, and the remarkable Abdullah Alkurd. Thank you to one of the best analysts of events, Peter Oborne, and in Europe and the US all those important sources who either wish to or need to remain anonymous.

The academics and writers who for decades have been recording the colonial intent of the state of Israel. For their diligence, their research, analysis and accounts. Particularly the extraordinarily brave Jewish and Israelis among them.

My friends, the author, Brian Conaghan and the journalist, Dion Fanning. Brian read a poor first draft, suggested a new structure but infused me with confidence to persist. Dion talked sense to me at a critical point when I was in Lebanon and offered valuable editorial advice later. Thank you Matt Cooper who also provided wise counsel at one critical point. Thanks also to those who read parts of early drafts: Tom Arnold, Bill Swainson, Gary Daly, Bríd Ní Chuilinn, Terry MacManus, Brian Cowen, John Ging, Christian Appy, Chris Gunness, and Fergus Mulligan.

The publishing professionals, chief among them my agent, Louise Dobbin, whose belief in the project never wavered. Her commitment, along with that of her Repforce colleagues, Bríd Ní Chuilinn and Nigel Carré, made the difference. Thank you to Jeremy Murphy and his editorial team at JM Agency for their exceptional work and to Adrian Robb, who created the cover that captured the narrative inside so well. And thanks to Peter O'Connell for his PR management.

Most importantly, my immense gratitude to Merrion Press. Síne Quinn saw the importance of the narrative and Conor Graham showed courage in backing me with the weight of Merrion's reputation in Irish publishing. In this part of the world, this is a contentious subject which many choose to avoid. Merrion Press took a leap of faith. Thank you.

My hope is that *Catastrophe – Nakba II* will be a credible and readable account of Israel's determination to wipe Palestine from the map and how it was sponsored in that endeavour by powerful nations in the West. I could not have set such an ambition without the support of all those mentioned but particularly Conor Graham, Síne Quinn, Jeremy Murphy and Louise Dobbin.

About the Author

Cover photo credit: IMEMC News

Fintan Drury is an author and opinion writer whose work has been widely published, particularly by *The Currency* and *The Irish Times*. He began his career as a news journalist with RTÉ (the Irish national broadcaster) in the 1980s, serving as a correspondent in Belfast and undertaking some overseas assignments, before going on to present Morning Ireland from 1985 to 1988.

Drury spent three decades in business, including a notably turbulent period between 2006 and 2010 – an experience he reflects on in his memoir, *See-Saw*, published in 2021. He returned to journalism in 2016, writing an extensive series for *The Irish Times* based on the diary of a Syrian refugee, following a short period volunteering in a refugee camp in Athens.

He currently serves as chair of SARI (Sport Against Racism Ireland) and lives in Dublin.